On Islamic Banking, Performance and Financial Innovations

On Islamic Banking, Performance and Financial Innovations

Edited by

Mondher Bellalah

CAMBRIDGE SCHOLARS

PUBLISHING

On Islamic Banking, Performance and Financial Innovations
Edited by Mondher Bellalah

This book first published 2014

Cambridge Scholars Publishing

12 Back Chapman Street, Newcastle upon Tyne, NE6 2XX, UK

British Library Cataloguing in Publication Data
A catalogue record for this book is available from the British Library

ISBN (10): 1-4438-5990-7, ISBN (13): 978-1-4438-5990-5

This book is written to better the understanding of the Muslim community around the world of Islamic economics and its importance, especially in these days of crisis. The book is also intended to be a reference manual for teaching the theory and practice of Islamic banking and Islamic financial innovations around the world. Islamic finance courses at universities are highly important since Islamic financial innovations remain very limited, and additional efforts have to be made in this area.

It is very important therefore to mention the unique efforts of the Tunisian Private Universities to enhance Islamic studies and in particular www.umlt.ens.tn.

Such efforts cover all fields in Islamic studies, including economics. No award will ever be given that denotes excellence in Islamic studies better than the award for Best Study in Field.

TABLE OF CONTENTS

FOREWORD

Despite the consequences of the latest global financial crisis, the slow process of international economic recovery, as well as the cautious positive outlook of recent international economy performance, Islamic Finance was able to maintain its position as one of the most growing sectors of financial services in the globe. Islamic Financial Services are actually shifting from the creation phase to widely and internationally tangible prevalence, constituting an integral part of the financial systems of many countries. By the end of 2013, total assets of Islamic Finance exceeded $ 1.6 trillion with apparent domination of Islamic Banking which amounted to "75-80" % of total Islamic Finance assets. By the end of 2014, total volume of asset is expected to exceed $ "2" trillion maintaining the growth pace seen in the last few years which was approximately "15-20"% per annum, so that total assets of Islamic Banks will be around $ 1.6 trillion. These positive prospects are enormously fostered by the positive economic outlook of the GCC and other emerging markets' Countries.

The process of transformation and restructuring implemented by many of the large Islamic financial institutions recently, as well as recent developments on the operational environment have contributed to the reduction of the profitability gap amongst Islamic and conventional banks. In addition, the continued positive outlook of the Islamic banking industry, encouraged many international banks to enter (or plan to enter) Islamic banking market. This, of course, in addition to the regulatory rules imposed by Basel III, increased competition and sophistication of Islamic Banking market. Therefore, it has become imperative to develop performance measurement and risk management techniques in light of an international economy overwhelmed by uncertainty. Furthermore, operational transformation has become a must in order to ensure responsiveness to a growing number of Islamic banking customers and their uninterrupted aspirations while taking into account cost cutting and to remain abreast with state-of-the-art technologies. Likewise, market sophistication imposes Islamic Banks to consider Shariah-complaint regularity clarity and governance regulations which performed a basic role in polishing the image of Islamic banking globally.

In light of all of the above, comes this book, with a solid scientific approach which practically clarifies Islamic banking systems, tools as well as methods for assessing performance in comparison with conventional banks. Using empirical evidences, the theoretical and practical foundations of these two banking types are also elaborated. In addition, the book illustrates the experience of smaller Islamic Banks growth in the last decade, the challenges they faced in terms of profitability and growth as well as up-to-date advanced mechanisms used in operational environment risk management.

We in **Kuwait International Bank (KIB)** deeply praise the efforts exerted in drafting this book in its current form. This book will eventually assist Islamic banks' staff; policy-makers, decision-makers as well as all those concerned with Islamic Banking in both Islamic and non-Islamic countries in the formulation of a clearer understanding of Islamic Banking in a systematic approach. This book can be used as an academic reference all over Arabic and Islamic universities.

—Mohammed Jarrah Al-Sabah
Chairman of Kuwait International Bank

PREFACE

Islamic banking has seen rapid growth during the last two decades. This is a result of the liberalization of financial regulation, the globalization of financial markets, technological changes, product innovation, the birth of several new Islamic States, and a growing Islamic presence in the West, among other factors. New innovations have allowed economists and religious scholars to bring new products to almost all areas of banking and insurance, products which would previously have been extremely controversial. There is no accurate data on the exact extent and volume of Islamic banking, but it is currently estimated that Islamic Banks' assets are between 500 and 800 billion U.S. dollars, and there are nearly 300 Islamic Financial Institutions worldwide, including "Islamic Windows" of conventional banks. The Islamic *sukuk* (bond) is the fastest growing product, estimated at USD 40 billion outstanding. In Pakistan and Malaysia, Shariah compliant funds have exceeded 50% of total market capitalization. Today, Islamic banking is growing at approximately 15% per annum. The growth of Islamic banking is a result of economic growth in the Islamic world, fuelled primarily by oil wealth. This growth created a large population of people with medium wealth, and hence made banking a necessary service for a large segment of the population rather than for just a few, as had been the case some 10 to 15 years earlier. The Islamic banking system is not only popular within Islamic banks, but also in international and other conventional banks. Nowadays, the majority of international banks are adopting Islamic banking in order to serve the specific needs of their new clients. Examples of such banks are Citibank and HSBC, both of which started up Islamic operations worldwide in order to expand their businesses.

Although interest in Islamic banking has grown considerably during the last decade, it is still an evolving industry today. The financial world has set conventional banking, driven mainly by the profit maximization principle, as standard practice. However, Islamic banking principles have been attracting increased attention from academic researchers and regulators, both in developing and developed countries, as a result of their distinctive micro-operating fundamentals. The prohibition of interest payments by Islamic Shariah (Islamic law) has made equity and profit sharing the cornerstones of its operational structure. This ban on interest does not mean that capital is free in an Islamic system. In fact, it recognizes funds as a factor in productivity, but it does not allow the providers of those funds to make a prior or pre-determined claim on any future interest. Theoretically, this risk sharing principle provides better long-term allocation of funds to investments with higher risk-return profiles, and subsequently, greater economic growth.

This book addresses the main issues of concern within Islamic banking (the conceptual framework and viability of interest-free banking) and provides an assessment of its performance and future. In a world where conventional interest-based finance is the dominant framework, Islamic banking faces many challenges that must be addressed. This book provides an excellent read for both researchers and practitioners globally, as it analyzes the past experiences of Islamic banks world-wide, and moreover, provides an objective assessment of their successes and failures, and discusses the contemporary issues and challenges confronting them.

—Adnan Ahmed Yousif
President & Chief Executive, Al Baraka Banking Group
President of Union des Banques Arabes.

INTRODUCTION

Islamic financial practices are founded on the belief that money is not an earning asset in and of itself, and therefore cannot earn interest. Unlike a conventional bank, which is basically a borrower and lender of funds, an Islamic bank is essentially a partner, in partnership with its depositors on the one hand, and also with entrepreneurs, employing depositors' funds in direct, productive investment. Islamic religious law – that is, Shariah – emphasizes ethical, moral, social and religious factors to promote equality and fairness for the good of society as a whole. Principles encouraging risk sharing, individual rights and duties, property rights, and the sanctity of contracts are all part of the code underlying the Islamic banking system.

Islamic banking has emerged as one of the most important industries worldwide. It is known for its interest free model and operates in many countries including Bahrain, Pakistan, Jordan, Iran, Sudan, the United Kingdom, Singapore and Malaysia. Islamic banking and finance have undergone rapid transformation and growth, from an industry striving to satisfy the needs of Muslim communities alone to a multibillion dollar industry upholding Islamic principles. Over recent decades the Islamic banking industry has emerged as one of the fastest growing and has spread to all corners of the globe, receiving wide acceptance from Muslims and non-Muslims.

The market for Islamic banking has grown rapidly over the past few years and is expected to continue to exhibit robust growth for the foreseeable future. In many markets, Islamic banking has evolved from being a niche offering to part of the mainstream financial services landscape. At the same time, the competitive landscape is being re-drawn, with more Islamic financial services institutions present in the marketplace than ever before. Incumbent banks and new market entrants are facing vastly different market conditions and need to develop new, unique features, beyond Shariah compliance, to compete successfully in the future.

Any future unique selling points that Islamic banks promote will likely revolve around the areas of product development and innovation.

Rapid innovations in financial markets and the internationalization of financial flows have changed the face of conventional banking, particularly since the recent financial crisis. Financial innovations led to increased market orientation and encouraged the use of financial products such as mortgages, automobile loans and export credits as backing for marketable securities; this is known as the securitization process.

As financial instruments and markets have become more complex and processing has been automated, the treasury function has also been made more complex. The conventional financial system focuses primarily on the economic and financial aspects of transactions. The Islamic system places equal emphasis on the ethical, moral, social, and religious dimensions, and seeks to enhance equality and fairness for the good of society as a whole.

This book discusses some conceptual features, and highlights the approach of Muslim economists on issues as controversial as the status of credit money, bank money and deposit money, the principle of compensation, etc. It studies the determining factors and measurement indicators of the performance of Islamic banks. It presents an overview of literature that deals with the concepts and determinants of banking performance. It investigates the different approaches and methodologies, as well as the main models, used by researchers when dealing with conventional banks.

The book draws attention towards the rapid development of Islamic finance and banking, their infrastructures and their supporting institutions in recent years. It sums up the different Islamic financial contracts and basic structures, and the derivative Shariah-compliant products used to offer a wide array of innovatively structured financing and investment banking products and services. Islamic banking intermediation lays out specific protocols both for the mobilization and the allocation of funds, and hence the balance sheet structure differs completely from that of conventional banks. Moreover, the current global crisis, which grew in the United States out of the subprime crisis, driven by an unethical attitude of greed and excessive speculation, has gradually engulfed the world. The financial crisis started with the development of an environment where the quantity of loans grew considerably, much more than the quality of those loans, and hence excessive risks were taken. In fact, the debt-based nature of interest delivery that has developed over the previous years, as well as poor and inadequate regulation and lax lending standards, have contributed massively to the augmentation of the gap between the real-world economy and the financial sphere. This book introduces some deregulated power markets by explaining the structure of these markets and the market products that can be used to sell the output of a power generator.

The book determines the potential economic benefits that an Islamic investor can enjoy through investment in power assets. It also presents the Islamic mechanisms that can be used to invest in power generation.

The book is organized as follows:

Part 1 describes the characteristics and performance of the Islamic Banking System.

Chapter 1 presents the fundamentals of the Islamic financial system and financial instruments.

Chapter 2 explains Islamic Banking Intermediation and financial instruments. This chapter also explains risk management issues and the capital adequacy regulations of Islamic Banks.

Part 2 deals with the Islamic banking system and financial Instruments. It provides some empirical results regarding performance measurement.

Part 3 compares conventional versus Islamic banks: Theory.

Part 4 is interested in the concepts of interest rates and profitability and the capital structure of Islamic institutions. Islamic finance has failed to capture the interest of Western writers. This deficiency is explained by references to Western literature regarding the prohibition of interest.

The Koran permits trade but forbids usury. This fundamental principle differentiates the Western from the Islamic banking system.

Islamic banks are involved in the process of implementing government monetary policy in addition to their important role in mobilization and allocation of resources.

Islamic teachings provide a better organizational system for bank operation. The practice of interest is condemned by many thinkers, like Aristotle, who described it as a "birth of money from money".

This part includes three chapters.

Part 5 is about advanced risk management techniques. The advanced analysis of the risk and return profile of Islamic products constitutes a challenge to Islamic financial institutions. Islamic financial institutions are obliged to keep a portion of their assets in equity investments. This part of the book talks about the dynamics of the specific risk profile that is central to Islamic equity investment in a Shariah compliant stock market. Therefore we investigate three Islamic equity indexes as classified by economic hubs (the Dow Jones Europe, Asia-Pacific and USA) in comparison to their conventional peers. Our risk profile analysis is based on the estimations of two well-known advanced risk measures, namely the Value at Risk and the Expected Shortfall.

PART I

THE ISLAMIC BANKING SYSTEM AND FINANCIAL INSTRUMENTS: DEFINITIONS, CHARACTERISTICS AND PERFORMANCE MEASUREMENTS

An Islamic bank is a financial intermediary institution which typically performs the functions of resource mobilization and revenue generation in compliance with Islamic Law. The Islamic banking system carries out two kinds of financial intermediary actions. The first is a payment action, where current deposits remain highly liquid and the aim is the safekeeping of money, and the second is an investment action whereby investments and saving deposits are treated as medium- and long-term savings. Unlike Western commercial banks, which pay interest on current and saving accounts, Islamic banks are prohibited from paying interest on any kind of financial product. Islamic banking converts the interest based banking system to an interest-free system, and the bank's conventional status of borrower and lender changes to become more of a partner status. In fact, the relationship between depositors and financial intermediaries becomes one based on the profit and loss sharing principle. Thus the terms of financial transactions reflect an equitable risk-return, shared between parties.

Along with the prohibition of interest and the upholding of the profit and risk sharing system, another unique feature of Islamic banks is that they are not allowed to invest in activities deemed illicit or featuring any kind of speculation or gambling, which provides a level playing field and protects the interests of all parties.

For the mobilization of funds, Islamic banks have developed two basic deposit products. Each of them is based on a Shariah-compliant intermediary contract. These deposit products are: current accounts, based on *Wadia* or *Amanah* contracts, and investment and savings accounts, based on *Mudaraba* or *Wakalah* contracts.

The assets division of an Islamic bank can carry a more diverse portfolio of heterogeneous asset classes than the liabilities division, representing a wider spectrum of risk and maturity profiles.

The growth of sukuk, or Shariah-compliant debt securities, is among the most significant developments within Islamic finance in recent years. Banks are subjected to a wide array of financial, operational and business risks in the course of their operating within the stipulations of the various Shariah-compliant financing and intermediation contracts, many of which involve highly complex interdependency between, and overlapping of, different kinds of risks.

Islamic finance features another component additional to those of conventional finance: the willingness to consider social welfare in the financing of a project. This links the investor's return to the performance of the underlying asset.

Islamic finance contributes to the funding of green energy projects throughout the world such as low carbon emission coal plants, gas power plants, wind and solar power plants.

Islamic financing can be brought into power asset developments worldwide by presenting the opportunities offered by different important markets (the US, Europe, Australia and India).

In this part of the book we will be dealing with the various issues related to the power generation industry, such as the different types of power assets and their investment risks, the structure of liberalized power markets in the US and Europe and finally, the Islamic financing mechanisms which can be used to finance power assets through investment deals.

CHAPTER ONE

FUNDAMENTALS OF THE ISLAMIC FINANCIAL SYSTEM AND FINANCIAL INSTRUMENTS

MONDHER BELLALAH AND RACHA GHAYAD

Introduction

Interest is prohibited by Islam, and it was the aspiration of Muslims to make this ban a reality in their economies that, over time, led to the creation of a number of Islamic financial institutions worldwide. These institutions included Islamic commercial banks, Islamic investment companies, Takaful (Islamic insurance) companies, leasing and Mudaraba companies, and other non-banking financial institutions.

This chapter discusses some conceptual aspects of Islamic banking and highlights the approach of Muslim economists on controversial issues such as the status of credit money, bank money and deposit money and the principle of compensation.

We will study the fundamentals of Islamic banking, the key feature being the non-recourse to the application of interest without waiving the return on capital. The purpose of Islamic banking should in no way deviate from the objectives of Islamic economics, which seek consistently to achieve the values of justice and charity: "Yes, God commands justice and charity."

Section 1. Currency in the Islamic economic concept

1.1. Revitalizing the normative branch of economics

The unique system of Islamic economics, as observed by Muslim economists, works in a way which allows for the prospect of revitalizing the normative branch of political economics. The idea that prevails nowadays, of economics as a positive science, detached from values, is in fact a recent phenomenon. If the distinction between positive economics and normative economics dates from the second quarter of the 19th century, theoretical developments since that time have focused specifically on positive economics. Nowadays, when social economy movements, which have traditionally supported the normative branch in debates over the economy, are faltering, Islamic economics purports to be the main cause of the revitalization of this branch of the economy.

1.2. The theoretical religious base for prohibiting interest (Riba) in Islam

Islamic banks have developed their specific, interest-free systems by applying the rules of the Koran, the holy book of Muslims. All Islamic banks, wherever in the world they operate, work on the clear basic principle of the prohibition of interest, based on verses of the Koran, for example The Sura Al-Baqarah (Cow Sura), verse 275: "… Those who live on usury will not rise up before Allah except like those who are driven to madness by the touch of Satan." That is because they claim: "Trading is no different than usury, but Allah has made trading lawful and usury unlawful." This prohibition of interest also includes any purely financial speculation. Islam considers money a mere means of exchange, without intrinsic value. Since its circulation does not reflect a real economic activity, therefore, it would be immoral for it to yield any premium whatsoever. Islam does not distinguish between secular law and religious law. It follows that the economic and financial practices of Islamic banks must comply with these guidelines, while retaining some flexibility in order to adapt to new economic situations.

1.2.1. Riba (usury) and hoarding

The Islamic approach has its own conceptions of the value of capital and labor. Instead of a simple lender and borrower relationship, the Islamic financial system is based on a more equitable sharing of risk between the lender and the business owner. This practice follows a central tenet of the Koran, which forbids *Riba*, that is to say the charging of interest payments.

As with the vast majority of precepts of Islam, there are historical explanations for this prohibition. The economy of the Arabian Peninsula in the seventh century was based, in effect, on merchant city-states in a hostile environment. Because of their isolation, they often suffered from a lack of liquidity that meant usury and hoarding were favored. Islamic teachings were aimed at curbing these undesirable social phenomena, because if the interest rates charged to dealers moving from city to city were too high, it discouraged trading and considerably increased the cost of goods. Islam had to create the moral obligation to use money only for the purposes of production, for oneself and for the good of the community by investing in profitable businesses. What is meant by "profitable" in this case, though, is something which makes an indisputable positive contribution to the community, and does not depend solely on the capital market for resource allocation. Muslim economists have noted that, in the Western system, available funds go mostly to the borrowers with the best financial guarantees and do not necessarily benefit the projects that do the most for the welfare of the community. In other words, when investing, one should at least consider the communal value of the project rather than just the economic gain. Finally, charging interest reduces the supply of venture capital and thus hampers growth.

1.2.2. The role of profit

There are also other arguments that justify the principle of prohibiting interest. Thus, there is no question of financing loans, but rather, lenders are offered an active involvement in the petitioner's company, which, in turn, offers a share of future profits. This is typically an equity investment in the form of allocations or shares. The economic rationale of profit is therefore not only that it is an opportunity for redistribution, but also that it is an opportunity for the efficiency, economic stability and company growth of which profit is just a reflection. Simply funding with interest may be very unfair if only the entrepreneur suffers loss, or conversely, reaps a disproportionately large profit.

The principle of compensation: Regarding "the *foulous*" (the money), we find in two Hanafi jurists, Abu Yusuf and Muhammad bin al-Hassan Chibani, the principle of compensation. Indeed, after the introduction of foulous (based on copper), they lost much of their value, while gold and silver retained some stability. Turning to the issue, the two jurists have accepted the principle of compensation by offering to link to the debts contracted in foulous with their equivalent in gold on the day of the transaction. In this case, the debtor will repay the equivalent in gold of the borrowed foulous. Thus we can deduce that the compensation is in line with the spirit of justice and fairness commanded by the Holy Koran Although contemporary jurists acknowledge the principle, the fact remains that they refuse to use this verse in deductive analogy (*qiyas*), with the justification that the context differs. They believe that as today's paper currency has totally replaced gold and silver, no compensation is therefore authorized by an analogy about a bimetallist society. This position seems to us inconsistent with the principle of justice stated in the verse quoted above. In the system of the gold standard, the creditor is not financially harmed. In the current system, however, he can be jeopardized to the extent that paper money loses its value entirely, especially in underdeveloped countries. In addition, the difference in context mentioned by contemporary jurists seems very insignificant. In fact the foulous, just like paper money today, is already a substitute for gold and silver. The changing nature of the monetary system is not a valid argument for disregarding the principle of compensation. It certainly has not prevented some scholars of Islamic economics from accepting it, if under two conditions: that the proposed compensation is as fair as possible, and that it should in no way resemble the application of interest. The principle of justice applies in all cases; inflation, deflation or stability.

In the first case, the compensation must take into account the inflationary phenomenon: the creditor receives more monetary units than he has lent.

In the second case (although very rare in modern economies), he will receive less. In case of stability in the value of the currency, the creditor will receive exactly the same as the amount of the original loan. When we talk about compensation, no reference is made to the interest that is received by the creditor, regardless of the level of inflation. Research studies in this area are still in their infancy, so here we will simply present previously issued proposals.

A. Using the Islamic Dinar

This proposal suggests the use of a constant unit, conventionally called the Islamic Dinar, for futures and loans without interest (Qard Al Hassan). This unit is equal to one gram of gold. Issa (1985) proposes that debts are contracted on the basis of this monetary unit, linked, of course, to a certain quantity of gold, and that repayment is made on this basis. This proposal may extend to wages, salaries and pensions. It should be subject to intervention by monetary authorities to determine the value of the Islamic Dinar, although it does not materially exist.

B. Using a (strong) reference currency

The second proposal is to take as a reference not, as previously suggested, an Islamic Dinar, but an international currency that is as constant as possible (Issa, 1985). Then the same scenario is repeated as in the previous proposal. In place of the Islamic Dinar, the unit used by this institution (which would comprise 45 Muslim countries) is equivalent to one Special Drawing Right (S.D.R.) of the International Monetary Fund. To guard against fluctuations in the currencies of member countries, the granted loans would be denominated in Islamic Dinar and refundable.

However, the two proposals we have just described have some drawbacks. Gold and hard currencies are themselves subject to fluctuations. Sometimes, strong variables in decline may ultimately jeopardize the creditor even when inflation is above zero. Therefore, our proposal consists of taking as a reference not the price of gold, nor a single hard currency, but a set of international currencies; a change upwards in one of them will be offset by falls in others. We would use the median price, which would be relatively stable. The fact is, though, that however good one's intentions, it is almost impossible to create a perfect compensation system. In this regard, the Koran is clear: "Therefore, fear Allah as much as you can." (Holy Koran, 64, 16)

Finally, it is worth mentioning that the best remedy for the deterioration of the value of money is balanced economic development coupled with a sound and effective monetary policy. If these two objectives are not achieved, inflation will continue to eat away at the values of national currencies, and any proposed compensation will be merely a soothing ephemeral which does nothing to improve the fate of the economy in question, nor that of creditors.

Having presented various aspects of the Islamic concept of currency, we will now discuss how funds are mobilized and allocated to different sectors of the economy in the absence of interest rates.

1.2.3. Financial intermediation in the Islamic system

In the absence of interest rates, how does the remuneration of financial capital occur? What is the nature of financial intermediation in the Islamic system?

To answer these questions, it is necessary to introduce the famous principle of the sharing of profit and loss, or Profit and Loss Sharing (PLS).

This principle bases itself on very simple logic: since nobody can predict the future, why should financier and entrepreneur not agree on the sharing of the outcome? In the Islamic system, and in order to be fair, both parties are paid downstream. This principle, of sharing the results of the company, positive or negative, is at the root of the Islamic financial system. Financial intermediation in the Islamic system, whether on the part of the depositors or the borrowers, is guided by the application of the PLS principle. Depositors are treated as if they were shareholders of the bank and are therefore assured neither of any par value guarantee, nor of any predetermined return on their deposits. If the bank makes a profit, the depositor receives an allocation under the Mudaraba contract; on the other hand, if the bank suffers a loss, the depositor is required to share that loss, also in accordance with the Mudaraba contract, and will therefore receive a negative return.

In terms of deposits made singly or for non-investment purposes, the bank guarantees the nominal value of the deposit, but does not pay liabilities. Thus they are considered equivalent to demand deposits or sight deposits in a conventional banking system.

Deposits for investment purposes are the main source of funds for the Islamic bank, but they are more like shares in a company than term deposits. The only contractual agreement between the depositor and the bank is about the manner in which losses and profits must be distributed. The ratio of sharing profits or losses should be discussed between the bank and depositors at the start of the operation, and may be modified by mutual agreement during the operation. The same principle of sharing of profit and loss applies to the use of funds. There are two contracts that fully meet the requirements of Shariah law in this area; Mudaraba and Musharaka contracts.

Under a Mudaraba contract, the bank finances an entrepreneur who invests effort and knowledge, as well as bank funds, in a productive activity, in exchange for sharing a percentage of the achieved profits. The losses are borne exclusively by the financier (lender), while the entrepreneur (borrower) only loses the time and effort invested in the company. This type of contract is equally concerned with human capital and financial capital.

Section 2. The Islamic Banking System

2.1. Definition of Islamic bank

In the relevant contemporary literature, there are no specific definitions of Islamic banking terms or Islamic banking activities. Instead, there is a flexible approach to defining such establishments and their business. For example, the International Association of Islamic Banks has described Islamic banking as follows:

> "The Islamic bank implements, basically, a new banking concept because it rigorously abides by the rules of Islamic Shariah in the field of finances and other business transactions. Moreover, the bank operated in this way

should reflect Islamic principles in its operations. The bank should seek to establish an Islamic society; therefore, one of its primary goals is to deepen the religious spirit among the people."

This description does not provide an accurate definition of "the Islamic bank"; it is more focused on the objectives of an Islamic bank than anything else. Based on this, however, we can say that an Islamic bank is a company that acts as a financial intermediary between depositors or investors, depending on circumstances, and users of funds, as well as providing various other banking services. Therefore the functions of this bank are parallel to those of a conventional bank or one based on the interest rate, because both act as financial intermediaries. However, in conducting banking activities, an Islamic bank must adhere to certain Islamic standards as well as to prudent standards for banking operations. Thus it is now appropriate to examine the meaning of the term "Islamic banking activity". Again, in this context, there is no clear definition. The Islamic Law of Malaysia, promulgated in 1983, defines Islamic banking operations as "banking activities whose aims and operations do not involve any element which is not approved by the religion of Islam." It turns out that the term "Islamic banking activity" has not been properly defined and perhaps has even been rather neglected. However, a recent Malaysian law dealing with conventional banking provided a more complete, albeit somewhat open, definition of banking operations.

The previous discussion has led us to try in this chapter to provide definitions of the terms "Islamic banking" and "Islamic banking activity". In this regard, we can define an Islamic bank as a company or corporation authorized by the necessary authorities to carry out Islamic banking activities under the rules and principles of Shariah law.

Islamic banking activities, on the other hand, comprise the acceptance of deposits or investments from clients and the provision of financing facilities to customers (financial intermediation) as well as the provision of other services for clients within the framework of banking practices. Nevertheless, all these activities must conform to Shariah law.

This definition, as it appears in existing laws and statutes, does not explicitly cover the activities of an Islamic bank as an investment bank or as an institution involved in fund management. However, the recent developments in Islamic banking operations seem to suggest that Islamic banks will assume a broader role as universal banks in the future. This means that they may be involved in fund management, as well as in the production of paper money or commercial paper, due to the process of securitization. So it would be appropriate for an Islamic bank to take on the role of a universal bank, covering most of the financing and investment contracts.

In conventional banking operations, the intermediation function has become more limited because of disintermediation, and we can expect this trend to be followed in Islamic banking activities. In contrast, the undertaking of universal banking functions would be of great significance. Modern statutes on Islamic banking operations must therefore address the issue of defining and redefining Islamic banks as their roles and functions change.

The one element that is made explicit by this definition is that compliance with Shariah is the essence of an Islamic bank and its activities.

Before the actual creation of the first Islamic bank, they existed only as theoretical models developed by a number of thinkers and intellectual Muslims. Today, both theoretical contributions and their practical implementations have clarified the picture of Islamic banks. So what is an Islamic bank? How does it differ from a conventional bank?

Before defining an Islamic bank, it is best to give a brief description of conventional banking. This differs from one country to another. In Anglo-Saxon countries, commercial banks are dominant, while in Germany, Switzerland, the Netherlands and Japan, it is the universal bank that prevails. Consequently, a comparison between these two banking models becomes inevitable.

The commercial bank model is based on the pure financial intermediation model, in which banks mobilize savings for lending to businesses and individuals. They profit from the difference between the interest rates payable and receivable. They offer a range of banking services such as letters of credit and bonds. A portion of their profit comes from cheap money that they collect in the form of demand or sight deposits. They are prohibited from doing business, and their own capital is limited to a restricted part of net assets.

This partial reserve system authorizes them to create derived deposits, thus allowing them to multiply their resources inexpensively. However, the process of offering bank loans is subject to some problems that render it ineffective. Borrowers are generally better informed about their own operations than funders, so when acting as creditors, banks often face a high level of information asymmetry. Borrowers are in a position that allows them to hide information from banks; therefore, they can use the loaned money for purposes other than those reported to the bank, thus exposing the bank to unforeseen risks. They can also provide erroneous figures or fraudulently declare a state of bankruptcy. These problems are described as moral hazards. The fulfillment of guarantees given to banks that they will be repaid depends primarily on the effective use of funds loaned for the agreed purposes in order to produce sufficient cash flow for covering debts. Even at a government level, several countries have been known to borrow billions of dollars and use them for unproductive purposes, leading to serious debt problems. Banks may ensure proper use of loaned funds by timely controls, but this does not appeal to customers and often results in additional expenditure, which goes against the goal of profitability. Therefore, the purpose for which the credit is allocated is of minimal importance to commercial banks. It is the credit rating or creditworthiness of the debtor which plays the most important role.

In contrast, universal banks are allowed to take equity capital, and to conduct business and insurance transactions, that go beyond the operations of a commercial bank. In comparison with commercial banks, universal banks are better equipped to overcome the asymmetry of information. They finance their customers through a mixture of *prêtage* (lending) and preferred equity. The equity stake enables universal banks to take places on the boards of directors of the funded companies, allowing them to monitor closely the use of funds which, in return, are offered at a lower cost. Reduction of control costs mitigates business failures and improves the efficiency of the banking system.

Adhering to this logic, many economists have shown their preference for universal banking because it is more efficient. Commercial banks are allowed to trade only up to their net worth. However, we cannot apply the same rule to Islamic banks, because as discussed above, several modes of Islamic financing are suitable to trading activities. It is possible for Islamic banks to fund business ventures involving the purchase of goods on credit or with fixed assets. These companies will buy these goods and assets to be sold on agreed terms to their customers. As such, this results in an equity stake. Thus we can say that Islamic banks resemble much more closely the model of universal banking than that of commercial banking. They are required to have a variety of ways to provide funding, including equity stakes. They can also develop financial packages by combining a form of equity participation with other modes of Islamic financing. Even when the formulae of trade or indebtedness are used, financing remains closely related to the real sector. The customer's creditworthiness remains relevant, but it is the productivity and profitability of the project that prevails in importance.

The comparison mentioned above leads us to the following definition of an Islamic bank: an Islamic bank is an institution which receives deposits and carries out all banking activities, with the exception of loan transactions and loans with interest. Its liabilities consist of funds raised in the form of Mudaraba or Wakala (agent contracts). It also accepts deposits on demand/at sight that are considered interest-free loans, from customers to the bank, and therefore they are guaranteed. Assets are constituted by funds offered on the basis of sharing profits and losses, or on the basis of indebtedness, in accordance with Shariah principles. These assets belong in the category of investment deposits. Furthermore, equity stakes and the financing of current assets (merchandise stock) and fixed assets also constitute an integral part of Islamic banking operations.

The Islamic bank shares its net earnings with its depositors depending on the date and in proportion with the amount of each deposit. Applicants must be informed from the outset of the profit sharing agreement they are entering into with the bank.

2.2. The history and development of Islamic banks

There are numerous indications of the current importance of Islamic Finance (IF). The value of the assets of Islamic Finance Institutions (IFI) was about five billion U.S. dollars in 1985 (Iqbal, 1997). Now, at the dawn of the third millennium, it is estimated at 100 billion U.S. dollars, which, for comparison, is equal to nearly a quarter of the external debt of developing countries (World Bank, 2000).

More than one hundred Islamic Finance Institutions are in operation (Khan, 1986). Most were created in the second half of the 1970s, predominantly in Muslim countries such as Saudi Arabia, Bahrain, Bangladesh, Brunei, Egypt, the United Arab Emirates (UAE), Jordan, Malaysia, Senegal, Sudan, Turkey and Lebanon. Although oil capital supports economic activities, and hence banking and financial operations, the structure of capital in Islamic banks does not depend on public initiative, but on private initiative.

2.2.1. The first experience of a rural savings bank

The idea of an Islamic bank dates back to the 1940s. The first Islamic bank was founded in 1948 in Pakistan; this was the Muslim Commercial Bank, an enterprise which was quickly extinguished (Quershi, 1967).

The second attempt at founding an Islamic bank took place in 1963 in Egypt with the establishment of the Mit-Ghamer rural savings bank in the Nile delta, inspired by a German savings bank. The operation of this bank had been adapted to the environment and the population; basically, rural and religious. Created by Al Nagar, the Mit-Ghamer was a savings bank that used financial techniques with particulars based on the principle of dual partnership; partnership between depositors and the bank and partnership between the bank and entrepreneurs. This principle was a result of the need to conform to the Islamic principle of avoiding usury. The funds, collected by the bank and corresponding to liabilities, were deposited either in savings accounts, opened with a minimum of five *piaster*, which received no interest and could be withdrawn at any time (Arab Republic of Egypt, 1972), or in investment accounts, opened with a minimum of one Egyptian pound, which produced a revenue proportional both to the size of the deposit and the profits made by the bank.

As for loans related to balance sheet assets, these were also of two kinds: common interest-free loans, granted to poor and middle class people, each of which was capped at two hundred Egyptian pounds and repayable in two years, and association loans that allowed the bank to join in a contractor's plans and subsequently to receive between 10% and 50% of the profits (and losses) achieved. These loans could be worth up to two thousand Egyptian pounds, and also had a maturity of two years.

Something which helped give the bank a reputation for legitimacy was the creation of the Social Fund for Alms, the *zakat*[1], contributions to which were calculated at 2.5% of the capital, and donations from which were given to the most needy amongst the general population through channels identified by various criteria specific to Islamic law (Seddik, 1986).

2.2.2. The institutionalization of the Islamic bank

2.2.2.1. The creation of the Nasser Social Bank in Egypt

The Nasser Social Bank in Egypt, which was the first State Islamic bank, was created in 1972. The bank was placed under the supervision of the Egyptian Ministry of Social Affairs; its activities did not follow the logic of profitability of the type generally used in banking. It escaped the control of the Central Bank and the various preventative rules imposed on other banks. Its goal was to help establish an Islamic microeconomy, in close coordination with the State and its other institutions. It had to be a practical instrument of state policy vis-à-vis the urban poor and small

[1] Zakat, or alms, constitutes the third pillar of Islam. It is a deed of worship of the financial category which purifies the soul and heightens its merits, as it purifies assets and increases wealth. It is not a morsel offered to the poor by the rich, but a right due to the poor from the assets of the rich: "Deduct a part on their assets for their purification and uplift their souls," says the Koran. It also says: "Perform prayer and pay Zakat."

entrepreneurs who were looking for means of production. In order to become that, it had to promote the two symbolic elements of such a policy, i.e. free social loans and alms. Unlike the Mit-Ghamer bank, the Nasser Social Bank did not set a minimum amount for opening accounts. The success of the Nasser Social Bank in terms of its social base, its amount of savings and the development of a small private sector allowed the Egyptian state to make a successful recovery from the experiences of the time of the Mit-Ghamer bank. This recovery took place in the context of a growing influence of religious discourse on civil society.

2.2.2.2. Generalization to the Gulf countries

The idea of Islamic banking attracted several economists and businessmen from Saudi Arabia, and we mention to this effect Prince Muhammed El-Faisal and Saleh Kamel. The first, considered the great promoter of Islamic finance, gave his name to the first private Islamic bank in Egypt.

Immediately, the ministries of foreign affairs and finance in Gulf countries and the peninsula formed a special committee, responsible for the preparation of joint agreements on the establishment and operation of Islamic banks. These agreements made possible the launch of the Islamic Development Bank in 1974/1975, which is the only Islamic bank supported by public authorities.

In the same year, 1975, the Dubai Islamic Bank (DIB) was established in the United Arab Emirates (UAE) on the initiative of businessman Said Loutha[2]. Its capital is primarily private, with the authorities in Dubai and Kuwait having taken just a minority stake in it. The bank operates primarily as a merchant bank, offering its depositors/investors equity investments in industrial and real estate projects, and remuneration based on the principle of sharing profits and losses as required by Islamic law.

In 1981, Muhammed El-Faisal founded the Dar Al Mal Al Islami (DMI) group, the first international network of Islamic banks. The Faisal Banks of Egypt and Sudan belong to this group. The Faisal network banks did not want to be confined to the role of merchant bank; they wanted to target a more diversified clientele, to whom they offered a range of operations and services comparable to that offered by conventional banks.

During the same period, the Saudi businessman Saleh Kamel created several Islamic investment banks. Later, these banks were part of what became the Al-Baraka Investment and Development Company group,

---

[2] The founder of the Islamic Bank in Dubai; he is among the people interviewed in Dubai as part of our case study.

which constitutes the other major international network of Islamic financial institutions.

In some countries, Islamic banks carry out their business side by side with conventional banks. Some Islamic banks, within and outside of the Muslim world, have opened branches and automatic teller machines (ATMs) or launched funds that offer Islamic banking and financial services.

2.3. Founding principles of the creation of Islamic banks

We will now deal with the founding principles that guided the establishment of the Islamic banking system, as well as other factors underlying the establishment of Islamic banks and their operations. To this end we will make a brief introduction of the characteristics of Islamic financial institutions.

The most interesting aspect of this research lies in shedding light upon the Islamic banking industry, which is an emerging and still little-known sector. The purpose of this section is to explain the basic elements of the Islamic banking system, and we will be discussing Islamic finance, its foundations, its theory and its reality.

"No profits, no sacrifice,"; "Money cannot create money on its own without the action of physical capital and labor … etc.". This is how some of the main players in Islamic finance have summarized it – this is the philosophy of Islamic banking.

Definitions of key concepts addressed by Islamic financial institutions are necessary, as well as definitions of traditionally used contracts. We shall also consider the implementation of these principles by Islamic banks. The major advantage of Islamic finance is its placement of equal importance on human capital as on financial capital. Thus the banks themselves, whose role is limited to existing as an outlet for savings and developing investments, systematically associate with their clients in two ways: Mudaraba and Musharaka.

The conventional banking model is based on the principle of interest rates, whereby it borrows, at a certain interest rate, from individuals who make their deposits at the bank, and it lends money and capital, at a more significant rate of interest, to individuals as well as to production and trading corporations. This model is inconsistent with the fundamental principles of Islamic banks for two reasons: the first concerns the practice of charging interest and the second is related to the mode of distribution of profits within conventional banking, which favors capital providers over workers.

In Islamic banks, we observe two characteristic principles. The first is respect for the prohibition of interest in all banking operations, which is the main constraint they face. Operations must not, under any circumstances, directly or indirectly, include a fixed or predetermined remuneration comparable to interest or Riba, because Islam prohibits Riba, an Arabic word meaning both usury and interest. The prohibition of Riba features heavily in Islamic law, and is the foundation of Islamic finance. Undoubtedly, the prohibition of interest in the context of the contemporary world significantly reduces an Islamic bank's margin of maneuver, and will affect the nature of its financial products and the structures necessary for the launching of its products.

The second principle is the application of stake or risk-taking, i.e. the sharing of profits and losses between lender and contractor. This principle involves the bank in non-banking activities (industrial, tourist, real estate, etc). It is supposed to provide the bank with a substitute for interest. According to the Islamic approach, the party that lends money for commercial and industrial purposes claims a share of the profit, because he becomes joint owner of the share capital and the business risk. He is a partner in the company and not a creditor. The remuneration of the lender should be proportional to the share of wealth created by his money.

To ensure compliance with the first principle, a religious oversight council should exist in the Islamic bank to ensure the compliance of banking activities and products, and the integrity of transactions in terms of their Islamic character.

With respect to the prohibition of Riba in banking operations, according to Islamic principles, banking operations should not in any way, directly or indirectly, involve a previously determined remuneration comparable to interest, or *rias*. The bank does not invest in activities that are considered immoral, such as commercial banks, insurance companies, distilleries, delicatessen businesses, financial instruments such as derivatives and especially options, futures and other forward contracts because of their speculative nature. At the structural level, this results in the creation of an entity whose mission is to ensure the compliance and integrity of banking transactions in terms of their Islamic character. Therefore, to ensure compliance with Islamic teachings, Islamic banks had to create new institutions. The Shariah council, whose role is to examine the transactions of the bank just like a credit committee and to deliver quietus with regard to noncompliance, is composed of doctors of Islamic law. This council may also suggest adaptations to the financial structure of transactions, irrespective of their nature, rendering them compatible with Shariah when they are not at first found to be so.

Islamic banks choose the members of this council from among Islamic jurisprudence experts who also have competence and knowledge in the field of banking and finance. The religious council has a very important mission within the Islamic bank concerning the compliance of banking activities with Islamic laws. They give their opinion on specific questions or current operations. The work of this council is to conduct a "religious audit" and draft an annual report certifying that the operations and activities of the bank have been carried out in accordance with religious precepts, and that the remuneration of bank deposits has indeed resulted from their direct investment according to the principle of participation in real economic projects.

The mission of the Islamic bank is considered a real service rendered to depositors, investors and developers, and remunerated to a fair value. The objective mission of the bank, besides the goal of building the economy through the operations of participation and partnership, is to facilitate participation, which is every Muslim's duty and required by Islamic law. Indeed, a bank under state supervision commits the funds deposited in its accounts to sectors of public authority. The process of capital accumulation is characterized by its social aspect, benefitting as it does all the dynamic forces of society. Furthermore, the Islamic bank should be limited to its essential role of an outlet for saving and investment planning. The Islamic bank will not lend its funds to its clients, but systematically associates with them to undertake and carry out satisfactory economic projects. (Nienhaus, 1982)

2.3.1. The Islamic bank: A partner bank

The principle of sharing profits and losses determines the behavior of the bank towards debtors. More than just a provider of capital, the bank becomes an active partner, with the right of to scrutinize the management of the financed company because its fate is directly linked to the performance of the latter. Thus the bank does not transfer to the company only money, but also expertise and advice. In other words, it provides funding and services: management consulting, information, new products, etc. It is clear that this kind of service is currently offered by traditional banks, but it is motivated by competition and the desire to profit from the borrower. In the Islamic system, the bank offers its services in order to help the partner company to perform better. As such, the bank/corporation relationship is a much closer one. The bank is not a passive funder, interested only in the reimbursement of its loan, but a partner, entitled to profits and even sharing in losses. This scrutiny on behalf of the banks may be interpreted as a disadvantage for entrepreneurs, who may see a reduction in their chances to dispose freely of borrowed funds, however, this is not always the case, since the intervention of the bank does not aim to replace the company's management but to consolidate it. In many cases, young entrepreneurs need advice and technical assistance from the bank. The intervention of the bank positively affects the decision-making process at the corporate level, as long as the bank's objectives converge with those of the company.

It is also worth mentioning that Islamic modes of financing require a rigor in keeping the accounts of operations carried out by corporations which is of vital importance in minimizing the risk of fraud. In the long term, a corporation that continues to produce bad results will be denied renewed financing. Long experience of working with and in the capitalist banking system absolutely does not mean that the importance of moral factors is relegated to second place. In fact, even experienced funders frequently stress the moral factor as the most important criterion in evaluating credit.

2.3.2. Characteristics of Islamic financial institutions

According to Islamic economic theory, which is essentially religious, the major objectives of economic activity are:

a. The increase of wealth, defined as the growth of productive capital, the engine of this growth being entrepreneurship
b. An increase in employment, which is fostered by the participation of all parties concerned in the establishment and good operation of production projects
c. Equitable distribution of wealth and income, the latter being reinforced by the compulsory practice of zakat or alms
d. The absence of waste, for example in the form of hoarding

The principles of Islamic finance, which arise more or less from these objectives, are (Qureshi, 1967; Khan and Mirakhor, 1987; Dar and Presley, 1999; Abdul Gafoor, 2000):

a. Profit (as determined ex post) as an expression of the company's performance should be encouraged
b. Interest is prohibited, and consequently, usury is also prohibited because it can be established ex ante and without reference to the aforementioned performance. As such, the practice of usury does not encourage the fund provider to be interested in the objective of

the investment that finances its savings. The danger then is that the latter may perform activities that produce goods whose consumption is condemned in Islam (wine, etc.) or even activities of a speculative nature, which is illegal, such as selling fish before fishing has occurred, selling wheat before the harvest, and gaming. In other words, the mere fact that a reserve of money has remained untouched for a certain amount of time does not justify a reward in the form of interest payments. Rewards cannot be associated with the passage of time, but must be related to the nature of the investment project, which is the case with profit.

c. Of course, there is also a risk attached to the profits, as there may be loss, but as the profit expresses the performance of the corporation, it is a lawful risk.
d. Since the supplier of funds, the investor, has the moral obligation to know how the funding he provides is being used, the profit (or loss) should be equally distributed between himself and the petitioner of funds or contractor.

Accordingly, the essential idea of establishing Islamic banks and financial institutions is to provide financial and banking services compliant with Islamic ethics. The establishment of Islamic banks is based on the prohibition of interest and its corollary, and on participation in the profits and losses system which, in the eyes of its promoters, rejects arbitrary rules and inequality in economic relations between individuals (Al Misri, 1975). This is how Islamic banks and financial institutions, whose ambition is to render the economic game respectful of this principle, came about.

The emphasis on equity affects the very nature of the banking techniques utilized and necessitates the existence of a service responsible for evaluating projects. The peculiarity of the funding methods of Islamic financial institutions lies in two aspects:

a. They encourage a cooperative system of participation that, according to its supporters, ensures better profitability and efficient fund allocation
b. They use methods of funding almost unknown to traditional banks and very rarely experienced by SMEs

The partnership system requires both parties to jointly assume all risks in sharing losses as well as profits, hence both parties must take into account the objectives assigned to them, which can be summarized in three points:

a. Promote and encourage respect for Islamic principles, laws and traditions in the world of finance and banking and analogous fields of activity through the creation and management of investment Mudaraba
b. Provide modern financial services to all Muslims in the region to enable them to conduct financial transactions while meeting the requirements of Islamic Shariah law and without violating the Koranic prohibition of Riba
c. Assist the Islamic community of the region in the collection and utilization of the resources necessary for true economic development while respecting Islamic principles

Islamic banks are generally established as anonymous companies with capital which is variable but often very high, supported mostly by the founding members, or by shareholders, generally Muslims, who register by signing a document called the Constituency Deed. A well-known example is Dar Al Mal Al Islami, a trust governed by the laws of the Commonwealth of the Bahamas and enjoying the tax benefits granted by that state.

The income of a bank in the Islamic financial intermediation system equals the difference between the money gained by the bank from corporations through profit and loss sharing and that allocated to savers.

Banks may use the formula of direct investment and thereby recover all profits. However, this approach has its limitations, since the vocation of a bank is primarily credit intermediation, i.e. the collection of the surplus credit of some parties on the one hand and the funding of unprofitable parties on the other hand.

This shows that the nature of financial intermediation in the Islamic system differs significantly from that which characterizes the conventional system. In the Islamic system, the bank continues to play the role of a provider of funds, but is not only interested in the guarantees offered by the borrower, instead becoming a true partner in the financed corporation. This is what we shall discover in the following section.

Section 3. Institutions and Mechanisms of the Islamic banking system

In this section, we will study various formulae that offer alternatives to a system of interest, before discussing the institutional side of the Islamic banking system.

3.1. Alternative formulae to the system of interest

We have seen that Islamic banks have their own vision for the raising and investment of capital. Existing Islamic banks operate in accordance with the principle of prohibition of interest and the allowances of the principle of Profit and Loss Sharing (PLS). However, the relationship between funders and the users of their funds is clearly defined in very specific contracts, which will be presented in this section. At the outset, it is worth mentioning that it was the differing natures of various financing and investment transactions which gave rise to each particular type of contract.

Despite their diversity, these contracts have in common the sharing of risk between the two parties; the party that relinquishes its funds and the one that utilizes them. The specific nature of each contract allows and facilitates a different mode of financing.

The remuneration of the Islamic bank: Within the framework of a conventional bank, remuneration is primarily based on the difference between the lending interest rates, earned through exploitation, and the borrowing interest rates, paid on account of the expenses incurred. As such, the role of the bank may be summed up as that of a trader who speculates on money and credit.

As we mentioned earlier, the Islamic banking system is based on the principle of prohibition of interest rates. So the question that arises at this point is the following: how does the remuneration of financial capital occur in the absence of interest? What is the nature of financial intermediation in the Islamic system?

To answer these questions, it is convenient to resort to the principle of sharing profit and loss, or Profit and Loss Sharing (PLS).

3.2. Financial sources of Islamic banks

In addition to its own capital, an Islamic bank has the typical external sources of any bank: different types of deposits.

3.2.1. Proper funds

As in the case of a conventional bank, the proper funds of an Islamic bank are made up of three categories:

a. Funds for general banking risks or sufficient funds

b. The basic proper funds which include the usual elements: capital, reserves and retained profits
c. Supplementary proper funds such as non-repayable grants, donations or bequests

3.2.1.1. The capital of an Islamic bank

The Islamic bank is considered a public law institution, with the same aims as merchant and investment banks: its capital must reach a certain level. Depending on the legal status chosen by the bank (partnership, cooperative, or joint-stock company) its capital can be accumulated either by shares or by issuing shares. This capital is gathered by the guarantors and divided into shares, the number of which is strictly limited in accordance with the requirements of Islamic law, which fears a concentration of wealth in the hands of a limited number of shareholders.

3.2.1.2. Provisions (Sufficient Funds)

With regard to conventional banks, bad loans can cause the most important provisions to become diminished. In Islamic banking, the establishment of reserves is of primary importance. As Islamic banking operates on the basis of profit sharing by providing risk capital, varied provisions must be made and added to regularly in order to cope with any eventuality.

3.2.1.3. Retained profits

A portion of achieved profit is allocated to capital accounts and can be used, along with the contributions of reported reserves, in the cash flow (self-financing) operations of the bank.

3.2.2. Islamic bank deposits

The Islamic bank offers three distinguishable kinds of deposit: deposits on demand/at sight, which serve to pay transactions, also known as current account deposits, savings deposits called Profit and Loss Sharing or simply PLS deposits, and term deposits referred to as return bearing deposits, which are invested on the basis of profit sharing.

3.2.2.1. Accounts on demand/at sight and current accounts

Just as in traditional banks, these accounts are not remunerated. They are managed in much the same way as those of other banks; the holders of these accounts are provided with a checkbook and can, at any time, claim their money.

Withdrawals cannot exceed the amount in the account, however, depending on the relationship between the bank and its customers, some account holders may benefit from interest-free credit facilities.

3.2.2.2. Savings deposits

In all their various forms, these deposits are of limited relevance in Islamic banks. They represent a transitory stage between current and investment accounts.

3.2.2.3. Investment deposits

When depositors make time or term deposits in a conventional bank, the bank is then indebted to them and responsible for the entrusted amounts and for paying customers interest at a rate previously fixed and declared. The Islamic bank does not guarantee a fixed income in advance; it acts as a placement and investment agent by investing these deposits in its chosen projects. In cases when profit is achieved, it is divided between the bank and the depositor according to a distribution key defined in advance. In cases of loss, and depending on the nature of the investment account, the bank may be relieved of any responsibility and the losses borne solely by the depositor/investor (Khan, 1986).

There are two kinds of term deposits:

Earmarked accounts

These accounts are created for customers who require that their money be invested in specific projects. Under these conditions, the account holders are the sole receivers of the results of these investment projects. Although the operation may be advantageous for the holders of these accounts, it is clear that, in case of loss, it can be offset by profits from other operations of the bank. Thus we can describe the holders of these accounts as risk takers.

Non-allocated term deposits

These accounts are the most commonly used by Islamic banks. In general, depositors, anxious to save their money, do not bother to expose themselves to unnecessary risk. Funds deposited in these accounts are used in various investment activities. They form a common fund that allows the bank to finance its various operations. However, in accordance with their fundraising policy, Islamic banks make available to the public a variety of short-, medium- and long-term accounts. Banks usually set a minimum amount below which it is not possible to open a long-term account. The remuneration of these accounts is obviously not carried out in the same way as that of others. The longer the duration, the more significant the remuneration. It is worth mentioning at this point that the bank is free to set different rates of return, a practice consistent with the principles of Islamic Shariah. Generally speaking, banks use this remuneration policy to encourage long-term investment, which is in turn capable of promoting economic development.

In addition to the contribution of the bank's shareholders, which may be public or private, funds collected through the three categories of account we have just described are the main resources of Islamic banks.

3.2.3. Social funds

These funds are collected under the legal and official alms commonly known as zakat which, according to the precepts of religion, is due on all held capital, investments and livestock as well as real estate, agricultural and commercial revenues. These funds are deposited into a special and autonomous account called a Zakat and Social Work account. Islamic banks manage this account entirely independently from other accounts. The bank distributes the funds collected in this account to the poor, the needy and the indebted.

3.3. The raising (mobilization) of funds by Islamic banks

Once funds are collected, the Islamic bank has a second important mission: the utilization of these funds in viable projects. Its financial intermediary position is that of a lender or a provider of funds, called on to finance various sectors of the economy.

How are funds raised (mobilized) and allocated to different sectors of the economy in the absence of interest rates?

According to the philosophical concept of Islamic banking, the bank's activities should be based on investment operations, which are intended to provide the bank with the necessary revenues for the production of these funds. These transactions are effectively accomplished by means of a financing contract by association (Mudaraba), a contract of association with participation (Musharaka) or a purchase-resale contract (Mudaraba).

In addition, the intervention sectors of the Islamic bank finance all sectors of the economy, provided they conform to Shariah. Islamic laws do not allow investments in certain activities that are prohibited, such as insurance companies, typical commercial banks, gaming or *Maisir*, distilleries, delicatessen businesses, financial instruments such as derivatives and especially options, futures and other future contracts because of their speculative nature (Shariah considers the uncertainty regarding these contracts illegal); naturally, this fundamentally limits the financial products that can be developed, as well as the corporate and business strategies of Islamic banks.

In the Mudaraba contract, the bank finances entrepreneurs who invest their effort and knowledge, as well as bank funds, in a productive activity, in exchange for a percentage of the profits. Any losses are borne exclusively by the financier (lender). As for the entrepreneur (borrower), he only loses the time and effort he has invested in the company. This type of contract treats the human capital and the financial capital involved in the project as equally valuable.

The Musharaka mode of financing involves several funders. All parties (entrepreneur, bank and other associates) invest in varying proportions, and the profits and losses are shared among them according to their respective financial contributions. If the division of results cannot be achieved, as with consumer credits or the finance of working capital at very short maturity, the banks have other methods of funding such as the Mudaraba contract, the *Baî as-Salam*[3], the *Baî bi Tadjil*, the *Ijara* or lease financing, the *Qard al-Hassan*, and others recently developed by Islamic financial institutions.

---

[3] The Salam may be defined as a sale contract under which the merchandise is delivered differently. Therefore, unlike under the Murabaha, the bank does not act as seller on credit of the merchandise acquired, but as acquirer with payment in cash of merchandise that shall be delivered to him by installment. The rules of Shariah prohibit in principle any commercial transaction whose objective is non-existent at the time of its conclusion. However, some commercial practices, although not compliant with this condition, are tolerated in view of their necessity in the lives of the people. This is the case of Salam sale which is authorized by the Prophet in the Hadith: "The one who makes the Salam, let him do it in a known size, a known weight and for a specified deadline."

3.3.1. The Mudaraba or work financing or "Passive Partner"

From a linguistic perspective, the Arabic word Mudaraba originated in the word "al-Dharb", which means moving on land, for travel or for business. In fact, there are two meanings in Koranic verses (4, 101) and (73, 20).

Mudaraba is also synonymous with the Arabic term "al-Kiradh" which means the divestiture of capital in order to benefit a third party.

The term Mudaraba is the word most commonly used by the people of Iraq, while in the Arabian Peninsula, the term al-Khirad is used instead. We use the term Mudaraba because it is the term used in intellectual circles, particularly among Muslim economists and bankers.

3.3.1.1. Definition of Mudaraba in banking

The Mudaraba is a consent reached between two parties, one, the financier or owner of capital, providing capital, and the other, the Mudareb, providing the work. The profit is shared in a ratio determined at the time of signing the contract. Of course, the parties each do not have some input on deciding the ratio, but an amount nor a percentage of capital is specified in the contract. It is left to the discretion of the parties according to the complexity of the task undertaken by the Mudareb.

If, after use of the funds, the transaction does not generate profits, the financier will have lost his capital, while the Mudareb will have lost his time and effort, and he is not permitted to try to make some gain by taking the capital of his partner.

The Mudaraba is a form of contract in Islamic law. Traditionally, it is signed by two people; the first person is one who has capital he wants to grow. This person is described as *Rabalmal* (owner of capital). The second person is the one who possesses professional qualifications and intellectual qualities; in a nutshell, the know-how. This person is called the Mudareb (the agent). To avoid the prohibited interest rate, Islam offers these two people, the owner of capital and the agent, the possibility of joining together under a legal contract, which is the Mudaraba.

It is a partnership agreement between two parties: the first, the owner of capital, provides all the capital and the second, the agent, provides the know-how. The Mudareb will manage and monetize the capital. The results will be distributed between the two parties at a predetermined percentage, which has to be based on the practical benefit of the operation. The principle is that loss is calculated on capital and profit is determined as customarily arranged. This is possible as long as there is no negligence from the Mudareb, because if that is the case, the latter may be held responsible for a larger part than is proportional, or all, of the losses.

In authorizing the sharing of the Mudareb in profits, and preventing him from bearing too much of any losses, the fouqaha, Muslim jurists, are instrumental in outlining the laws upon which the Mudaraba contract is based, because the owner of the capital's expected benefit is in the form of the remuneration of his capital, while that of the Mudareb is the funding of and assistance in his work. In other words, in case of loss, the Mudareb cannot withdraw anything in return for his effort, and so he will have lost the time and effort he has invested in the company. Under the Mudaraba contract, he is considered a partner and therefore earns revenue only on the basis of achieved profits. If he chooses to receive a salary, he is considered a wage-earner and if that is the case, a Mudaraba contract is no longer appropriate.

The Mudareb, who by definition does not have sufficient financial resources, may not be asked to financially bear part of the loss. This is required only under the Musharaka contract, where the enterprising party also owns part of the capital, and is thus expected to bear a part of the loss that is in proportion with his capital contribution.

3.3.1.2. Conditions for Mudaraba

Like any other form of contract, the Mudaraba is lawful only if certain clauses are met.

3.3.1.2.1. Terms of the contracting parties

The contractors must be in good mental condition, otherwise the contract is declared null and void. It is not required that both sides are Muslim.

3.3.1.2.2. Conditions relating to capital

For the Mudaraba contract to be valid, the invested capital must meet certain conditions including:

A – Determination of the amount of capital

The amount of capital must be known by both parties in advance, otherwise it will be difficult to calculate the profits before any incurred costs are taken into account. Knowledge of the invested capital also helps protect the contracting parties against the risk of conflict or *Gharar*[4].

B – The capital must be in monetary form

However, some fouqaha, or Muslim jurists, have relaxed this rule by accepting other forms of capital (physical stock, for example) as long as it will not complicate the calculation of results.

C – Payment of capital must occur at the time of signing the contract so as to enable the Mudareb to initiate his activities

D – The capital may be in the form of debt to the Mudareb

If these conditions are not met, the contract is considered illegal by all fouqaha without exception. Some Muslim jurists refuse to allow the mixing of capital and collected investment, on the grounds that this contract, Mudaraba, is a unilateral contract between a provider of funds and a speculator. They recommend that funds intended to finance a single project should originate from a single person. According to them, the combination of capitals may create a situation of joint ownership, which is more likely to make it difficult to share the profit fairly among all investors. Thanks to the mediation of the Islamic bank, however, this opposition is moderate.

3.3.1.2.3. Conditions for profits

In the Mudaraba contract, profits represent the earnings of the parties, and exact amounts are known only a posteriori. So in order to eliminate any possibility of disagreement, the fouqaha require that certain conditions relating to benefits are satisfied:

a. Determination of the benefit sharing rate occurs upstream and not downstream.
b. The sharing rate on achieved profits should in no way, directly or indirectly, refer to the invested capital, because the Mudaraba amount is based primarily, if not exclusively, on profits.
c. The agreement must be for a fixed amount, even if that amount is modified by the realization of profits.
d. The agreement of the two parties may be accompanied by additional conditions, aside from the benefits owing to each party.

[4] The prohibition of Gharar is because, as speculation, it introduces uncertainty and risks.

However, neither party may demand the provision of services that are usually billable for free.

3.3.1.2.4. Conditions relating to the contract

For the legality of the contract to be guaranteed, the nature of the project must be clearly defined in writing, and it must be signed by the provider of funds and the contractor. Any contract risks being deemed void if it relates to the production or trade of goods and services whose consumption is forbidden for Muslims. The contractors would in this case be entitled to terminate the contract and their association. This termination must occur in the presence of both parties and before the entrepreneur commences work. If one of the contractors disappears, the contract is automatically cancelled.

3.3.1.3 The practical obstacles

Although the formula of the Mudaraba may be considered a viable alternative to the system of interest rates that links a conventional bank with its depositors, the experience of Islamic banks has revealed that there are some practical obstacles which require adequate solutions. One of these challenges is the recognition of the benefits due to depositors. Traditional banks consider interest payments a financial burden and therefore they are deducted from net income and thereby not taxable. A second problem concerns the issue of insurance for Mudaraba funds. The fouqaha do not require the Mudareb to insure the funds he receives, unless he misuses them.

Is it not too risky for banks to advance funds without getting any guarantee?

This may be one reason why banks do not, in practice, resort very often to Mudaraba, generally preferring the Murabaha, where the risks incurred are minimal. Although the opinion of Sami Hamoud, i.e. that the Mudareb should be required to provide guarantees in exchange for the offered funds, has not been enthusiastically received by Muslim jurists, it is imperative to find a solution that will protect depositors and banks against anything which may lead to negligence and laxity manifesting in the debtor's actions. One way or another, it is necessary to develop this notion of "institutional *Fiqh*" if we really want to put the rules and principles of Shariah into practice.

3.3.1.4 Use of the Mudaraba by the Islamic bank

The Mudaraba is used by the Islamic bank:

a. as contract between a client depositor and the bank
b. as a contract between the bank and a Mudareb

3.3.1.4.1. The Mudaraba between a client depositor and an Islamic bank

Under their contract, the client depositor, the contributor of funds, is the Rabalmal, and the Islamic bank, with its market experience and the competence of its staff, is the provider of the know-how and so becomes the Mudareb. Therefore the relationship that binds the Islamic bank to its customers, especially those who have deposits to be made, will be based on a Mudaraba contract. In other words, the remuneration that goes to the depositing client is not interest at the rate set by the authorities, but instead, as agreed between the bank and its client, it will be based on the shared results of the Islamic Bank (IB). The bank employs all its resources (capital plus deposits) in investments of all kinds and shares the profits and losses of these investments with the depositors. Thus it is in compliance with the terms of profit and loss sharing.

3.3.1.4.2. The Mudaraba between Islamic bank and Mudareb

The Islamic bank seeks clients with the know-how, and lacking the capital, to enter with them into a Mudaraba contract in which the bank becomes the Rabalmal and the client becomes the Mudareb. The Mudaraba covers several kinds of professions and Mudareb may be craftsmen and doctors. The Mudaraba helps develop creativity and encourages innovation because the Mudareb is not exposed to any risk. In reality, bank/Mudareb relationships under Mudaraba are a very small proportion of the working relationships of most Islamic banks. For example, it represented only 3% of all the funding of the Faisal Islamic Bank of Sudan in 1983. On a practical level, the Mudaraba is used primarily in client depositor/Islamic bank relationships, and only incidentally in bank/Mudareb relationships. In the latter case, financing by Musharaka is preferred.

3.3.2. The Musharaka

The Musharaka is the association of a source of capital with another source of capital, with the aim of sharing the profits and losses that may result from their joint enterprise. It is based on the concept of participation (used in a very broad sense of the term) and the principle of Profit and Loss Sharing (PLS) also applies.

In this type of contract, the client and the bank, for example, jointly participate in the financing of an operation and jointly assume the risk in proportion with their participation. This can be done either by a cash contribution from both parties or by a contribution in kind by either party. The losses are distributed between the client and the bank on the basis of each party's contribution. Regarding the sharing of profits, two opinions have been developed: that benefit should be determined by agreement (this is the opinion of the Hanbalite or Hanafi School); and that benefit should be determined by the contribution of each party (the view of the Maliki and Chafite Schools). The capital of the Musharaka can be a cash contribution plus a cash contribution, or a cash contribution plus a contribution in kind. The management of Musharaka can be overseen by all associates or by one or several associates, or by one or several third parties. Losses must be apportioned in proportion to capital.

3.3.2.1. The commitment of funds

The commitment of funds under a Musharaka contract takes three different forms:

- A permanent participation in corporate capital
- A lesser participation in corporate capital
- A temporary participation in just a specific operation

3.3.2.1.1. Participation in the capital of emerging companies

This participation can take many forms, for example, the bank's participation in the capital of a company being created or the purchase of shares in a company that already exists. Either way, a joint venture is formed between the bank and the owner of the company. The bank and the company will share profits according to the capital contribution of each. In Islamic jurisprudence, this type of company is referred to as a limited co-management company. The associates are personally responsible for the company and its debts, so they are interdependent. Only two conditions can terminate this contract: the dissolution of the corporation, or the sale by one of the associates.

3.3.2.1.2. Digressive participation

Digressive participation is when, as stipulated as a condition of the Musharaka contract, the bank sells its shares in the capital to the entrepreneur in installments, thereby gradually but definitively withdrawing from the project. The settlement of the shares purchased by the entrepreneur may be in cash or on credit. The bank uses one of three modalities for the transfer of its shares:

A – Assignment by hire purchase

In this case, the entrepreneur refunds to the bank the amount of capital contributed in the creation of the company, several times over and at fixed intervals. Upon signing the contract and paying the first installment, the right of ownership is transferred entirely to the entrepreneur, but in case of default by the buyer, the bank may recover this right (Khan, 1986).

B – Assignment by leasing

Under this type of contract, the entrepreneur pays the bank a lease, which is considered a partial payment of the price charged by the bank for its shares. Several factors should be taken into account in determining this price, among which are the following: first, the real value of the company; secondly, that of the lease on the still unpaid portion and finally, the risk of default by the purchaser. The bank transfers the ownership of the company to the entrepreneur when it receives the final lease. According to Ali Mohamad (1984), the leasing contract must expressly state:

- The total sale price
- The term of the lease
- The amount of rent
- The guarantees

C – Sale by assignment of capital

As for a Musharaka with digressive participation, in fact it will create two different contracts: the first related to the foundation of a company, and the second to the gradual sale of that company. By purchasing shares in the bank, the entrepreneur can set the price of those shares by assigning to them either a portion of his profits or all of them.

3.3.2.1.3. A temporary participation in a specific operation

This is a commitment among several partners, chosen by the bank from individuals or from private or public companies in the business sector. The participation contract usually covers a specific operation and ends with the completion of that operation. The bank diversifies its partners in order to minimize the risk of loss and compare profitability by category and status.

3.3.2.2. Use of the Musharaka by the Islamic bank

Just like the Mudaraba, the Musharaka may be used in both directions; in the Islamic bank/client direction, where the bank funds a client entrepreneur, and also in the client/Islamic bank direction, where the client depositor's funds are used for the bank's investments.

3.3.2.2.1. The Musharaka: Islamic bank-client entrepreneur

The Islamic bank can finance its clients using the Musharaka (under the PLS principle) in several ways:

- Participation in the equity of existing businesses or businesses to be created; all shareholders of a capital-intensive company are bound by a Musharaka contract
- The funding of one operating cycle
- Funding for import

3.3.2.2.2. The Musharaka: Client depositor – Islamic bank

In this case, the client is a depositor, who becomes a semi-shareholder in the Islamic Bank and participates in its results.

The Islamic bank (IB) thus becomes a company with variable capital. Deposits will increase the capital whilst giving the depositor the right to share in the profits and losses, and any withdrawal will decrease the capital and lead to a decrease in profit sharing.

The client depositor is not paid according to an ex ante interest rate, but he participates in the bank's annual results based on the amount that he deposited and the time his funds were withdrawn. He receives an ex post interest rate. In fact, only some Islamic banks use Musharaka in their client/Islamic bank relationships; most use the Mudaraba.

3.3.3. Leasing or Tajir

A company may apply to an Islamic bank to finance the purchase of equipment or materials indispensable for its activities and make that equipment or material available to it. The company agrees to pay a lease, fixed in advance, for a specified period. Upon expiry of the contract, as in a normal case of hire purchase, the entrepreneur is not obliged to acquire the property, but he may if he wishes.

From the time of receipt of the equipment and/or materials, the entrepreneur bears all mandatory costs for their maintenance and all the risks inherent in their use. However, the bank may have to deal with people who fail to pay.

3.3.4. Ijara wa Iktina

Under this contract, the bank finances equipment, a building or a factory as a turnkey via payment of a lease, convened by mutual agreement between the parties, with the client committed to paying the lease payments into an investment account which will eventually allow him to buy the financed property. The profits from the lease payments deposited into this investment account are for the client's benefit. With regard to buildings, the difficulties encountered by the bank are in the high costs incurred by double modification work.

3.3.5. Deferred sale: The Bai-Muajjal

In this case, the Islamic bank purchases the equipment or materials from the supplier and resells them by installment to the entrepreneur under terms of payment agreed in advance. It is a type of leasing, but in the medium term.

3.3.6. Qard Hassan: The free loan

This is an exceptional free loan, granted, in general, to a loyal client who encounters difficulties. The bank does not profit and the client, therefore, only reimburses what the bank has granted him. This product represents only 1% of the transactions of Islamic banks.

3.3.7. Salam

The *Salam* is a contract in which the price is paid in advance upon signing the contract, while delivery of the goods/service is carried out on a specified future date. The Salam contract does not suit all goods. Generally speaking, it is applicable only to fungible goods. Islamic banks can finance operations through the Salam technique using one of two separate contracts: the first, a basic Salam contract, and the other a contract of sale by instalments. The bank may, for example, buy goods by paying an advance to the supplier while fixing the date of delivery according to the desire of the client. The client may then resell the goods to a third person on the basis of a Salam contract by instalments. If both operations are based on the Salam contract, the second contract will include the same terms of delivery for the same quantity of goods, the same specifications, etc. as those mentioned in the first Salam contract. The second contract is often concluded after the first contract because the price must be paid immediately after the signing of both parties, i.e. the bank and the supplier. To be valid under Shariah, the second contract should be independent of the first, particularly in the delivery of the goods. If the second contract is an instalment sale, the date must be after the receipt of the goods by the bank. With the exception of Mudaraba, and sometimes Musharaka, with their agricultural variants, most Islamic methods of financing exist also in conventional finance (sale with deferred payment, deferred delivery sale, and lease with option to purchase).

Since the beginning of their activities, Islamic banks' most used contract is Murabaha, followed by Ijara and then Iktina, or lease with possibility of acquisition, all of which are primarily used to finance short-term trade operations. In some agricultural countries, for example Sudan, there is also significant use of *Bai-salam* which, for all practical purposes, is rural, short-term credit. Methods of finance under profit-sharing agreements, for the establishment of investment projects for long-term production, traditionally receive only a meager portion of the financial resources of Islamic banks.

Appendix 1: Islamic Swap Term sheet

Structure Overview

Its Sharia Compliant Protection Transactions cover the Profit Rate Protection transaction, the Sharia compliant alternative for the Interest Rate Swap. The transaction is based on the Murabaha Finance and Investment transactions.

Indicative Terms:

Terms of Swap

Notional:	USD 1000,000,000.00
Start Date:	27 March, 2010
Maturity Date:	27 March, 2015
Fixed Rate:	5.75%
Fixed Rate Basis:	Actual / 360
Fixed Rate Payer:	Client (Party B)
Floating Rated:	'Murabaha Investment Return' Benchmark
Floating Rate Payer:	Bank A (Party A)

Payment Details

Party A Pays:	6 Month MIR x (n / N) x Notional on the formula: n = the number of calendar days in the Financing Period (6 month); N= 360.
Payment Dates:	To be adjusted as per Business Day Convention.
Party B pays:	5.75% p.a. x (n / N) x Notional as per attached schedule at each reset period for entire tenor of the swap on the formula: n = the number of calendar days in the Financing Period (6 month); N= 360.
Payment Dates:	To be adjusted as per Business Day Convention.
Rate Source:	Murabaha Investment Benchmark.
Calculation Agent:	Bank.
Business Day Conv:	Modified Following, Adjusted.
Business Days:	
Documentation:	Customer Treasury Agreement, Murabaha Financing Agreement and Murabaha Investment Agreement.

Advantages:

- Islamic Mode of Hedging.

- Eliminates uncertainty due to fluctuations in financing rates.
- Guarantees a rate for the tenor of the swap (price assured).
- Allows for much better financial forecasting.

Risk/disadvantages:

- Immediate Negative Carry.
- If rates remain stable of fall further, there is an opportunity loss

Terms and Conditions

General Terms

- ➢ This term sheet is an integral part of the Customer Treasury Agreement
- ➢ Currency Exchange process shall be done on spot basis.
- ➢ Amounts owed shall be paid in full, time value for money shall not be a condition for calculating settlement amount.

Transaction Specific Terms

- ➢ In the case of protection against fixed rate, the Bank shall provide a revolving Murabaha Finance for periods defined in the confirmation having fixed profit mark-up for each period.
- ➢ In the case of protection against variable rate, the Bank shall provide a Murabaha Finance for the protection period defined in the confirmation having fixed profit mark-up for the period. The financed amount shall be invested in a revolving Murabaha investment for periods defined in
- ➢ The Customer shall not be entitled to receive the value of the Murabaha Finance.
- ➢ The protection transaction shall not be cancelled before the maturity date defined in the confirmation.
- ➢ When paying the profit mark-up for the Murabaha Finance and the Murabaha investment at the end of each of the periods defined in the confirmation, netting may be performed where the difference between the Murabaha Finance profit mark-up and the Murabaha investment profit mark-up shall be paid.
- ➢ At maturity of the protection transaction, netting shall be performed where the difference between the amounts the Customer shall pay to the Bank and the Bank shall pay to the Customer is determined and paid.

Appendix 2: Convertible forward based on Wa'ad 9 at maturity

Structure Overview

This product provides the client with 100% protection against Euro appreciation. It provides the opportunity to participate on lower levels limited by each respective lower trigger.

If a particular trigger is traded at maturity of the cash flow, then client is locked at the protection rate.

Indicative terms:

Party A:	Client
Party B:	Bank
Notional Amount:	
Trade Date:	To be determined, TBA
Expiry Dates:	Two Business Days Prior to Settlement Date
Party A Sells:	USD equivalent amounts
Party A Buys:	EUR as per Schedule
Settlement Dates:	
Business Days:	London, New York, Frankfurt
Spot Reference Rate:	Current Market
Par Forward Rate:	XXXX
Protection Rate:	XXXX
Lower Trigger:	XXXX

Exchange of USD and EUR

Amounts:

- If at Expiry, EUR/USD is trading higher than the Protection Rate the client will be protected at protection rate.
- If at Expiry, EUR/USD is trading below the Protection Rate and never touched the Lower Trigger, client will buy EUR/USD at the prevailing market price.
- If at Expiry EUR/USD is trading below protection rate and the lower trigger was touched during the life of the Wa'ad, client will buy Euro at the Protection Rate.

Advantages:

- The client is provided with 100% protection against any appreciation in the Euro rate against the USD.
- This structure provides the opportunity to participate on lower market levels up to the Lower Trigger which is observed at maturity only.

Risk/disadvantages:

- Protection rate is set above the current market forward rate
- If the Lower Trigger is traded at maturity, the client must purchase full amount at the Protection Rate

Required documentation:

CTA, Wa'ad 1, Wa'ad 2 where:

Wa'ad 1	Party B promise to Party A unconditionally and irrevocably to SELL Underlying Asset to Party A at the Protection rate if the Underlying Asset trades above Protection rate on Expiry Date.
Wa'ad 2	Party A promise to Party B unconditionally and irrevocably to BUY Underlying Asset from Party B at the Protection on Expiry Date if the Underlying Asset touches the barrier at any time.

General Terms

- This term sheet is an integral part of the Customer Treasury Agreement
- Currency Exchange process and the barter will be done on spot basis.
- Amounts owed shall be paid in full, time value for money shall not be a condition for calculating settlement amount.

Transaction Specific Terms

- The Bank may promise the Customer (or the Customer promises the Bank) to sell/purchase (the "Promise") certain currencies, commodities, mutual funds units or, Shari'ah compliant basket of shares or currencies (the "Underlying Assets") at a specific date(s) and price(s).
- Upon the issuance of the Promisee, promise shall pay to the promisor a non-refundable mutually agreed upon fixed fee (the "Promise Fee").

- The date(s), price, exchange rate and promise fee shall be specified in the Term Sheet, which shall also specify the promisor and the promisee.
- In case promise decides to execute the Promise, promisor shall sell/purchase the Underlying Assets as detailed in the Term Sheet. The sale/purchase of the Underlying Assets shall be in accordance with the terms specified in the Term Sheet. The promisor is entitled to enforce the Promise on the date(s) and in accordance with terms specified in the Term Sheet.
- The promisee shall have the right to claim from the promisor any sum from the amounts due to it.
- All the accounts regardless of their type that are opened under the name of the Customer or the accounts that will be opened with the Bank or at any of its branches shall mutually secure one another regardless of their names.
- The Bank and the Customer shall not have the right to transfer their obligations resulting from this transaction to any party without a per-written The Islamic Banking System and Financial Instruments: Definitions, Characteristics and Performance Measurements approval of each other.

CHAPTER TWO

ISLAMIC BANKING INTERMEDIATION AND FINANCIAL INSTRUMENTS: ON RISK MANAGEMENT ISSUES AND CAPITAL ADEQUACY REGULATIONS

MONDHER BELLALAH AND ZEINEB CHAYEH

Introduction

Islamic banking, as a concept or a business, is about more than simply avoiding charging interest and conforming to legal requirements regarding Islamic financial products. As a system it also aims to contribute to the fulfillment of socio-economic objectives and the creation of a just society.

Respect for the tenets of Shariah changes the classic scheme of banking intermediation.

Islamic banking intermediation has specific procedures for both the mobilization and the allocation of funds, and therefore the structure of its balance sheet differs completely from that of conventional banks.

Section 1. Islamic Banking Intermediation: Mobilization and Allocation of Funds and Profit Distribution

A. Dusuki[1] (2008) identifies the fundamental distinctions between Islamic Banks and Conventional Banks:

[1] Asyraf Wajdi Dusuki, "Understanding the Objectives of Islamic Banking: A Survey of Stakeholders' Perspectives", International Journal of Islamic and Middle Eastern Finance and Management, Volume 1, Issue 2, 2008.

Islamic Bank	Conventional Bank
Financing products are based on either asset-backed trading contracts or profit and loss sharing contracts.	Financing products are based on charging interest.
Deposit products are based either on free interest charging or the profit and loss sharing concept whereby depositors are treated as investors.	Deposit products are interest oriented and the depositors are assured of a pre-determined rate of interest along with a guaranteed repayment.
Theoretically, Islamic banks strategies aim to balance profit maximization and social responsibility	Theoretically, conventional banks focus mainly on profit maximization.
No penalty to defaulters[2].	Charging compound rate of interest in case of default.
Islamic banks are banned from financing economic activities that are unethical under Shariah.	Conventional banks have no restrictions and finance any profitable activities.
Corporate governance is based on a stakeholder-oriented model. Property rights and contractual frameworks are crucial principles.	Corporate governance is based on a shareholder-oriented model.
Islamic banks have a Shariah board which is the key player in guaranteeing compliance with Islamic law.	Conventional banks do not have a Shariah board.
Paying Zakat to charity (2.5% out of income) as well as tax is mandatory for Islamic banks.	Conventional banks pay only tax.

[2] Some scholars allow the charging of small late payment penalties, but only for reluctant defaulters. The amount has to be channeled to charity and not treated as business income.

1. Fund Mobilization

Islamic banks have developed two basic deposit products for the mobilization of funds. Each of them is based on a Shariah-compliant intermediary contract. These products include current accounts based on Wadia or Amanah contracts, and investment and savings accounts based on Mudaraba or Wakalah contracts. Although the former are considered liabilities and their holders are not entitled to any kind of return, the latter would not be listed under liabilities, nor would they be included in banks' equity, though they could be considered a form of limited-term, non-voting equity (Iqbal[3] et al, 2011).

These investment and savings accounts are considered one of the earlier unique innovations of Islamic banking. While conventional banks hold debt and deposits with fixed interest rates, Islamic banks rely on funding with a cost linked to the return of its assets and to which, theoretically, no guarantee of return is provided (A. Hassoun[4], 2007).

The second source of Islamic banks' funds is their shareholders, a source of funds shared by conventional and Islamic banks. The owners provide the banking firm with funds in the hope of acquiring a competitive return on their invested funds (Rosly[5] et al, 2008). The mobilization of a bank's capital is based on a Musharakah contract, where funds are raised through the sale of common shares to the public.

No preferred shares are issued by Islamic banks because holders of these shares are paid a fixed dividend, which is prohibited by Shariah. Although Islamic banks' equity funds, like those of conventional ones, are supposed to be set aside in order to cover unexpected credit and market risk losses, they are subjected to many risks that may erode the value of the funds but may also increase their value if the firm performs very well. The kind of risks faced by Islamic bank owners depends on the financial instruments the bank uses, its management and level of transparency as well as its performance.

---

[3] Z. Iqbal and A. Mirakhor, "An introduction to Islamic Finance: Theory and Practice", 2011, Wiley Finance.

[4] A. Hassoune, "Islamic banks' profitability in an interest rate cycle", *International Journal of Islamic Financial Services, Vol.4, No.2.*

[5] Rosly et al, "Risk-return analysis of Islamic banks' investment deposits and shareholders' fund", Managerial FinanceVol. 34 No. 10, 2008pp. 695-707.

1.1. Islamic Banking Deposit Products

1.1.1 Current Accounts

Islamic banks' current accounts are similar to those of conventional banks. Holders of this type of account do not receive any kind of return, and revenue generated from investing the funds deposited in them is the exclusive right of the shareholders because, in the case of loss, the account holders will be paid from the shareholders' funds. These accounts are generally based on one of two basic trust contracts, namely the Wadia and Amanah contracts. Current accounts allow their holders to benefit from transactional services such as withdrawing their funds on demand.

1.1.2 Investment and saving accounts (ISAs)

An overview

ISAs usually constitute a bank's largest source of funds. In fact, according to a study (Sundararajan[6], 2008) based on the investigation of a sample of Islamic banks in 12 countries in the Middle East and South East Asia, ISAs constitute about 62% of assets.

These accounts are neither liability nor equity funds. Under profit sharing based Mudaraba or Wakalah agreements, Islamic banks are allowed to invest money deposited in these accounts. AAOIFI (1993)[7] classified investment accounts into unrestricted and restricted accounts.

Unrestricted investment accounts count toward an Islamic bank's overall financial position and it has been proposed that they should be classified into a third category lying between liabilities and equities. These accounts are based only on profit sharing contracts.

Restricted investment accounts are considered an element of the off-balance sheet, as investments financed by deposits in them are managed by the bank, which does not have the right to use or dispose of these investments except within the conditions of the contracts between the bank and the holders. These investments are not the assets of the bank and should not be reflected in its balance sheet. They are based on Wakalah or Mudaraba contracts.

Under the Mudaraba contract, financial and credit risks linked to investments financed by ISA deposits are borne exclusively by Investment

---

[6] Sundarajan V. (2008) "Issues in Managing Profit Equalisation Reserves and Investment Risk Reserves in Islamic Banks."

[7] The Statement of Financial Accounting No. 2 "Concepts of Financial Accounting for Islamic Banks and Financial Institutions" issued in 1993.

Account Holders (IAH) except if losses are caused by either management misconduct or negligence. These latter risks are known as operational risks and were identified by the AAOIFI as fiduciary risks which are borne exclusively by the Islamic bank.

Profits should be shared with IAHs by the Islamic bank, which acts as a fund manager, in accordance with the pre-agreed profit sharing rate and on the basis of the actual return generated by assets, rather than in accordance with a fixed interest rate.

Visser[8] (2009) also describes the distinction between an investment account and a savings account. While the nominal value of the former is not guaranteed, that of the latter is considered to be in the custody or safekeeping of the bank. Both involve profit sharing based on a pre-agreed sharing rate. The revenue attributed to savings account holders is not considered Riba because it is not predetermined, nor based on an interest rate.

According to Al-Deehani et al (1999)[9], an increase in investment deposits results in an increase in both the Islamic bank's market value and its shareholders' rates of return, with no increase in financial risk. This assertion is based firstly on the fact that Islamic banks are continuously facing commercial risk due to the redeemable nature of these funds and so deserve a higher return rate. Secondly, as long as these accounts are based on the profit and loss sharing principle whereby no return is guaranteed, higher amounts of deposits are not perceived to incur any extra financial risks.

Displaced Commercial Risk

However, this rationale strays away from making sense when confronted with the practices of Islamic banks. In fact, the ability of Islamic banks to transfer the financial risks to its IAHs, known as the pass through mechanism, seems to be an illusion. In order to uphold and develop their market shares under strong pressure to mitigate any liquidity risk stemming from potential depositors' withdrawal due to negative or lower returns than expected, Islamic banks have opted for some specific practices. These practices have contributed to the rise of a special kind of risk very specific to Islamic Banking, called Displaced Commercial Risk, which consists of a transfer of financial risk from IAHs to shareholders.

---

[8] H. Visser, "Islamic Finance: Principles and Practice", 2009, EEP Ltd.

[9] Al-Deehani et al. (1999), "The Capital Structure of Islamic Banks under the Contractual Obligation of Profit Sharing" International Journal of Theoretical and Applied Finance.

This is contradictory to the spirit of the Mudaraba contract and the profit and loss sharing mechanism.

The Islamic Financial Services Board[10] (2005) identifies Displaced Commercial Risk as "the risk arising from assets managed on behalf of IAHs which is effectively transferred to the shareholders because the Islamic bank follows the practice of foregoing part or all of its Mudareb share of profit on such funds, when it considers this necessary, as a result of commercial pressure, in order to increase the return that would otherwise be payable to the IAHs".

The Accounting and Auditing Organisation of Islamic Financial Institutions (1999) defines displaced commercial risk as the risk resulting from the volatility of returns generated by assets financed by investment accounts.

Profit disbursement smoothing may also be required and even encouraged by the supervisory authority in order to avoid any increase in systemic risk caused by particularly large withdrawals of ISA funds. This involves rate of return paid to IAH being smoothed by drawing upon profits that would otherwise be payable to shareholders. This transfer of risk has resulted in the emergence of the Displaced Commercial Risk.

In practice, special reserves emerged to absorb a proportion of the losses normally borne by IAHs, caused by either a negative rate of return or lower than expected returns. Islamic banks implemented income smoothing for IAHs based on the Profit Equalization Reserve (PER) along with a reduction in the rate of profit shares taken from Mudareb to a level below that contracted. These two practices are used to level the returns actually paid to IAHs, so that an expected return can be provided. Another kind of special reserve, the Investment Risk Reserve (IRR), is used to cover potential losses on assets invested with IAHs' funds. As long as the IRR and the PER are sufficient to avoid income being taken from shareholders to give to IAHs, the Islamic bank is not exposed to Displaced Commercial Risk.

Profit Equalization Reserve

The Profit Equalization Reserve is taken from the profits before distribution between shareholders and IAHs begins, although this reserve too is actually apportioned out to IAHs and shareholders at the pre-agreed profit sharing rate. Should investment returns decline, Islamic banks draw

---

[10] IFSB (2005), "Guiding Principles of Risk Management for Institutions (other than Insurance Institutions) offering only Islamic Financial Services (IIFS)", standard 76.

upon the PER in order to smooth the payout to both IAHs and shareholders. A part of accumulated PER belongs to shareholders, and this can also be drawn on to smooth payouts to IAHs; thus the PER may be considered a contributor to displaced commercial risk. At the same time, such a reserve may also mitigate DCR if sound provisions, based on the entire future profile of expected losses, are put in place. These reserves contribute largely to the decrease or even elimination of return rate variability, and allow returns aligned with market rates to be offered on conventional deposits and other benchmarks. (R. Karim et al, 2007)[11]

PER is used as an indicator of deterioration in Islamic banks' earnings. The determinants of PER are important in assessing an Islamic bank's financial stability along with depositors' confidence. Net non-performing financings, net income before provision and capital ratio all significantly affect decisions about PER, which have to be based on a forward looking strategy and thus on the entire future profile of expected losses of all fund investments. (A. Ismail, 2006)[12]

Investment Risk Reserve

The Investment Risk Reserve is set aside from the profits available for distribution to the IAH, but after paying the Islamic bank's share of profits as a Mudareb. These reserves belong entirely to IAHs and are maintained specifically to absorb periodic losses, in whole or in part, and also to smooth the rate of return actually paid out over time.

The following figure illustrates the link between Displaced Commercial Risk, the PER and the IRR:

[11] R. Karim et al, "Islamic Finance: the regulatory challenges", 2007, Wiley Finance.

[12] A. Ismail, 2006, "Profit Equalization Reserve Decisions: An Empirical Analysis of Islamic Banks in Malaysia", Islamic Economics and Finance Research Group.

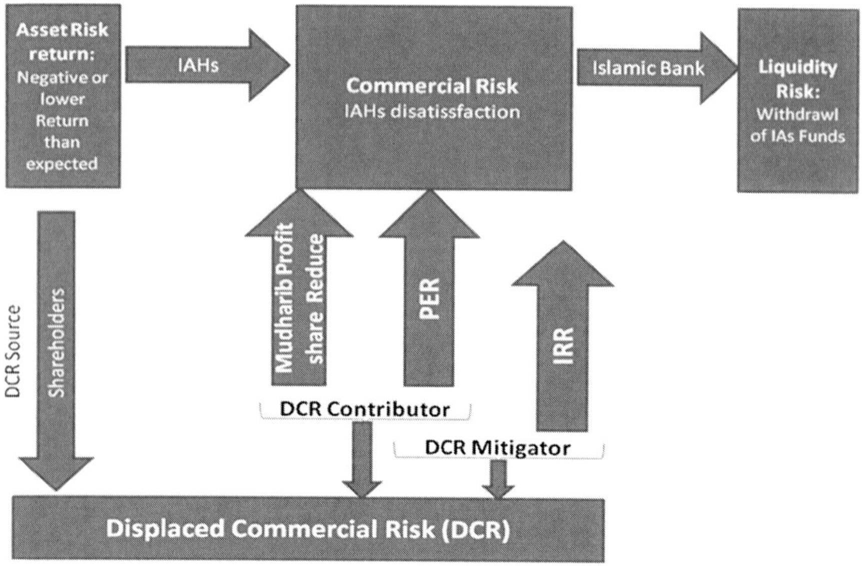

Figure 1: DCR, PER and IRR

The IAs and Capital adequacy

As far as capital adequacy regulation of investment and savings accounts is concerned, the IFSB (2005)[13] proposed including an amount proportional to credit risk and market risk weighted assets financed by investment accounts (as a measure of Displaced Commercial Risk) in the calculation of the capital adequacy ratio. The higher the Displaced Commercial Risk, therefore, the higher the amount.

The IFSB allowed for the deduction of the PER and the IRR from the risk weighted assets funded by IAs before the application of the relevant capital requirements.

Therefore, Displaced Commercial Risk requires additional regulatory capital (Sundararajan, 2008)[14] and the value of the added Alpha-proportional amount indicates the extent to which these ISAs are considered able to carry the financial risks linked to the underlying assets. In fact, if the Alpha score is low, IAHs bear any downturn linked to investments made with ISA funds, and thus risks on assets financed by

[13] Capital Adequacy Standard for Institutions offering Islamic Financial Services (IIFS).

[14] Sundarajan V. (2008) "Issues in Managing Profit Equalisation Reserves and Investment Risk Reserves in Islamic Banks".

ISAs do not involve any capital requirements. However, when the Alpha score is near 100%, ISAs can be treated the same as conventional deposits. In these cases, the nominal amounts as well as the associated returns are guaranteed and thus the Islamic bank bears the entirety of any losses.

In practice, the Alpha score is usually between these two extremes and depends on the volatility of investment returns.

Adopting a forward-looking approach based on the development of an internal model is more appropriate for assessing the regulatory capital charge linked to DCR.

Section 2. Fund Allocation

The assets side of an Islamic bank represents a more diversified asset portfolio with a wider range of risk and maturity profiles than the liabilities side (Iqbal[15] et al, 2010).

As far as the maturity profile of an Islamic bank's financing and investment assets is concerned, they may offer three kinds of maturity assets:

Short-term maturity assets generally include trade financing contracts, mainly the Murabaha (a.k.a the cost plus sale), the Salam (the deferred delivery sale facility), and the Bai-Muajjil (the deferred payment facility). This kind of financing instrument is considered a limited risk investment as the financial claims are backed by the commodity financed asset.

In terms of medium-term assets, Islamic banks finance *Istisna'a* transactions or manufacture sale transactions, operating as a lessor. Islamic banks may also invest in medium-term sukuk based on Ijara or Istisna'a, along with medium-term Mudaraba and Musharaka. Medium- as well as short-term profit sharing arrangements are used as solutions to finance companies' working capital.

For longer term maturity investments, Islamic bank generally use equity based financing products comprising Mudaraba, or trustee partnerships, Musharaka, or joint ventures through investment in quoted and unquoted Shariah-compliant equity investments, as well as investments in associations which give the bank the ability to exercise significant influence over operations through representation on the Boards of Directors, and Musharaka *Mutanaqisah*, or declining partnership facilities, often proposed as a solution to house financing. Islamic banks may invest in Islamic funds similar to sukuk.

---

[15] "The stability of Islamic Finance: Creating a resilient financial environment for a secure future", 2010, Wiley Finance.

Other assets may include property investments, assets held either for leasing or trading, cash and balances held by other Islamic banks and Islamic financial institutions. Islamic banks have mandatory reserves in the Central Bank which are not available for the bank's day to day operations, just as conventional banks do.

Figure 2 presents a stylized Islamic bank balance sheet, displaying different activities and financial instruments and illustrating the composition of a typical bank's balance sheet. The structure of a typical balance sheet displays current deposits and investment accounts, along with reserves and equity capital, on the liability side and Islamic financing and investing instruments with different maturity profiles on the asset side.

Assets	Liabilities
Short Term Trade finance (Murabaha, Salam)	Current Accounts (Amnah, Wadia)
	Investment and Saving accounts (Mudarabah)
Meduim Term Investment (Ijara, Istisna'a, sukuk...)	Reserves (IRR, PER...)
Long Term partnership (Musharakah, Mudarabah...)	Shareholders ' Equity

Figure 2

Figure 3 presents and summarizes the dynamic of an Islamic bank's fund mobilization and allocation, and identifies the different transactional and intermediary contracts used to carry them out.

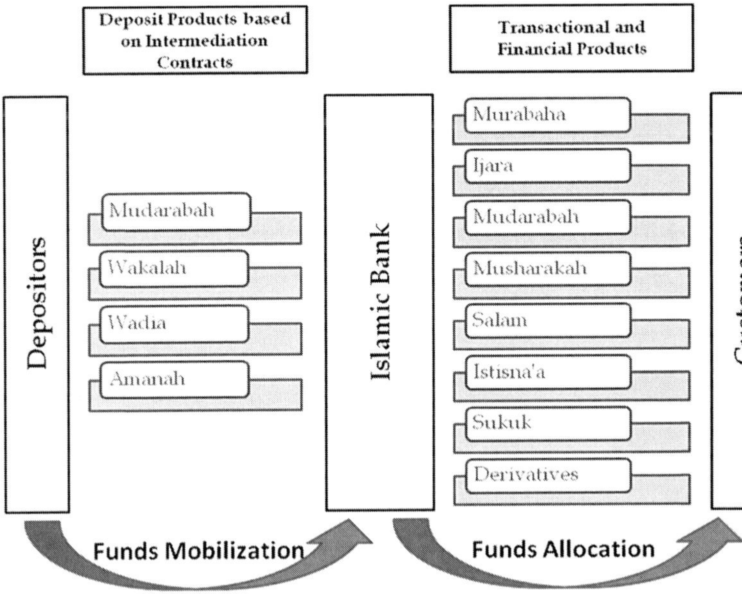

Figure 3: Typical mobilization and allocation of funds in an Islamic Bank

2.1. Limited Maturity Asset Structure and Asset Liability Management Issue

2.1.1. The Lack of Appetite for Profit and Loss Sharing Assets

An investigation of the composition of the assets sides of the top five Islamic banks, ranked by the level of ROA (The Banker[16], 2009), shows that Islamic banks' first preference is for trade financing instruments, arranged using sales contracts, and leasing instruments, which tend to be of shorter maturity, and less risky as they show less uncertain returns than partnership based instruments.

Figures 4 and 5 provide empirical evidence that on average, trade financing assets (Murabaha, Salam, and Istisna'a) and leasing (Ijara) constitute about 67% of Islamic banks' assets, in comparison to investment assets such as Musharaka and Mudaraba, which count for only 19.6%. Local and international Murabaha assets represent on average about 80% of asset backed financing, which implies that Islamic banks rely heavily on Murabaha in carrying out their financing and investment transactions.

[16] Top Financial Islamic Institutions listing, The Banker, 2009.

Although Islamic banks should, theoretically, be more involved in profit and loss sharing agreements and equity sharing securities, empirical evidence has pointed out a real reluctance on the part of Islamic banks to engage in profit and risk sharing arrangements, which represent one of the cornerstones of the Islamic financial system's plans to achieve its true potential. Our results corroborate the estimations of Iqbal (1997)[17] which have shown that in the mid-1990s, Murabaha contracts made up three quarters of Islamic bank financing and Ijara some 10% – profit and loss sharing arrangements are far from dominant. The obvious question to ask is: why does this trend still continue in spite of the growth of Islamic finance?

Iqbal et al (2008) believe this preference is due to the fact that sales related financing instruments have actually got lower risk profiles than partnership agreements, but is in fact more to do with the fact that their risk return profiles resemble conventional fixed income securities. With this in mind, it is worth pointing out that Islamic financial institutions often imitate conventional institutions and tend to use financial instruments similar to those offered by conventional finance. Financial engineering in Islamic Finance is limited to reverse engineering, which mainly involves replicating conventional financial instruments or finding the closest substitutes within the basic set of Islamic instruments, which may involve some misidentification. The adoption of this kind of financial engineering stemmed from a great desire to rapidly acquire a certain legitimacy and to facilitate integration into the conventional system.

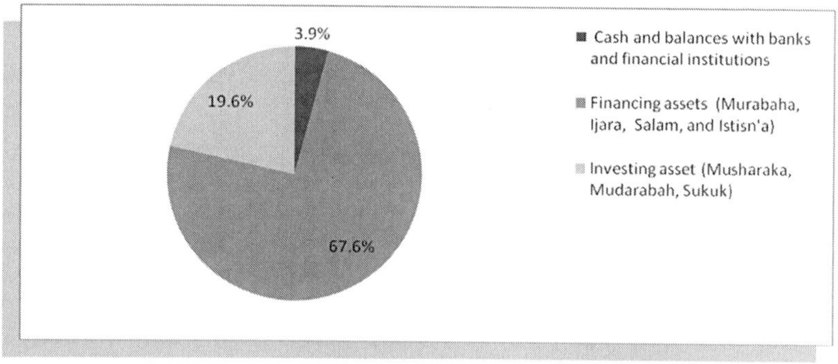

Figure 4

[17] Z. Iqbal, 1997, "Islamic Financial Systems" Finance and development.

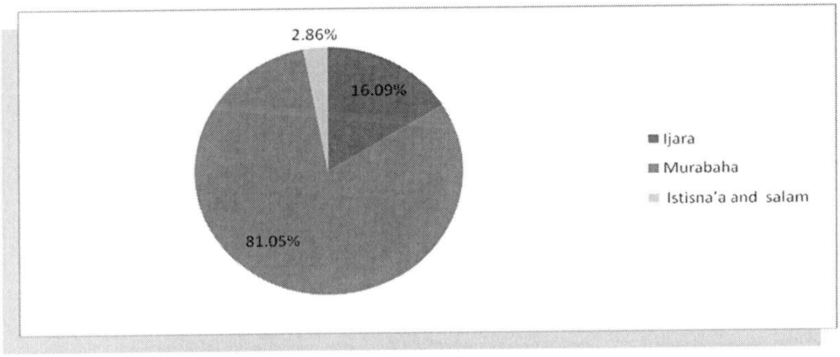

Figure 5

2.1.2. Asset and Liability Management Issues

Despite the fact that Islamic banks can, in theory, carry a diversity of asset classes that allow them to participate in a panoply of maturity and risk structures and obtain the benefits of a diverse portfolio, Islamic banks' preference for trade and commodity financing instruments has in practice limited their asset portfolios to short-term maturity products. A large percentage of Islamic banks' assets (68.8 %) have short-term maturity (of less than a year), 9.8% have a maturity of 1 to 3 years, and the remaining 31.4% mature after three years (Khan and Ahmad, 2001)[18].

Short-term maturity financial instruments are considered more appropriate for Islamic banks as they evolve in environments where secondary markets are not developed and thus the liquidity of different claims still depends almost exclusively on their maturity, rather than on the ability to sell them. Hence Islamic banks tend not to invest in longer maturity assets, due to their lack of liquidity. Because of their reliance on short-term maturity, Islamic banks are often very limited in the long-term investment opportunities they offer. (Iqbal et al, 2008)[19]

2.2. Risks Profile Analysis of an Islamic Bank's Assets

Banks are subjected to a wide array of financial, operational and business risks in the course of their utilization of the different Shariah-

---

[18] Khan, T. and Ahmed, H,2001, "Risk management: An analysis of issues in Islamic financial industry", *Occasional Paper No. 5*, IRTI, Islamic Development Bank, Jeddah.

[19] Z. Iqbal and H. Greuning, 2008, "Risk analysis for Islamic banks", The World Bank.

compliant financing and intermediation contracts, which involve complex interdependency and overlap between different kinds of risks. The figure below illustrates the different kind of risks linked to the basic Shariah-compliant financing contracts.

	Short Term Trade Financing		Meduim Term Investment			
					Long Term Partnership	
Major Risk	**Murabaha**	**Salam**	**Istisna'a**	**Ijara**	**Mudarabah**	**Musharakah**
Credit Risk	√	√	√			
Market Risk						
•Mark up Risk	√					
•Price Risk						
•Rate of return Risk					√	√
•Leased Asset value Risk				√		
•Currency Risk	√	√	√	√	√	√
•Liquidity Risk						
Agency Risk					√	√
Delivery Risk		√	√			
Operational Risk	√	√	√	√	√	√
	Financing Assets				Investment Assets	

Figure 6: Risks Profile Analysis of Islamic Bank's Assets

2.3. Fund Allocation Models

Iqbal et al (2007)[20] identify two main theoretical fund allocation models within the structure of Islamic banks: the two tier Mudaraba model, and the two windows model.

The two tier Mudaraba model is based, naturally, on two tier Mudaraba contracts. The first tier Mudaraba contract forms the structure of the relationship between the Islamic bank, acting as fund manager, and the depositors, considered here investors. However, the second tier is a Mudaraba agreement between the Islamic bank acting as a financier and

[20] Z. Iqbal and A. Mirakhor, "An introduction to Islamic Finance: Theory and Practice", 2011, Wiley Finance.

clients as Mudareb, or fund managers. In this fund allocation model, an Islamic bank does not distinguish between funds mobilized from current accounts, investment and saving accounts and shareholders' funds. The Islamic bank's funds are pooled and invested based on the two tier Mudaraba agreement. Under this model, the assets and liabilities are completely integrated and there are no reserve capital requirements.

The two windows model refers to fund allocation methods that do make distinction between the sources of an Islamic bank's funds. Under this model, current accounts are considered Amanah, or in custody, and may not be used in banks' investment activities, although in many cases current account holders may be charged a service fee for the safekeeping of their money. Hence the first window on the liabilities side of an Islamic bank's balance sheet contains reserve requirements. The second window refers to investment and savings account funds, which are fully available to be used and invested by Islamic banks on behalf of their holders. Scholars prefer this kind of fund allocation model as it adheres more to the Islamic conception of property rights, which imposes severe restrictions on the use of someone's money when it has been placed in safekeeping.

Section 3. Profit Distribution in Islamic Banks

According to the AAOIFI[21], when a bank commingles its own funds with IA funds, the net income of the Profit Equalization Reserve is first allocated between shareholders and the investment account holders, then to the Islamic Bank as its remuneration as a Mudareb, as well as the amount of the IRR being deducted from the share of profits allocated to the IAHs. The cost of non-equity funds (IAs) is precisely what distinguishes Islamic banks from conventional banks (A. Hassoune, 1999).

[21] Financial Accounting, Standard 6.

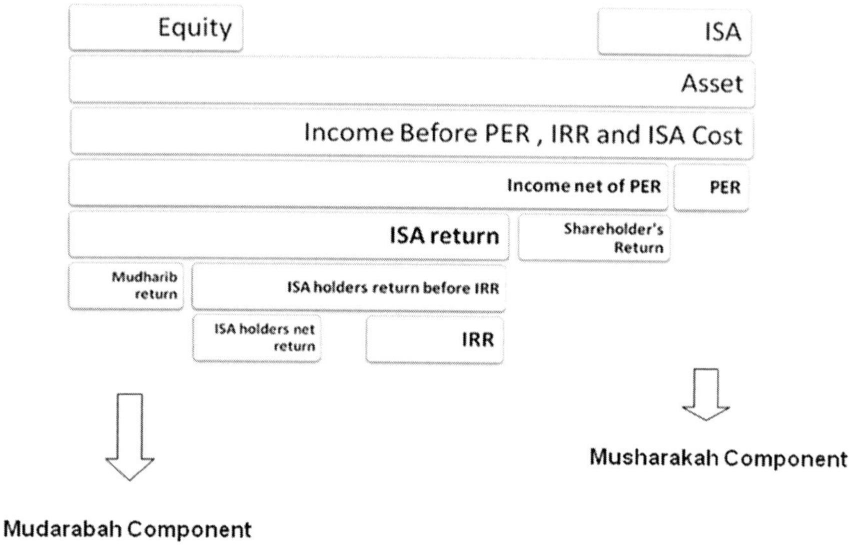

3.1. Profit Allocation Methods

In practice, Islamic banks have implemented two methods of profit allocation.

The first method is the pooling method, by which all of the Islamic bank's revenues and expenses are shared between shareholders and IAHs with no differentiation made between the natures of the revenues and expenses. This method is based on the idea that depositors should be seen as participants in the bank, and should therefore share the revenues and expenses of other banking operations.

The second method is the separation method, by which the Islamic bank does distinguish the revenues and expenses of investment activities from those of other banking services. Under this method IAHs share only the revenues and expenses related to the investment activities in which their specific funds are involved.

The method used depends on the level of restriction stipulated by the Mudaraba agreement. Unrestricted Mudaraba contracts are more suited to the pooling method, while restricted contracts are more consistent with the separation method.

3.2. The Mudaraba Profit and Losses Allocation System and Agency Issues

The mechanism of profit and loss sharing that distinguishes the Mudaraba agreement, whether it is between the Islamic bank and its IAHs or the Islamic bank and its clients who need financing, throws up extensive agency problems and involves a higher risk profile (Iqbal et al, 2007).

Visser (2009) described how, inside an Islamic bank which operates with very little of its own funds and higher risk taking, incentive to increase the expenses borne by IAHs for the benefit of the shareholders may rise. This may be facilitated when the Islamic bank opts for the pooling method. Such a profit allocation system needs a higher level of transparency and information disclosure. Iqbal et al (2007) raise the question of the governance rights of IAHs and highlights the important role of regulators, as well as the Shariah board, in this respect. Although investment accounts constitute a large part of mobilized funds, the holders do not enjoy any participation in the governance or monitoring processes.

As far as the Islamic bank's asset side is concerned, the partnership agreement once again does not seem to be preferred to debt-like financing contracts (Iqbal et al, 2007). This preference is due to the fact that partnership contracts create in practice particular informational and moral hazard issues that require thorough investment screening in advance, and intensive monitoring throughout.

Under the PLS agreement, banks need more information than under conventional banking agreements in order to mitigate the high risk profile that distinguishes such investment instruments (Visser, 2009). As the Islamic bank's profitability under Musharaka contracts is directly linked to future cash flows and the profit generated by the financed project, the screening process is not limited to assessing the borrower's creditworthiness, as in conventional finance, but puts emphasis on the evaluation of the project's potential profitability.

The Musharaka contract is a particularly unpopular selection. In fact, as potential losses are borne only by the financer, and the entrepreneur would be free from any responsibility, this contract may interest the entrepreneurs of projects with poor potential for profit. At the other extreme, in highly profitable projects, the entrepreneur is more likely to choose conventional loans as interest based remuneration becomes lower and thus they become more appealing than profit sharing remuneration.

Close monitoring is also required to ensure that disclosed information about profits from the entrepreneur is regular. Hesse et al[22] (2008) point out that standardizing the monitoring process effectively is almost impossible, which puts larger banks in particular at a disadvantage. Hence the PLS agreement actually seems to be quite expensive for Islamic banks, requiring more investment of managerial expertise and skills for the screening and monitoring of investment projects (Iqbal et al, 2007). For the sake of enhancing partnership based financing and investment and reducing Islamic banks' reluctance to engage in profit and loss sharing arrangements, it should be possible to establish institutions to work on the development of a systemic specifically for performing the collective monitoring of economic agents, thereby reducing monitoring costs for Islamic banks. M. Chapra[23] (2007) proposes the development of private credit rating agencies to facilate the task of Islamic banks in choosing their clients/partners. These private credit rating agencies, along with the chamber of commerce and the trade association, may contribute largely to this field and permit a widespread implementation of PLS instruments.

References

Al-Deehani et al. (1999), "The Capital Structure of Islamic Banks under the Contractual Obligation of Profit Sharing" International Journal of Theoretical and Applied Finance, Volume 02, Issue 03.

Askari, H et al. (2010), "The stability of Islamic Finance: Creating a resilient financial environment for a secure future", Wiley Finance.

Chapra, A. (2007) "Challenges facing the Islamic financial industry", Chapter 21 in M. Kabir Hassan and Mervyn K. Lewis(eds.), Handbook of Islamic Banking (Edward Elgar, 2007).

Cihak, M and Hesse, H. (2008), "Islamic Banks and Financial Stability: An Empirical Analysis", IMF working paper.

Dusuki, A. (2008), "Understanding the Objectives of Islamic Banking: A Survey of Stakeholders' Perspectives", International Journal of Islamic and Middle Eastern Finance and Management, Volume 1, Issue 2.

Hassoune, A. (1999), "Islamic banks' profitability in an interest rate cycle", International Journal of Islamic Financial Services, Vol.4, No.2.

Iqbal, Z. (1997), "Islamic Financial Systems, Finance and Development."

---

[22] M. Cihak and H. Hesse, 2008, "Islamic Banks and Financial Stability: An Empirical Analysis", IMF working paper.

[23] A. Chapra, "Challenges facing the Islamic financial industry", Chapter 21 in M. Kabir Hassan and Mervyn K. Lewis(eds.), Handbook of Islamic Banking (Edward Elgar, 2007).

Iqbal, Z. and Greuning, H. (2008), "Risk analysis for Islamic banks", The World Bank.

Iqbal, Z. and Mirakhor, A. (2011), "An introduction to Islamic Finance: Theory and Practice", Wiley Finance.

Ismail, A. (2006), "Profit Equalization Reserve Decisions: An Empirical Analysis of Islamic Banks in Malaysia", Islamic Economics and Finance Research Group.

Karim, R et al. (2007), "Islamic Finance: the regulatory challenges", Wiley Finance.

Khan, T. and Ahmed, H. (2001), "Risk management: An analysis of issues in Islamic financial industry", Occasional Paper No. 5, IRTI, Islamic Development Bank, Jeddah.

Rosly, S and Zaini, M. (2008) "Risk-return analysis of Islamic banks' investment deposits and shareholders' fund", Managerial Finance Vol. 34 No. 10, pp. 695-707.

Sundarajan, V. (2008) "Issues in Managing Profit Equalisation Reserves and Investment Risk Reserves in Islamic Banks".

Visser, H. (2009), "Islamic Finance: Principles and Practice ", EEP Ltd.

Appendix 1: Convertible Forward Protection based on Wa'ad (at maturity)

Illustrative term Sheet

Structure Overview:

This product provides the client with 100% protection against Euro appreciation. Moreover it provides the opportunity to participate on lower levels limited by each respective lower trigger. If a particular trigger is traded at maturity of the cash flow, then client is locked at the protection rate.

Indicative terms:

Party A:	Client
Party B:	
Notional Amount:	See Appendix
Trade Date:	TBA
Expiry Dates:	Two Business Days Prior to Settlement Date (See Appendix)
Party A Sells:	USD equivalent amounts (See Appendix)
Party A Buys:	EUR as per Schedule
Settlement Dates:	See Appendix
Business Days:	London, New York, Frankfurt
Spot Reference Rate:	Current Market
Par Forward Rate:	XXXX
Protection Rate:	XXXX
Lower Trigger:	XXXX

Exchange of USD and EUR

Amounts:

- If at Expiry, EUR/USD is trading higher than the Protection Rate the client will be protected at protection rate.
- If at Expiry, EUR/USD is trading below the Protection Rate and never touched the Lower Trigger, client will buy EUR/USD at the prevailing market price.

- If at Expiry EUR/USD is trading below protection rate and the lower trigger was touched during the life of the Wa'ad, client will buy Euro at the Protection Rate.

Advantages:

- The client is provided with 100% protection against any appreciation in the Euro rate against the USD.
- This structure provides the opportunity to participate on lower market levels up to the Lower Trigger which is observed at maturity only.

Risk and disadvantages:

Protection rate is set above the current market forward rate
If the Lower Trigger is traded at maturity, the client must purchase full amount at the Protection Rate

Required documentation:

CTA, Wa'ad 1, Wa'ad 2 where;

Wa'ad 1	Party B promise to Party A unconditionally and irrevocably to SELL Underlying Asset to Party A at the Protection rate if the Underlying Asset trades above Protection rate on Expiry Date.
Wa'ad 2	Party A promise to Party B unconditionally and irrevocably to BUY Underlying Asset from Party B at the Protection on Expiry Date if the Underlying Asset touches the barrier at any time.

General Terms

- This term sheet is an integral part of the Customer Treasury Agreement "CTA", any conflict between the terms of the CTA and this term sheet, this term sheet shall prevail.
- The defined terms used in this Term Sheet have the meanings ascribed to them in the CTA.
- Currency Exchange process and the barter will be done on spot basis.
- Any Penalty is to be paid to Samba Shariah Supervisory Board approved charity organizations.

- Amounts owed shall be paid in full, time value for money shall not be a condition for calculating settlement amount.
- Any amendments and supplements to the CTA by the Saudi Arabian Monetary Agency should not conflict with Shariah Laws.

Transaction Specific Terms

- The Bank may promise the Customer (or the Customer promises the Bank) to sell/purchase (the "Promise") certain currencies, commodities, mutual funds units or, Shariah-compliant basket of shares or currencies (the "Underlying Assets") at a specific date(s) and price(s). Upon the issuance of the Promisee, promise shall pay to the promisor a non-refundable mutually agreed upon fixed fee (the "Promise Fee"). The date(s), price, exchange rate and promise fee shall be specified in the Term Sheet, which shall also specify the promisor and the promisee. The Promise is binding to the promisor only, and is deemed rightful & optional to the promisee. The promisee may sell/purchase the Underlying Assets in accordance with the terms specified in the Term Sheet, or may forgoes Sale/purchase as dictated by its own interest, and that it assumes no responsibility in the event of such action, except for the Promise Fee already paid up.
- In case promise decides to execute the Promise, promisor shall sell/purchase the Underlying Assets as detailed in the Term Sheet. The sale/purchase of the Underlying Assets shall be in accordance with the terms specified in the Term Sheet. The promisor is entitled to enforce the Promise on the date(s) and in accordance with terms specified in the Term Sheet.
- In case the promisor fail to fulfill his obligations, promisor shall compensate the promisee for the loss caused to him due to such failure. Compensation shall be determined based on the market price of the Underlying Assets agreed upon in the Term Sheet.
- The promisee shall have the right to claim from the promisor any sum from the amounts due to it. Any lapse in silence from claiming on maturity date shall not be interpreted as a grant of respite or condescension on the part of the promisor from taking any precautionary measures or inflicting a seizure on the money of the promisor. The promisor shall acknowledge and agree that the promisee shall have the right to take any measure to collect his rights including the right to confiscate his dues with the private institutions and government departments for amounts equal to the debt or to request the amounts even after the lapse of the fixed dates.

- All the accounts regardless of their type that are opened under the name of the Customer or the accounts that will be opened with the Bank or at any of its branches shall mutually secure one another regardless of their names. In the event the Customer fails to fulfill his obligations, the Bank shall have the right to merge or consolidate all or some of these accounts and deduct the debit balance in settlement of the debt or to freeze the debit balance until the Customer fulfills all his obligations to the Bank.
- The Bank and the Customer shall not have the right to transfer their obligations resulting from this transaction to any party without a per-written approval of each other.
- In the event the Customer fails to fulfill his obligations, all the funds, commercial and financial papers and the precious metals that are deposited under the name of the Customer with the Bank or at any of its branches shall be considered a security and insurance against all the obligations of the Customer to the Bank without the need for any special acknowledgement in this regard. The Bank shall have the right to fulfill his debt directly from the above funds.

Appendix 2: 2 Years Capital Protected "Bai Al-Arboon" on Illustrative Term Sheet

Pick & Drop on Dow Jones Islamic Markets Indexes

1. Dow Jones Islamic Markets US Titans 50
2. Dow Jones Islamic Markets Europe Titans 25
3. Dow Jones Islamic Markets BRIC Index
4. Dow Jones Islamic Markets Japan

This Islamic Investment is through Bai Al-Arboon linked to four of the Dow Jones Islamic Markets Indexes.

The Dow Jones Islamic Market Indices

The DJIMI provide guidance to investing in accordance with Islamic guidelines. The DJIMI tracks Shariah-compliant stocks globally. The DJIMI consists of companies that are compatible with Shariah law.

The DJIMI family of indexes includes the broad DJ Islamic Market US Index, the DJ Islamic Market UK Index, the DJ Market Europe Index, the DJ Islamic Market Technology Index, the DJ Islamic Market Extra Liquid Index, the DJ Canadian Index, and the DJ Islamic Market Asia/Pacific Index.

A Shariah Board of Islamic scholars advise Dow Jones on matters pertaining to the Shariah compliance of the indexes' eligible components.

Producers of alcohol and pork-related products, providers of conventional financial services and providers of entertainment businesses are incompatible with Shari`ah law. The DJIMI include only actively-traded companies with "acceptable" Shariah financial ratios.

Historical Performance Charts before financial crisis

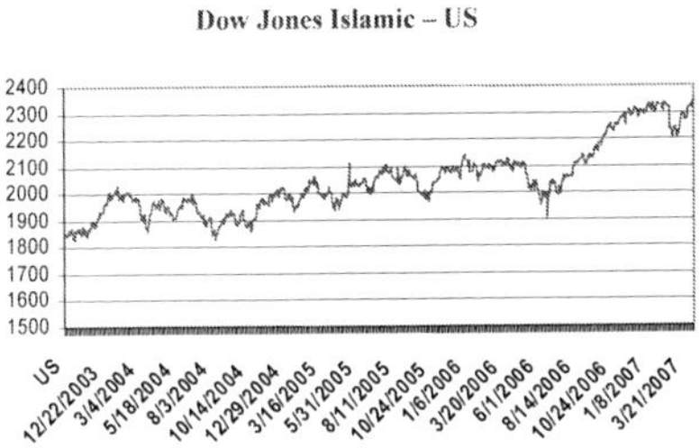

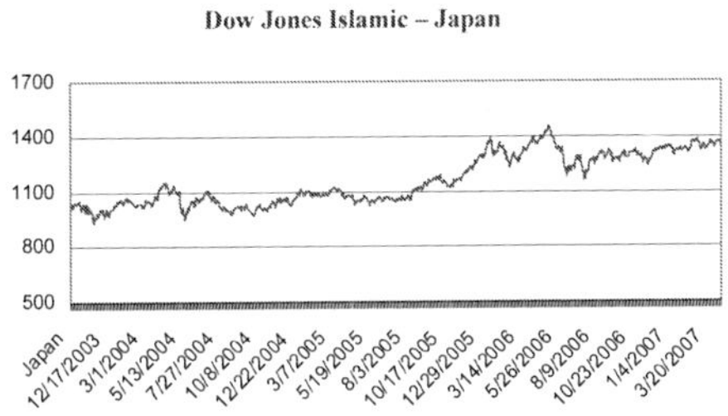

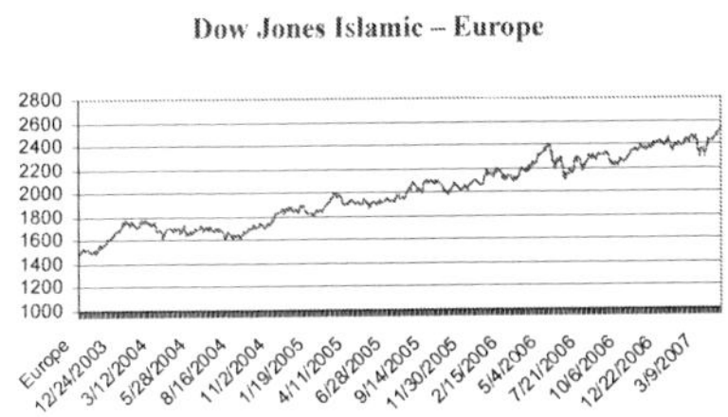

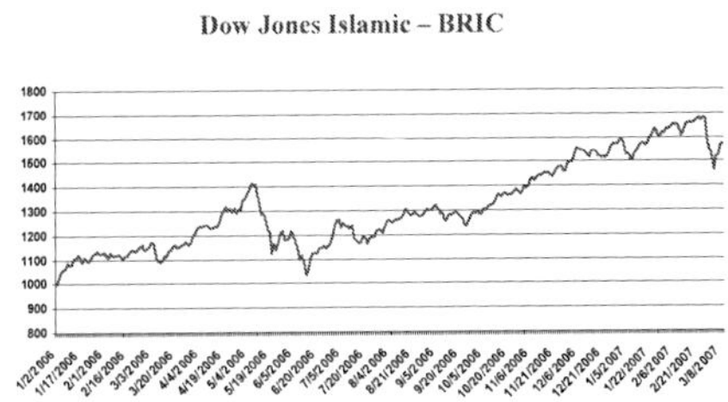

Indicative Term Sheet: Saudi Ryal, SAR, 2 Years 100% Principal Protected Bai Al-Arboon on Islamic Indexes

Seller	:	Bank A
Calculation Agent	:	Bank A
Buyer	:	Customer
Currency	:	USD
Notional	:	To be determined, TBD
Trade Date	:	TBD
Strike Date	:	TBD
Maturity	:	Strike Date plus 2 Years
Maturity Date	:	Last observation Date plus 2 Business Days
Settlement Date	:	2 business days from Maturity Date
Observation Frequency	:	Semi-Annually starting after 6 months
Coupon Payment Date		2 business days after the corresponding Observation Date

<table>
<tr><td>Underlying</td><td>:</td><td>Underlying Basket j= 1…4; an equally weighted basket of 4 of the Dow Jones Islamic Markets Indexes:
Index Name
5. Dow Jones Islamic Markets US Titans 50
6. Dow Jones Islamic Markets Europe Titans 25
7. Dow Jones Islamic Markets BRIC Index
8. Dow Jones Islamic Markets Japan</td></tr>
<tr><td>Payoff at Maturity</td><td>:</td><td>At Maturity date, client shall receive an amount in USD equal to :
$$N \times \left[Part\% \times Max\left\{ 0\%, \frac{1}{4} \times \sum_{i=1}^{i=4} BestPerf(t_i) \right\} \right]$$
Where:
BestPerf(ti) :
The best performance on Valuation Date 'ti' amongst the 4 indexes which constitute the Basket on date ti. The corresponding Index will not be considered as part of the basket in order to determine the BestPerf on following Valuation Dates
$\frac{Under_j(t_i)}{Under_j(t_0)} - 1$ Performance of Index j on date ti
$Under_j(t)$ Closing value of Index Index j on Date t
$t_{1 \le i \le 4}$ 4 Valuation Dates, every 6 months
t_0 Strike Date
P = 70% Participation</td></tr>
<tr><td>Risks</td><td>:</td><td>The structure is to hold to maturity. Principal is 100% protected if held to maturity.</td></tr>
<tr><td>Documentation:</td><td>:</td><td>Market Linked Investment Master Agreement, Iqrar, Customer Risk Tolerance Profiling</td></tr>
</table>

Scenario Analysis:
Determination of Performance and Return on Investment

Basket Details	Observations								
Baskets	Initial Strike	6M	Perf	1Y	Perf	18M	Perf	2Y	Perf
DJIM US	2,330	2,400	3.00%	2,600	11.59%	2,800	20.17%	3,000	28.76%
DJIM Europe	2,535	2,650	4.54%	2800	10.45%	3100	22.29%		
DJIM BRIC	1,720	1,830	6.44%	1996	16.57%				
DJIM Japan	1,344	1,450.0	7.89%						

Participation = 70%
Basket Average Performance = (7.89% + 16.57% + 22.29% + 28.76%)/4
= 18.87%

Payout = Performance * Participation
= 18.87 % x 70%
= 13.21%

Redemption is = Principal + (Principal x Payout)

Termination Clauses
Following the announcement of a non-Shariah compliance ("Disruption") of a basket member, the Calculation Entity will in good faith apply one of the following alternatives respectively:

- substitute any Basket member affected by such event or Shari'a constraint with another compliant stock; or
- re-allocate the relevant weighting among the remaining Basket members; or
- Terminate this transaction immediately.

Appendix 3: 2 Years 100% Capital Guaranteed Investment Linked to Islamic Infrastructure Basket (Selected from Dow Jones Industrial DJI Basic Materials Index & Dow Jones Industrial Utilities Index)

The investment is linked to the Islamic Infrastructure Basket. A Basket of Stocks is selected from Dow Jones Islamic Markets Utilities Basket and form the Basic **Materials Index**

Dow Jones Islamic Market Indices

Dow Jones Islamic Market Indices provide guidance to investing in accordance with Islamic guidelines.

The indexes track Shariah compliant stocks globally. They consist of companies that are compatible with Shariah law. Included in the Islamic Market family of indexes are the broad Dow Jones DJ Islamic Market Index, the DJ Canadian Index, the DJ Islamic Market US Index, the DJ Islamic Market Technology Index, the DJ Islamic Market Extra Liquid Index, the DJ Islamic Market UK Index, the DJ Market Europe Index, and the DJ Islamic Market Asia/Pacific Index.

A Shariah Board of Islamic scholars advise Dow Jones on matters pertaining to the Shariah compliance of the indexes' eligible components.

Producers of alcohol and pork-related products, providers of conventional financial services (banking, insurance, etc.), and providers of entertainment businesses are incompatible with Shariah law. Tobacco manufacturers, defense and weapon companies are also incompatible investments. The Dow Jones Islamic Market Indexes include only actively-traded companies with "acceptable" financial ratios.

Rationale

The above indices consist of over 300 stocks combined together and all of them are not liquid rendering the trade on these indices non-feasible. Bank picks select stocks from the basket, which follow the Dow Jones selection criteria of being Islamic, and are traded in the market (liquid)

The Basket

The basket consists of stocks of companies engaged in sectors of Electricity, Water and Construction Supplies, Energy, Exploration, etc that partly contribute to the overall infrastructure development across the world. The companies are from different geographical areas and are selected based on their past performance, future expectations in the market and health fundamentals like (Volatility Price Earnings Ratio, Dividend Yield, etc)

The basket constitutes of Large, Mid and Small cap companies. Some of these companies' stocks may be more volatile than those of more established companies. These stocks may have returns that vary, from the overall stock market. In general, smaller and medium capitalization companies and the industries in which they are focused are still evolving, and while this may offer better growth potential than larger, more established companies. It may make them more sensitive to changing market conditions.

Utilities like Energy, Electricity and Water have a direct correlation with Urbanization and Population accentuating the fact that these commodities would continue to be in demand.

Stocks and References

#	Company Name	Country	Activity
1	Syngenta AG	Switzerland	Agriculture Technology
2	PPG Industries Inc.	USA	Industrial Materials, Optical, Chemicals
3	International Flavors & Fragrances Inc.	USA	Flavors & Fragrances
4	Air Products & Chemicals Inc.	USA	Technology, Energy, Healthcare
5	Lonza Group AG-REG	Switzerland	Chemicals & Bio-Technology Solutions
6	Praxair Inc.	USA	Industrial Gas Supply
7	Nan Ya Plastics Corp.	Taiwan	Fiber Glass, Polyester Films
8	Koninklijke DSM N.V.	Netherlands	Health, Personal Care, Human Nutrition
9	Avery Dennison Corp.	USA	Pressure sensitive Materials
10	Valspar Corp.	USA	Coatings & Paints
11	Formosa Chemicals & Fibre Corp.	Taiwan	Paints, Wood Pulps and Rayon
12	Rohm & Haas Co.	USA	Electronics, Packaging, Personal Care
13	Enel S.p.A.	Italy	Electricity Supply
14	Hong Kong Electric Holdings Ltd.	Hong Kong	Electric Supply and Technical Services
15	Hong Kong & China Gas Co. Ltd.	Hong Kong	Gas Production, Distribution
16	Gas Natural SDG S.A.	Spain	Gas Production, Distribution
17	Gaz de France	France	Gas Production, Distribution

18	Exelon Corp.	USA	Electricity Generation and Distribution
19	AGL Energy Ltd.	Australia	Sales & Dist of Gas and Electricity
20	Fortum Oyj	Finland	Energy Generation & Distribution
21	Questar Corp.	USA	Gas exploration and Production
22	Cez A.S.	Czech Republic	Electricity Production

2 Years Bai Al-Arboon – Investment Deposit linked to Islamic Infrastructure Basket

Seller	:	Bank A
Calculation Agent	:	Bank A
Buyer	:	Customer
Underlying	:	Islamic Infrastructure Basket (Selected from Dow Jones Islamic Markets Basic Materials Basket and Dow Jones Islamic Markets Utilities Index)
Currency	:	USD
Notional	:	To be determined, TBD
Trade Date	:	TBD
Strike Date	:	TBD
Maturity	:	2 Years
Maturity Date	:	2 Years from Strike Date
Settlement Date	:	TBD
Observation Dates	:	4 observations semi-annually: Observation (1) at 6M: TBD Observation (2) at 12M: TBD Observation (3) at 18M: TBD Observation (4) at 24M: TBD
Payoff at Maturity	:	On Maturity Date, the buyer receives the payoff: 100% + P * Max [(Basket Average / Basket Initial)-1,0] where: P = 70% Participation $\text{Basket}_{\text{Average}} = \frac{1}{4}\sum_{j=1}^{4} \text{Basket}_j$ Basket Average = arithmetic average of basket Levels on basket observation Dates (4 observation), Basketj = Basket value on the observation Date j BasketInitial = Structure Strike at the Strike Date

Settlement	:	Cash
Capital Guarantee	:	100% Capital Guaranteed if held to maturity.
Risks	:	The structure is intended to be held to maturity. Principal is 100% protected only if held to maturity. Premature termination would lead to capital losses
Business Day Convention	:	Exchange Business Days – Modified Following
Documentation	:	Bank A Market Linked Investment Master Agreement, Iqrar, Customer Risk Tolerance Profiling

Scenario Analysis: Determination of Performance and Return on Investment

Scenario 1

Period	6M	12M	18M	24M
Basket Initial	Obs 1	Obs 2	Obs 3	Obs 4
2700	3300	3500	3750	3875
% Change	22.22%	29.63%	38.89%	43.52%
Average of four observations				33.6%

Principal =	**100%**
Participation =	**70.0%**
Performance =	**33.6%**

Payout=	Participation	x	Performance
Payout=	70.0%	x	33.6%
Payout=	**23.5%**		

Redemption=	Principal +	Payout +
=	100%	23.5%
Redemption=	**123.5%**	

Scenario 2

Period	6M	12M	18M	24M
Basket Initial	Obs 1	Obs 2	Obs 3	Obs 4
2600	2500	2400	2450	2400
% Change	-3.85%	-7.69%	-5.77%	-7.69%
Average of four observations				-6.25%

Principal =	**100%**
Participation =	**70.0%**
Performance =	**-6.3%**

Payout=	Participation	x	Performance
Payout=	70.0%	x	-6.3%
Payout=	**0.0%**		

Redemption=	Principal +	Payout +
=	100%	0.0%
Redemption=	**100%**	

Termination Clauses

Following the announcement of non-Shariah compliance ("Disruption") of a basket member, the Calculation Entity will in good faith apply one of the following alternatives respectively:

- substitute any Basket member affected by such event or Shari'a constraint with another compliant stock; or
- re-allocate the relevant weighting among the remaining Basket members, or
- Terminate this transaction immediately. The Calculation Entity calculates the actual performance of the value of the Basket by reference to the value for the underlying constituents of the Basket as at that termination date as determined by the Calculation Entity in accordance with the formula for and method of calculating the value of the basket last in effect prior to the Disruption, but using only the value of the underlying constituents of the basket immediately prior to that Disruption provided that if at the termination date:
  a) the final value of the basket is higher than the initial value of the basket, the buyer receives the actual basket performance; or
  b) the final value of the basket is lower than the initial value of the basket, the buyer receives no performance.

PART II

ISLAMIC BANKING SYSTEM AND FINANCIAL INSTRUMENTS: SOME EMPIRICAL RESULTS REGARDING PERFORMANCE MEASUREMENTS

The concept of performance as used in business can be easily understood when we consider the multiple dimensions that characterize the overall performance of a company. The main objective of this part of the book is to identify the determining factors in, and measurement indicators for, the performance of Islamic banks. This chapter will be devoted to the analysis of research covering the performance of both conventional banks and Islamic banks. It presents an overview of literature that deals with the concept of banking performance and the determinants of banks' performance. This chapter investigates the different approaches and methodologies, as well as the main models, used by researchers dealing with conventional banks.

The Islamic banking industry, characterized by banking operations with no use of interest, has emerged and flourished only during the last four decades. This explains the limited number of studies and the general lack of literature on the performance of Islamic banks. At this point it is worth mentioning that literature on the performance of conventional banks emphasizes the importance of internal and external variables and their effects on the financial performance of those banks; this does not mean that the same variables cannot influence the performance of Islamic banks. Further review of these variables is necessary, however, to ensure their applicability in the context of Islamic banking operations. This is necessary because of doctrinal differences between Islamic and conventional banks.

CHAPTER THREE

THE MEASURING AND EVALUATION OF BANK PERFORMANCE: SOME EMPIRICAL RESULTS

MONDHER BELLALAH AND RACHA GHAYAD

Introduction

The chapter identifies the determining factors in, and measurement indicators for, the performance of Islamic banks. It is devoted to the analysis of research covering the performance of conventional and Islamic banks. It summarizes literature dealing with banking performance and the determinants for that performance. It investigates the different approaches and methodologies, and the main models, used by researchers dealing with conventional banks.

The first section is devoted to the definition of "banking performance". An analysis of the traditional indicators of performance, such as profitability ratios and efficiency, as well as relatively new indicators such as the shareholding value (EVA or Economic Value Added), is of vital importance. These indicators can all be used when considering the performance of Islamic banks.

The objective is to find indicators for the measurement of performance. There are many indicators utilized by researchers studying the performance of conventional banks, and they are analyzed here in order to choose from among them those that can best be utilized for measuring the performance of Islamic banks.

Section 1. Definition of Banking Performance

The concept of performance is commonly used in business but it remains difficult to give it a simple definition. We can more easily understand the concept when we consider the multiple dimensions that characterize the overall performance of a company (Mathé, 1999).

Financial market participants, namely depositors, bank management and regulators, are naturally interested in measuring banking performance. The importance of measuring performance increases within competitive financial markets, because performance indicators send positive and/or negative signals to depositors and investors, potentially encouraging them to make an investment or to draw their funds from the bank. Moreover, assessments of performance send signals to bank executives indicated whether they ought to increase their deposit or loan services, or both simultaneously. Regulatory bodies are also interested in this knowledge for their own purposes.

The idea of performance is related to obtained results and the primary use of the idea has always been to assess it through various financial indicators. Nevertheless, if we seek to deepen the concept of performance, other dimensions appear. A. Bourguignon (1997) identifies three main dimensions:

- Performance is the action, i.e. a process corresponding to "the enactment of a jurisdiction that is merely one possibility"
- Performance is also a result of the action "understood as the ex post evaluation of the findings
- Performance is successful, according to the representations of success, and variable depending on the players. De La Villarmois (1998) distinguishes two key dimensions: On the one hand, objective dimensions, both economic (efficiency) and systemic (sustainability of the organization), and on the other hand, subjective dimensions, both social (value of human resources) and societal (legitimacy of the organization). "Performance" refers to the evaluation of the object (the company) by the subject (shareholder, official or wage-earner) of a given project.

The researcher chooses the indicators by which he or she will measure performance depending on his or her chosen level of analysis. A company's performance can be measured simply by its profitability, market share or productivity. Researchers analyzing the performance of conventional banks take bank performance to mean the financial performance of that bank. To evaluate the profitability of banks, we can use either an assessment by the market or an estimate based on accounting measures. These measures are not, strictly speaking, equivalent to each other. Accordingly, different types of measures possible a priori are presented, and the choices that have been made are justified. Some measures are either inappropriate for the Islamic banking sector or simply impractical.

Section 2.
Profitability ratios as a measure of banking performance

1. The profitability of banks: A risk-return couple

Profitability is defined as the ability of capital placed or invested to provide income, expressed in financial terms. The profitability of a credit institution is its ability to achieve sufficient earnings through exploitation, after deduction of the costs necessary for this exploitation, in order to continue its sustained activity.

If we look into the etymology of the word profitability, we see that it is the ability of a company, a working tool, or an investment to yield profit. This leads to the measurement of profit actually achieved compared either with activity, or with capital used. The concept of profitability is of course linked to profit and, in general, we can define the profitability of a company as its ability to produce a profit. These definitions express the fact that the profitability of a business (financial or non-financial) is calculated as the difference between its income and the expenses it has incurred to generate this income. Profitability is measured using a rate of return, which is the ratio between the value of income and the amount of capital:

Rate of Return = Income / Capital .100.

Analysis is carried out with reference to current financial schools of thought and the "risk-return couple". This consideration of risk becomes all the more necessary upon exploring the relationship between banking strategy and performance.

2. Accounting Measures of Profitability

Out of the various options available, the income-capital pair is often used for sheer convenience. The stratification of capital is essential because each component of capital will match one and only one level of income. There are two main sources of capital:

- Invested capital, which includes all invested funds regardless of their nature (tangible, intangible, financial, etc).
- Shareholders' capital, representing committed financing; the counterpart of the invested capital. This is classified as either internal equity, external equity or debt capital.

The position of income depends on the type of capital used to define the ratio.

Profitability, if thought of as the ability of the company to produce a profit, can be expressed as a ratio, of the results to the invested capital, and that ratio then assessed in terms of economic efficiency. It can also be expressed as a ratio of result to committed capital, in which case we talk about financial profitability. The position of income depends on the type of capital used to define the ratio.

Is this notion of Return on Invested Capital (ROI) suitable for studying the performance of banks?

This measure provides a good estimate of profitability only if the depreciation accounted for is a good reflection of existing physical capital. This is not often the case. DAPs often appear in amounts that correspond more to tax considerations than economic ones. This poor estimate of depreciation, together with the practice of valuing investments at their historical costs, renders this measure of profitability not much more than a biased estimation of the firm's performance. Because of the low portion of tangible assets in the bank's balance sheet, this indicator should not be accepted as a measure of banking performance.

Instead, other measures, such as Return on Asset (ROA) and the Profit Margin (PM), are used in the banking sector as an indicator for assessing the profitability of banks.

2.1. The measure of profitability by ROA

ROA is the ratio of net income to total assets; it expresses the efficiency with which assets have been used within the bank:

R.O.A = net income after taxes / total assets
= profit after tax / total assets.

ROA is a traditional measure of the performance of a financial intermediary; it measures the ability of a bank to make optimum use of borrowed funds, i.e. the strongest performance. This ratio is the indicator most watched by financial analysts and bankers themselves. It is frequently used for international comparisons of bank performance.

Insofar as strategic choice is partly about the distribution of assets, ROA is an appropriate measure of performance which, moreover, offers the advantage of being comparable to the performance measures used in previous empirical studies of this nature. ROA is a measure of performance which takes into account the relationship between the strategic choices made by banks and their performance. The performance of banks is shown in three ratios; two of the ratios are the aforementioned ROA and ROE. However, the demands of shareholders, the work of financial analysts and more generally, the banking and financial markets have developed and grown in complexity in recent years, calling for increasingly sophisticated indicators in the banking sector. The most common indicator is known as the Risk Adjusted Return on Capital (RAROC) methodology and is a good indicator of shareholding value.

2.2. The measure of profitability by RAROC

RAROC is the yield of activities as compared to their capital requirement. Its calculation involves subtracting a risk premium from the accounting return. The risk factor can be estimated in different ways, and regularly gets recalculated in the light of new empirical research based on recent occurrences. The Bankers Trust Group introduced the RAROC ratio to the United States, where it is now extensively used within the profession. In fact, most large international banks are currently using this ratio, which considers three main sources of risk: market risk, credit risk and operational risk (Ory, 2002).

2.2.1. RAROC logic in banking activity

The RAROC method assists bank administrators in:

(1) Pricing their various products and services
(2) Measuring the performance of clients, products, transactions and business portfolios
(3) Structuring their own funds optimally by allocating proportionately more capital to profit centers or liabilities that produce the highest adjusted returns relative to risk
(4) Reducing or eliminating activities whose yields are consistently under a predetermined minimum yield or over a maximum cost of capital

- This method can be used by the management of a bank in a dynamic way in order to determine the worth of different activities, increase revenues and moderate risk.

RAROC methodology is based primarily on the need to assess and cover the losses inherent in banking activity. The various parameters described above are derived from the RAROC measure. It can be expressed as the equation:

RAROC = income – costs – average losses / economic capital

This approach has its limitations. RAROC assumes that it is possible to measure the risk-adjusted return for the entire banking establishment, as it is for each of its components. In fact it is very difficult to recognize the benefit in a given period, e.g. one year or fraction of a year, of certain bank loans whose risk and return (as compared to those of trading operations) can be effectively gauged only at the final maturity of these loans, a period of time which may extend over several years. To the extent that these credits are not negotiable or securitized, it is advisable to use relatively high capital. The other challenge posed by RAROC is to allocate fixed costs and set valid transfer prices of various banking products and services within each single establishment.

Section 3. Efficiency as a measure of banking performance

The concept of efficiency has become more important in the work of researchers with the liberalization and globalization of financial markets, which has led to an increase in the number of mergers and acquisitions.

Efficiency uses as its criteria both comparisons between organizations, and comparisons between organizations and markets, for establishing their respective performances, as well as the transformation conditions of organizations, the relationship between organizations and the placement of these organizations in the market. As the object of this research focuses on the performance of Islamic banks, this is not the type of efficiency that we shall address; we will be looking at banking efficiency. Therefore we limit ourselves to explaining how the efficiency of a bank is calculated. At this stage, it is important to note that in most recent works, the topic of measuring banks' efficiency is rarely addressed. It seems important for us to address the theoretical fundamentals and the empirical data as part of this line of research, however, the efficiency of any financial or non-financial firm is determined by the allocation of resources, economies of scale and of scope, costs and the volume of transactions.

We can measure bank efficiency using various different techniques and indicators. In general, experts consider the cost or result ratios as the best indicators of efficiency. Methods based on estimating a cost or profit function take into account all these differences. However, in the context of our research, we will not address in detail these two methods.

According to Berger and Mester (1997), measurement of efficiency requires two steps: first, we must specify the efficiency frontier for the sector, and then we must measure the difference between that boundary and the efficiency of the observed bank. A review of literature available on this matter presents two important concepts of efficiency:

- Efficiency of profit/standard (standard profit efficiency)
- Efficiency of cost (cost efficiency)

While the efficiency of profit/standard measures whether a bank realizes the maximum profit for a given price using inputs, outputs and other variables (Berger and Mester, 1997), the measure of the efficiency of cost (cost efficiency) indicates how close a company is to specific production targets.

Section 4. Shareholding value as a measure of banking performance

If financial globalization has resulted in heightened competition among stock exchanges, it has also emphasized the need for companies to convince investors of their ability to pay back committed capital. This need requires a redefinition of the measures of business performance, particularly the EVA (Economic Value Added) concept and even the MVA (Market Value Added).

The relevant specialized press and literature make EVA a primary criterion in assessing performance. In economic literature, performance is nowadays translated almost directly as EVA. It is a measure of performance that was created in the 90s by the firm Stern and Stewart and is directly linked to operational economic results. Since the creation of this indicator, a growing number of large groups (for example, Total, Danone, etc.) evaluate the performance of their operational managers using this indicator.

Alfred Marshall developed the concept of economic income. This concept implies that a company is making profits as soon as its revenues are sufficient to cover its operating costs and capital.

Concerning the cost of capital, a fundamental concept must be introduced, and it can be summarized as follows: opportunity cost deciding an economic cost by calculation of the difference between it and accounting cost. This economic cost includes all production costs, valued at market prices.

EVA is a tool that objectively measures the performance of the company and constitutes an internal and external communication tool (to shareholders and bondholders). This concept is derived from the notion of value creation. The objective of a firm is the maximization of profit, i.e. the difference between the revenue of the firm and its costs. In other words, it is necessary to take into consideration all production costs on top of accounting costs, and in particular, to take into account the cost of capital for which remuneration, at least, is guaranteed.

The various methods of calculating shareholder value are mainly based on the concepts of residual income, Internal Rate of Return (IRR) and net present value.

The concept of residual income is measured by "… the difference between the exploitation result and the financial burden representative of the cost of employed capital".

The IRR is the maximum rate at which it is acceptable to borrow for financing a project. It depends only on the sequence of cash flows generated by investment. For example, if the Internal Rate of Return on an investment is less than the rate of interest on the market, the equity holder may be more interested in placing his or her funds on the market than on investing. As for the net present value, or NPV, this is measured by discounting the expected future earnings at a rate equal to the return offered by comparable assets. We often call this rate of return the discount rate or the opportunity cost of capital.

EVA is calculated by those who use it as follows:

EVA = Operating profit after tax – weighted average cost of capital

A key component for calculating EVA is the weighted average cost of funding resources. This is the actual price paid by the company to support its investment plans, which must include the cost of capital (the remuneration of shareholders) and the cost of debt (namely the remuneration of bankers).

A number of precautions are inherently necessary in determining EVA. We will not detail our recommendations in regard to these; let us simply emphasize that the weighted cost of capital should use the economic value of debt and capital, not the historical value. In addition, prior to the calculation of EVA, accounting restatements are necessary. These adjustments are intended to approximate market values and use them to find an economic result.

A review of literature on this matter shows that, in studies on the determinants of banking performance, researchers prefer not to use shareholding value as a criterion for measuring banking performance. In empirical studies on the determinants of performance in Islamic banks, the Return on Assets (ROA) and Return on Equity (ROE) have instead been used as indicators for measuring financial performance. However, most researchers who study the determinants of performance in conventional banks measure banking performance by using the usual accounting profitability ratios. Therefore, studies dealing with the financial performance of Islamic banks are now opting for this too.

Within the framework of our research, we also intend to measure the financial performance of these banks with the use of the usual accounting ratios. The difficulty of obtaining sufficient data dictates our choice, and the calculation of these ratios requires data easily accessible, contrary to the calculation of indicators such as shareholding value (EVA, Economic Value Added) and RAROC, which requires confidential or proprietary information.

Section 5. Other indicators for measuring banking performance

Some empirical studies on banking performance use the Price-Earnings Ratio (PER) as a performance indicator. The PER can be defined by the formula:

PER = stock price / earnings per share (EPS)

Empirical studies that aim to include the performance of banks placed on the stock exchange often use the PER as an indicator of performance as it reflects the stock market capitalization of banking establishments. As part of our research on the determinants of the performance of Islamic banks, and because the Islamic banks in this study are not publicly traded on the stock exchange, PER cannot be used as a performance indicator.

Other researchers have evaluated banking performance using a measuring index, which is a series of indicators. They assess the effects of internal and external variables on the performance measuring index through a canonical correlation analysis. A measuring index for the performance of a new bank would take into consideration the following elements: profitability, the average interest rate on loans and deposits and market share.

Hirtle (1991) used a set of indicators to assess the performance of 51 international banks and investment companies. Five measures have been implemented to predict banking performance: ROA, ROE (net income after tax/total equity capital), productivity (the ratio of total revenue to expenses not bearing interest), funding (proper funds and PER) and size (the level and rate of growth in assets).

CHAPTER FOUR

PREDICTORS OF THE PERFORMANCE OF CONVENTIONAL AND ISLAMIC BANKS: SOME EMPIRICAL RESULTS

MONDHER BELLALAH AND RACHA GHAYAD

Introduction

Our goal is to explain the dimensions and indicators, as identified in literature that determine the performance of conventional banks.

To this end, we first provide an overview of different approaches and then explain the variables (internal and external) most used in the literature on this matter. We present results obtained in the main empirical studies on conventional banking. With the aim of presenting the main theoretical underpinnings of our research, we will quote some theories explaining what determines banking performance. Finally, we will present empirical results for each predictor variable, indicating whether the variable has a positive or negative impact on the performance of conventional banks.

Section 1. The theoretical basis

Literature shows that studies explaining conventional banking performance can be grouped into two categories. The first category includes works analyzing theories related to the competition variable and its effect on the banking sector. These theories include the following:

- The "Structure – Conduct – Performance" (SCP) model
- The Efficient Structure or Relative Efficiency theory
- The theory of Economies of Scales
- The theory of Economies of Scope
- The theory of Contestable Markets
- The theory of Efficiency – X (or X-Efficiency)

The second category concerns more general studies that do not seek to test any particular model.

The studies we consider generalist tend to be conducted by international institutions (cf. The World Bank). These studies have a mainly descriptive purpose (see for example Barth, Nolle and Rice, 1997; Demirgüç-Kunt and Huizinga, 1997).

When using certain approaches, banking performance is explained by internal and external variables. In this context we often find empirical works based on the Structure – Behavior – Performance model and the theory of efficient structures or relative efficiency. Some studies that we refer to as generalist explain banking performance in the same way. As for studies testing the theories of economies of scale, economies of scope and X-efficiency, banking performance is explained either by internal variables alone, or by both internal and external variables.

However, there are certain studies which explain the performance of conventional banks using internal or external variables.

Internal variables used to explain banking performance are listed below:

- Capital structure
- Adequacy of proper funds
- Structure of assets
- Liquidity and/or cost efficiency

Moreover, in some studies on government banks, researchers seek only to understand internal factors – namely the level of "managerial equity ownership" – and the effect they have on the profitability of the bank (for example: Hirschey, 1999). Research focusing on external variables is primarily designed to explain the impact of the regulatory and economic environment on banking performance. The latter also aims to explain the determinants of banking crises in both developed and developing countries (for example Demirgüç-Kunt and Detragiache, 1997).

Section 2. Studies in the framework of conventional banks

Our literature review shows that the methodology adopted to explain banking performance differs depending on the objective of the study. Studies on the performance of conventional banks primarily use one of two approaches to assessing performance.

In some studies, the researcher represents banking performance as an accounting ratio, affected by a number of internal and external variables.

In this approach, researchers use a regression equation to test the correlation between bank performance and the chosen variables.

Using a second approach, conventional banking performance is gauged by the level of efficiency of the bank in question. In this context, assessments of banking performance are based on an estimate of cost and profit function, established from inputs and outputs.

This section presents these two approaches to banking performance research: measuring performance by calculating accounting ratios and by examining efficiency.

2.1. Studies opting for an approach based on accounting ratios

Regarding the conventional banking sector, empirical research on performance carried out by studying accounting ratios is generally carried out using a methodology based on the following equation:

$$\mathbf{P = a + bCR + cMS + \Sigma dZ + e}$$

Where:

P: performance measurement (often the profitability of assets, return on equity or rate of interest margin to total assets)
CR: market concentration (Concentration Ratio)
MS: market share
Z: vector of control variables (statement ratios of the bank and environmental indicators)
e: error term

As in the case of conventional banks, empirical studies on the determinants of the performance of Islamic banks measure these using accounting ratios as part of an econometric model to examine the relationship between performance and internal and external variables. Let us mention as an example of this a study by Bashir (2000) and Harron (1994).

Once the equation has been constructed, it is up to the researcher to find the significance level coefficients associated with each variable using regression methods. This methodology is mainly used in studies designed to test the Structure – Behavior – Performance model and the theory of relative efficiency. In these studies, the main objective is to discover the impact of key variables relating to market structure, such as market concentration and market share. Other variables, internal or external, are control. The regression model is not only used in empirical studies testing a particular hypothesis; it is also used in generalist studies. These studies are usually conducted by researchers from major international organizations. In this type of study, they tend to treat the explanatory variables as of equal importance; in other words, there are no key variables in their analyses. Indeed, the aim is to find which variable or variables are responsible for performance. These studies present banking performance in terms of accounting ratios; they do not favor any one variable. Accordingly, we do not differentiate between key and control variables. Also, these studies look at far more variables at a time than studies with the objective of testing a single, particular theory.

2.2. The efficiency approach

Efficiency is measured by the amount of resources used to produce one unit of goods or services. It is an internal measure of performance, and related to the formal aspects of a corporation. Some factors which may affect efficiency are economies of scale, experience, purchasing costs and the processes of production and design.

Within the research area of the performance of conventional banks', there are researchers who still use efficiency as an indicator, using cost or profit functions to measure that efficiency. This methodology has often been implemented for the testing of theories, such as those of economies of scale, economies of scope and X-efficiency.

We present this approach here without detailing the econometric subtleties, because we will not be using this approach in our own empirical study.

In defining the concept of efficiency, we will rely on the study of Berger and Mester (1997). Cost efficiency measures whether a company is far from its specified production target under current conditions. To measure efficiency, we separate the factors of inefficiency and random error from the other terms of the function, and then we perform a logarithmic calculation.

Concerning the definition and selection of input and output, there are two different theoretical approaches which deal with the operations of a banking firm: physical (production) and financial (intermediation). For the purposes of the first approach, the bank "produces" transaction and information services. "Banking products", therefore, refers to accounts opened by the bank to manage deposits and loans. As banks are firms that use two factors, physical capital and work, to offer different types of deposits and loans, the costs come exclusively in the forms of personnel and physical capital. These operating costs are related to the management of deposit and loan accounts, especially the debit and credit on these accounts.

According to the production approach, output is measured in physical units (in other words, by the number of accounts or transactions), so we measure it by the number of deposits and the number of loans (including operating costs and excluding financial charges).

The financial, or intermediation, approach, on the other hand, measures banking products in monetary units. In the language of this approach, a bank produces amounts in currency, not in number of accounts, of loans and deposits.

The objective of the bank, according to those using the second approach, is to use the resources of physical capital and work to transform deposits into loans and investments. This approach measures input and output in loans, investments and deposits as opposed to in production levels, i.e. the number of accounts. The costs include both financial costs and operating expenses.

Within studies on the conventional banking sector, researchers tend to prefer the intermediation approach because financial charges are included in the calculation of bank costs. These charges represent a significant portion of the total costs incurred by a bank, and so they must be considered to avoid biasing the results of empirical studies. Deposits must be considered input, as they are by the intermediation approach, and not output, as in the production approach. In reality, after all, deposits are used in conjunction with other sources of funding to make up loans and investments. Finally, the production approach requires data that is not readily accessible to measure efficiency, such as the number of lines of loans. In the intermediation approach, knowledge of the number of accounts is not necessary to measure efficiency, although it is in fact possible to use data from the balance sheet to calculate the total amount of accounts. Regarding the Islamic banking sector, there are only two studies on performance that use efficiency as an indicator.

2.3. Study results

In this section, we present the results of various studies, each conducted using one of the two approaches that we have called the accounting ratios approach and the efficiency approach. As our own case study falls into the category of accounting ratios studies, we will start with the results of these. The purpose of this section is to discover the determinants of conventional banking performance, whether internal or external. This aim forms the theoretical basis of our research work. As we have already mentioned, we will verify the applicability of each variable to Islamic banking corporations. We will try to analyze the relationship between each variable and banking performance. It is worth remembering at this stage that there are two types of variables that can affect banking performance, namely internal variables and external variables.

2.3.1. The results of studies that take the "accounting ratios approach"

In the following sections we will present the variables that affect banking performance, and then explain in further detail the impact of these variables. There are two types of variables affecting banking performance: internal and external variables.

- **Internal variables:** These are the variables controlled by the bank's management and they also reflect its characteristics. They are:
  * Capital structure
  * Asset structure
  * Liquidity
  * Cost efficiency

- **External variables:** These variables reflect the environment, and are as follows:
  * Market structure
  * The economic and regulatory environments, including the taxation system

These variables are included in several empirical studies based on the SCP theory or the theory of efficient structure. They are also found in some studies that we have called generalist, i.e. in studies not designed to test a specific theory.

2.3.1.1. The impact of internal variables on banking performance

In studies that take the accounting ratios approach, internal variables of banking performance were measured by indicators of a quantitative, or quantifiable, nature. These indicators are primarily financial in nature. They express various dimensions of the financial structure such as:

- The structure of capital
- The structure of assets
- The structure of liquidity

- Efficiency and the ownership of capital

We represent the correlation that exists between an indicator and banking performance as an accounting ratio.

2.3.1.1.1. The structure of proper funds

The proper funds of a bank represent risk capital and are characterized by three attributes: relative stability, no legal obligation to produce a dividend payment and, finally, a residual legal position after satisfying the interests of depositors and other creditors (including employees and tax authorities). The term "capital" generally includes capital stock, participation certificates or bonus certificates (without voting right) and other similar instruments of ownership, open reserves and hidden reserves.

In a bank, equity has three core functions:

- To absorb unexpected losses or lessen the probability of losses occurring
- To secure depositors and other donors
- To make the investments necessary to launch and develop profitable businesses for the bank

The profitability of a conventional commercial bank varies depending on the cost of borrowed funds such as deposits and funds borrowed in the short- and long-term. Indeed, the financial autonomy of a bank depends on the level of its equity interest; as the level of capital secured by the bank progressively grows, the need for long-term funding decreases.

In addition, well-capitalized banks are considered less risky, so they can access funds under better conditions (Berger, 1995). Banks whose capitalization is prominent can be considered conservative institutions.

The role of capital as a variable determinant of banking performance has been asserted in most of the empirical literature on this subject (Demirgüç-Kunt and Huizinga, 1999; Molyneux and Thornton, 1992). It is worth mentioning that a positive relationship exists between the ratio of equity to total assets and return on assets.

Most researchers calculate the level of capital using the following information: social capital and possible reserves as compared to total assets. Since this ratio does not take into account the level of risk of assets, and in order to better reflect the level of risk, the Basel Committee, whose purpose is to recommend appropriate balance sheet structures to banks, created a ratio called the Cooke ratio in July 1998. This ratio does not comply directly with the law but is transcribed by local regulatory authorities. In Europe, it is the European Community which is responsible for enforcing the recommendations of the Basel Committee through the CAD (Capital Adequacy Directive). To arrive at this ratio, we refer to the solvency, or adequacy, ratio of proper funds. Indeed, the balance sheet of a company is divided schematically as follows: firstly, the liabilities, which are sources of funding (more or less just capital and long-term liabilities) and secondly, assets, which include everything that the company has accomplished with the funding provided and everything it possesses; the tangible assets (buildings) and intangible assets (shares in other companies), inventories and receivables. The results are presented so that the total assets equal the total liabilities.

Equity comprises all resources "running the risk" of the company, i.e. those which will be refunded in principle only with the liquidation of the company (equity), or those that will be reimbursed only in the very long-term (semi-equity).

Net assets are equal to the total assets of the company subtracted from all its real or potential commitments:

$$\text{Net assets} = \text{Fixed assets} + \text{Current assets and financial} - \text{All debts}$$

The solvency of a company, whatever that company may be, is its ability to repay, in full, its commitments in the event of liquidation. It depends on the quality of its assets, especially the ease with which they may be liquidated, and the amount of its liabilities (debts).

$$\text{As Assets} = \text{Liabilities}$$
$$\text{Equity} + \text{Liabilities} = \text{Fixed assets} + \text{Current and financial assets}$$
$$\text{Equity} = \text{Net Assets}$$

In conclusion, solvency, which intuitively corresponds to the debt:net asset ratio, may also be measured by the debt:equity ratio.

Debts consist primarily of demand and sight deposits, and financial assets consist of granted loans. It is the purpose of a bank, of course, to distribute credit.

The solvency of a bank can therefore be defined as its ability to meet the withdrawal requests of all its depositors. It is part of the responsibility of regulating authorities to ensure that banks are able to meet their obligations, because it is so important to the maintenance of stability, even that of the entire economy of a country, that they can do so.

In view of the equity mentioned above, we see that in order to distribute additional credit, the bank must either raise more deposits, at the risk of not being able to repay them, or strengthen its equity. However, a company is more secure if some of its current assets are financed by resources which will not expire within the year. Assets are always random in nature and therefore risky (especially when they consist primarily of receivables, as for banks) while debts, on the other hand, are unavoidable. This is why at least a part of the assets must be funded not by debt but by capital.

On the other hand, if we require a bank to raise its own funds, it has more to lose in case of bankruptcy and will therefore tend to engage in less risky activities.

The level of proper funds is the guarantor of a company's financial soundness. Thus proper funds guarantee the bank's solvency against the losses that risks on assets are likely to generate. Indeed the international solvency ratio is calculated by the ratio of proper funds to risk weighted assets. The minimum ratio that must be adhered to is 8%. The risk weighted amount is obtained from the commitments in the balance sheet and the off balance sheet. The calculation is done by applying a different weighting of risk to each different type of commitment.

As in conventional banks, the capital of an Islamic bank usually consists of four accounts: the corporate capital, surplus, reserves and retained (non-distributed) earnings. The capital consists mainly of the par or stated value of all non-amortized shares, subscribed and paid for by members (usually in the form of ordinary shares). The retained earnings are usually derived from the value of surplus premiums at which ordinary shares were sold to the public. The reserves comprise various funds established by the bank to fulfill the conditions of a monetary authority, or for other specific purposes such as those mandated by municipal orders or by the bank's management. The retained profits, or undistributed surplus, are the net profits from previous years.

The capital held by a conventional bank allows that bank to achieve two goals: first, it represents the stake of owners in their companies and it assumes and thereby ensures that the bank manager will undertake careful policies, not only to insure that capital, but to ensure adequate returns to the owners. Secondly, capital constitutes a protection for depositors; in case of loss or liquidation, the claims of depositors are met (by drawing upon this capital) before those of shareholders. The higher the level of capital a bank has, therefore, the higher the level of confidence in that bank and the more likely customers are to deposit larger amounts of money.

Modigliani and Miller (1958) examined the capital structure of companies. They thought that, with the existence of complete transparency of information and complete markets, capital structure has no influence on the value of the firm. Other researchers studying the link between capital and bank profitability have found results that decidedly conflict with this.

One theory of banking assumes that there is a positive relationship between the performance of a bank and its capital. This means that the bank should realize a high level of return on its assets if it holds a high level of capital. This theory applies to Islamic banks for two reasons. First, no predetermined rate of return is given to depositors, in contrast to the conventional banking system. Most Islamic banks offer savings and investment accounts based on Mudaraba. Under this contract, the depositors instead share with the bank any profit realized by activities invested in with their funds. In the case of loss, depositors must also bear the losses and the bank has no obligation to reimburse the funds.

From the outset, Islamic banks operate in a manner different from that of conventional banks which can combine the funds of shareholders with those of depositors. They use two methods to deploy these combined funds.

The first method is the grouping system, in which the capital of depositors and the funds of shareholders are combined together and used in a particular project. The profits from this project will be shared between the depositors and shareholders.

Using the second method, the bank finances a specific project with the funds of depositors. In this case, the project's yields go directly into the accounts of depositors. The bank receives some of these returns in the form of commission. Based on these arrangements, a hypothesis arises that the volume of an Islamic bank's capital is unrelated to its profitability.

In his empirical study on the determinants of the performance of Islamic banks, Harron (1994) tested the correlation between capital structure and financial performance. It is worth noting at this stage that he equated performance with profitability. Harron used the ratio of capital and reserves to total assets as a measure of capital. Beshir (1993) shows a positive correlation between the level of capital and the profitability of Islamic banks. In other words, a high level of capital implies high profitability.

2.3.1.1.2. Asset structure

Most empirical studies addressing the determinants of conventional banks' performance show that the composition of assets has an impact on banking performance. It seems useful to now present the various elements that make up a bank's balance sheet, with the aim of studying the impact of each component on performance.

In a conventional bank, income is generated mainly through loans granted by the bank. Assets, therefore, can be measured in terms of the lending rates on them. The relationship of this ratio with to actual profitability depends on the risk inherent in the loans (default risk) as each loan's generated profit has an impact on the overall profitability of the bank.

Credit risk is the risk that a debtor will default, or that the economic situation will deteriorate to the point of devaluing the claim that the institution has on him. To measure the credit risk we must apply a weighting to the total amount of the debt, which we call the "outstanding quality" of the debtor. The Basel Committee identifies many types of exposure to credit risk, with each different category having an associated weighting, which ranges from 0% for sovereign states, which amounts to saying that loans to sovereign states are considered risk-free, to 150% for lower-rated parties.

The rate of return that the bank charges on a loan is related to the risk level of that loan. The higher the risk associated with the loan, the greater the rate of return required by the bank. However, at the same time, the higher the risk is, the more significant the possibility of default by a bad debtor. Outstanding (non-reimbursed) amounts have a direct influence on profitability and may endanger the very existence of the bank.

Consequently it is assumed that, in a weak macroeconomic situation, the link between the profitability of banks and the ratio of loans to total assets is negative. A study using data from 180 banks (including commercial banks, savings banks and cooperative banks) from 13 European countries confirms that the negative impact of interest rates on total assets on the return on equity is negative. This analysis also supports the results of a study by Molyneux, Lloyd-Williams and Thornton (1992) on European banks. Another study, by Demirgüç-Kunt and Huizinga (1999), shows a positive correlation between the ratio of loan rates to total assets and net interest margin. However, this correlation is negative if the profit in question is that before tax. This last result needs to be taken into account when considering the studies mentioned earlier.

Unlike conventional banks, which are free to grant loans to all sectors and invest in all types of project in both primary and secondary capital markets, the financing activities of Islamic banks must comply with Shariah, which specifically prohibits investing in activities that have to do with interest. In other words, the instruments associated with interest which are issued and sold on the primary and secondary markets are strictly forbidden to Islamic banks. Therefore they are investment activities with which an Islamic bank will not involve itself.

Shariah law allows three types of banking operations, based on:

- The principle of sharing profit and loss
- The principle of fixed costs
- The principle of zero charge, which is a principle adopted by Islamic banks in their financing of certain activities

Of the above, Mudaraba and Musharaka come under the category of profit and loss sharing, while Murabaha, Baii Mouazzal, Ijara, and Iktinaa come under fixed cost or profit margin. Correspondingly, the Qard Hassan belongs to the category of zero cost.

Islamic banking revenues are generated through financing and investment. As such, these revenues are related to the volume of funds allocated through operations from the three categories listed above. Activities conducted under the principle of profit and loss sharing are risky and uncertain, therefore the yields of these activities are also unpredictable and uncertain. It is not only the owner (the user) of the funds that benefits from achieved profits, but also the bank. The principle of fixed costs, on which Murabaha contracts are based, is very similar to the activities of conventional banks in terms of simplicity, minimal risk and a predetermined, fixed rate of return. The benefits of these activities are easily quantifiable.

Harron (1993) tested the impact of the ratio of funds invested according to the principles of sharing profit and loss to total assets on the performance of Islamic banks. He used this variable as an indicator of the ability of the assets owned by the bank to create and maintain activity and/or obtain, protect, and enhance its competitive advantage.

On a similar note, we can also cite a study by Beshir (2000). After compensating for macroeconomic variables (the structure of financial markets, taxes etc.), Beshir showed that a high ratio of loans to assets implies a high profitability.

The second component of the balance sheet is the assets. This category includes buildings (e.g. headquarters, branches) and technological equipment. In principle, the assets should generate interest in the bank, otherwise they represent a cost. Based on the study of Demirgüç-Kunt and Huizinga (1999), we can conclude that the possession of assets that do not generate interest contributes to a reduction in net interest income as well as profitability. According to these authors, this is true to an even greater extent when the bank operates in a rich country. In addition to the ratios that relate to the structure of assets, the overall size of assets, i.e. the total size of the balance sheet, also has an impact on banking performance.

Concerning the impact of size on banking performance, there exist in literature two very distinct approaches. The first uses the theory of options (option pricing model) to consider the problems of moral hazards in banking. The second works within the framework of the new theory of intermediation that focuses on market imperfections, including those relating to information (Goyeau, Sauviat and Tarazi, 1998, p 342). The impact of size on banking performance will be discussed in later sections, both in the context of option theory, where it will also be addressed in the context of the regulatory environment, and the new theory of intermediation, in the section where we will also be discussing the impact of efficiency.

For now, however, we will continue to concern ourselves with researchers analyzing the effect of asset structure on banking performance. These researchers must not fail to take into account off-balance sheet accounts. Several types of operation are recorded in the off-balance sheet. These include letters of credit, letters of guarantee, the sale of options, foreign currency transactions, and repurchase transactions (repurchase agreements). While these processes do not involve cash movement, the level of uncertainty, and hence of risk, is high.

The number of existing Islamic banks has been used by Beshir (2000) to measure the effect of competition on their profitability. Total assets were used to compensate for the cost differences related to the differing sizes of the banks and the ability of each to diversify. The first factor can have a positive effect if there are significant economies of scale, while the latter can have negative effects if increased diversification leads to greater risks and lower profitability. Ultimately, the results obtained indicate a strong positive correlation between profitability and general expenses.

2.3.1.1.3. The structure of liquidity

Within banking, liquidity is defined as all monetary assets of the bank (banknotes, balance accounts open at the Central Bank and current accounts payable from its associates and the public treasury).

Regarding the impact of liquidity on banking performance, there exists within the literature a general suggestion that the higher the liquidity, the higher the cost of assets, especially if this liquidity is in the form of minimum reserves required by the government. Indeed, liquidity in the form of banknotes or accounts open at the Central Bank (i.e. the mandatory reserve) provides no benefit to the bank. In addition, liquidity in the form of Treasury bills, although they are normally held for investment purposes, has a lower return than investments with more associated risk.

Regarding the relationship between liquidity and performance, there are several empirical studies that test it. We cite a study by Bourke (1989) on 90 banks in 12 countries (European, South American and Australian) over the period of 1972-1981, and the study of Çanakçi (1996) on banks (public, private and foreign) in Turkey over the period of 1986-1995. Both authors observe a positive relationship between liquidity ratio and profitability of assets. This result is due to the rise in the shares of Treasury bonds, whose income is high in the portfolio of banks. The impact of liquidity level on banking performance depends, however, on the banking context.

When considering impact of liquidity on the performance of Islamic banks, it is important to note that they, like their conventional counterparts, must pay out the funds deposited in savings accounts when depositors demand it. For investment accounts with notification, a short time is normally required before withdrawal can take place. The non-fulfillment of customers' withdrawal requests by the bank may damage confidence in the bank, thus placing it in a difficult situation.

At the same time, Islamic banks are based on the principle of sharing profits and losses with their enterprises. For this reason, the objective of the bank is to increase shareholder returns and those of investment depositors. Having a sufficient amount of capital provides good returns. Islamic banks must have an adequate level of liquidity, but also need to achieve high profits in the long term.

Most of the research work carried out within the framework of conventional banking shows that the performance of assets (ROA) tends to change inversely to the degree of liquidity and safety. As such, the higher the level of capital a bank has to help meet its liquidity needs, the less this capital contributes to the prospective revenues of the bank, and vice versa. The application of this theory in the context of Islamic banks allows us to say that an Islamic bank holding excessive amounts of liquid (available) assets can meet all its commitments, but is getting fewer benefits. If an Islamic bank uses most of its funds in long-term investments, non-liquid and risky, it will achieve more profits, but then it might not be able to repay money to depositors who request it. The impact of liquidity on performance in Islamic banks has been analyzed in a study by Harron (1993). He suggested that the effect of liquidity on bank profitability can be measured by the following ratios:

- Available assets to total assets
- Total loans to total deposition

The ratio of liquid assets to total assets is inversely correlated to profitability. In contrast, there is a positive correlation between the ratio of total loans to total deposits and profitability. In the case of Islamic banks, the value of financing (loans) and deposits are all that is available. For this reason, Harron chooses the second ratio as his indicator of the effect of liquidity on performance. He uses the total deposits to total funding ratio as a measure for liquidity.

The term "financing" refers to the total amount of funds available to Islamic banks; in other words, the funds from PLS ventures, trading operations based on Murabaha and interest-free loans.

2.3.1.1.4. The structure of deposits

Like conventional banks, Islamic banks also offer the public three types of accounts:

- Current accounts
- Savings accounts
- Investment accounts

However, the Islamic bank does not reward the holders of current accounts. The rewards of savings accounts and investment accounts are generally influenced by two elements:

- The predetermined rate at which profit and loss are shared
- The annual profit earned by the bank

a. The current account: As in conventional banks, these accounts cannot be remunerated. They are managed in much the same way as those of other banks. The holders of these accounts receive a checkbook and they can at any time claim their money and withdraw their funds without notice.

b. The savings account: There is a difference between conventional banks and Islamic banks in the case of the savings account. In conventional banks, depositors will automatically be rewarded for the placement of their funds; the reward for savings accounts in Islamic banks depends on the principle of Shariah that their particular bank has chosen to adopt. Returns are based on two factors:

- A pre-agreed rate of profit sharing
- The profit earned by the deployment of the deposited money

c. The investment account: The investment account offered by Islamic banks is fairly consistent with fixed equipment or term deposits in conventional banks, with one exception; the fact that there is no predetermined interest rate attached to deposits. In general, two types of investment accounts are available in Islamic banks:

- Investment accounts requiring notice (notice must be given by customers before any withdrawal)
- Specific investment accounts or deposits for specific projects. All these investments are governed by the Mudaraba contract

Current account funds are considered funds without cost. Indeed, the more money deposited in savings accounts and investment accounts, the more significant the cost to the bank.

The results of empirical studies using data from conventional banks have shown that savings deposits are inversely related to profitability (Hester and Zoeliner, 1966, and Heggested, 1977). The more funds deposited in current accounts, the higher the profits made by the bank. In his study in 1993, Harron included the variable structure of deposits in his model. He used the following ratios as measures of the structure of deposits:

- Total deposits in current accounts to total deposits
- Total deposits in savings accounts to total deposits
- Total deposits in investment accounts to total deposits

2.3.1.1.5. Efficiency

The efficiency of a bank is an important performance criterion. We can use different techniques and indicators to measure the efficiency of a bank. As part of the previous section, we showed how efficiency was measured using the cost function.

The link between banking performance and efficiency ratio depends on the chosen ratio. For example, if one takes the level of expenses over income or assets, then it is to be expected that this may negatively affect banking performance. Bourke (1989) and Molyneux and Thornton (1992) used the cost of personnel as a measurement indicator of total expenditure. Bourke (1989) finds a weak negative correlation between the ratio of personnel expenses to total assets and return on assets (before taxes). However, we find in corresponding literature banking studies that hold the total size of the bank's assets to be a better indicator for measuring the efficiency of scale.

The positive impact of the size of total assets on banking performance can be explained by the new intermediation theory. This focuses on market imperfections, particularly those relating to information. Large financial intermediaries may be more profitable because their generated information can be reused within the same institution. These institutions can therefore exploit the yields associated with production more than smaller banking establishments. Consequently, the efficiency and profitability of these operations increase.

Regarding the effect of efficiency on the performance of Islamic banks, the empirical study conducted by Harron (1993) also dealt with this relationship. He used the ratio of total expenditure to total assets as an indicator of efficiency.

2.3.1.1.6. Capital ownership

Most empirical studies using regression models to explain banking performance also use variable ownership of capital. It may be useful here to observe that within the structure of capital, capital ownership is an independent variable of binary gender (a dummy). Studies show that the relationship between public ownership and banking performance is negative. This is due to the fact that the priority of public banks is not always to maximize profits. Thus the financing of certain sectors to support their development may be entrusted to public banks.

Results found by Molyneux and Thornton contradict the generally accepted results. They suggest that state-owned banks generate a return on equity greater than that of their counterparts in the private sector.

However, insofar as the Government implicitly covers transactions made by state-owned banks, they generally keep a ratio of proper funds lower than their counterparts in the private sector. This explains the positive correlation between the public ownership of a bank and the profitability of its assets.

2.3.1.2. The impact of external explanatory variables on "banking performance"

Studies on performance of corporations, financial and non-financial, must take into account the effects of the environment, or the external factors, which are of paramount importance in this field. Almost all research works studying the determinants of banking performance use values that represent the environment, such as market structure, the economic environment and the regulatory environment.

Regarding the effect of external variables on the performance of Islamic banks, Beshir (2000) shows that favorable macroeconomic conditions exert a positive influence on performance.

2.3.1.2.1. Market structure

The effect of market structure on the performance of conventional banks has been examined in several studies. Indeed, indicators of market structure are the key indicators used in empirical studies which apply the model of Structure-Behavior-Performance, or the theory of efficient structures, in which profitability is retained as a performance criterion. Most studies use two ratios as indicators of market structure. These ratios are concentration ratios and market share ratios. The calculation of concentration indices is usually performed on all banks. The concentration indicators are the Cx index and the Herfindahl index. The most widely used technique for measuring the concentration ratio (Cx) in the banking sector is presented in the following manner:

C = (total assets of X banks) / (total assets of all banks in the sector)

The *Herfindahl index* is defined as the sum of the square of the size of firms in an industry. The size of each bank is expressed as the percentage of assets held by the bank over the sector's total assets.

Meanwhile, the market share of each bank in terms of assets, deposits or credit, can be measured using the following ratios:

ai = (total assets of bank i) / (total assets of all banks in the sector)
di = (total deposits of bank i) / (total deposits of all banks in the sector)
ci = (total loans of bank i) / (total loans of all banks in the sector)

Studies with the objective of testing the Structure-Behavior-Performance model and the theory of efficient structures use indicators of market structure, in particular, as key explanatory variables. At this point we can outline that the results of studies testing the Structure-Behavior-Performance model show a positive link between concentration ratio and profitability.

These include, for example, work by Bourke (1989) who found that concentration is positively, if moderately, correlated with the rate of return on assets before taxation. This study also validates the hypothesis of the preference of expenditure made by Heggested and Mingo (1976). According to these authors, a high concentration level indicates a low personnel cost. According to Molyneux and Thornton (1992), there exists a positive relationship between the level of concentration and return on equity.

Studies testing the theory of efficient structures show a positive link between market share and profitability. Beshir (2000) used the ratio of total bank deposits to GDP as an indicator for measuring the financial market. It is worth mentioning that the financial markets of some countries included in his study sample are still in the development phase. The size of the banking system was used, by calculating the ratios of total assets and bank deposits to GDP, to measure the relative importance of other financial competitors in the economy. Both variables negatively impact upon performance.

Nienhaus (1983) tested the relationship between the performance of Islamic banks and market structure. In his model, he postulated that the rate of sharing profit and loss in Islamic banks is positively associated with the credit rate in conventional banks. Nienhaus (1983) suggested that Islamic banks actually use interest rates as a basis for calculating their profit sharing rates. He also argued that the rate of profit sharing is equivalent to the interest rate offered by conventional banks. In a related study, Khan (1983) also suggested that the ratio of profit sharing is positively correlated with the rate of interest. Unlike Nienhaus, Khan assumes that the rate of profit sharing is not necessarily equal to the market rate. However, neither Nienhaus' nor Khan's work has been empirically verified.

2.3.1.2.2. The economic environment

In most studies on the determinants of banking performance, the indicators for measuring the economic environment are: economic growth, inflation and interest rates. In this section, we summarize the theoretical approaches and the empirical works dealing with links between banking performance and each indicator of the economic environment.

A – Economic growth

As part of the conventional banking system, the influence of financial intermediaries on economic growth has been addressed by several researchers. Most empirical studies show that financial development has an important influence on economic growth. Some authors dispute this, assuming that the development of financial markets is due to economic growth.

In terms of our research, this issue is important, however, at this stage it seems important to point out that neither of these two opinions has been empirically proven correct. Indeed, the results of studies concerning the impact of economic growth on the performance of banks, which are the major players in financial markets, are highly varied and in some cases, insignificant. While according to Barth, Nolle and Rice (1997), the annual change in the real gross domestic product (GDP) has a significant positive impact on the profitability of proper funds, Demirgüç-Kunt and Huizinga (1999), testing the banking data of 80 countries, found that the impact is not significant. Researchers observed that gross domestic product (GDP) per person have a positive influence on the profitability (before taxation of assets).

B – Inflation

In the case of Islamic banks, price risk may come from either transient changes in the prices of certain goods and/or non-financial assets, or an increase in the general level of prices due to inflation. As such, inflation generates risks linked to the nominal value of debts (claims) from Murabaha transactions. However, in case of inflation, it is expected that the prices of goods and merchandise purchased by banks as part of a Salam contract will appreciate. (Khan and Ahmed, 2002, p. 156)

The relationship between inflation and economic growth has been the subject of several empirical studies. The results of these have shown a negative relationship between the two studied variables, especially in cases of high inflation. In other words, inflation is a factor that affects growth. A reduction in inflation, and even the reduction of its volatility, allows economic growth. However, an increase in inflation or its volatility, whilst reducing the average maturity of contracts, diminishes the efficiency of the pricing policy and therefore creates a slowdown in economic growth. A summary of the findings of research testing not only the relationship between inflation and economic growth but also the correlation between economic growth and the development of financial markets allows us to conclude that an increase in the inflation rate has a negative influence on growth; in other words, on the performance of financial markets, including the banking system. However, several researchers have addressed the effects of inflation on banking performance and their studies have shown a variety of different results. An increase in inflation could, in fact, have a positive impact on net interest margin and performance.

However, regression results show that the correlation coefficients between net interest margins and performance are insignificant. The authors of studies that reached this conclusion explain the obtained results in two ways: firstly, the volatility of inflation and the late crediting of client accounts have a positive impact on profitability, and secondly, inflation increases the number of transactions, and also personnel costs. Moreover, this increase in the number of transactions can also have an impact on the number of branches per capita. Regression results show that inflation has an impact on profitability, but as the regression coefficient is not significant, we can state that this impact is extremely limited.

C – The rate of interest

The existence of different types of interest rates (the nominal interest rate, the real interest rate, the lending interest rate, the borrowing interest rate etc.) means that the researcher needs to accurately specify the kind of interest rate referred to when dealing with its impact on banking performance. Moreover, this variation in interest rates may itself have an impact on banking performance.

The nominal interest rate is regarded by researchers as an indicator of the scarcity of capital. Molyneux and Thornton (1992) also found a positive relationship between the nominal interest rate and return on assets. They point out a positive link between the real interest rate, profitability ratios and the net interest margin.

As for the impact of changes in interest rates on banking performance, empirical studies show that it is usually negative.

D – Regulatory environment

The banking sector is amongst the most heavily regulated industries. Banks generate assets using the funds of depositors. Knowing that the rate of return on equity that they can offer depends on the volume of investment projects they accumulate, they aim to mix the little money they have with as much money as they can raise from depositors. Therefore, the projects a bank is associated with will far exceed its own resources. When assets are much more important than proper funds, any loss, however small, may be fatal and may assimilate all the equity of the bank, hence causing its collapse and damage to its depositors. The contagion effect that afflicts the process of regulation can lead to systemic instability if one bank should collapse. Islamic banks are no exception to this systemic phenomenon. The primary aims of regulatory standards and banking supervision are to establish a systematic stability, protect the interests of depositors and promote public confidence in the financial intermediation system.

The better market discipline that the Islamic banking system has the potential to introduce to the financial system would not eliminate the need for regulation and control. Nevertheless, the regulations would not need to be too tight, nor global to the point of increasing the overall costs of its implementation and excessively setting back innovation and creativity. The connection between stability and efficiency should not be overlooked. There are important reasons for the imposition of regulations on the banking sector. First, they are designed to maintain the strength of the bank. Public confidence in a particular bank and the strength of the global banking system is critical to an economy. Indeed, any perceived increase in the likelihood of the imminent failure of a small bank may interrupt the whole payment system. This would lead to a financial crisis, a decline in the value of assets already in place, a weakening of the economy's productive capacity, a decrease in economic welfare and social instability. Secondly, the bank must carry out efficient intermediation, and ultimately provide the specific products and services that are desired. To achieve these goals, regulations are imposed on the management of the banking system. These regulations cover loan policy, deposit policy, interest rates and liquidity conditions, and include conditions for entry, the establishment of new businesses, mergers and acquisitions. One wonders if all the regulatory measures established by the Basel Committee are also necessary for Islamic financial institutions. Since the holders of investment deposits participate in risks, Islamic banks should probably not be subject to more regulations than normal corporations. However, there is a significant difference in the regulations that are required.

First, there are systemic considerations. While the bankruptcy of a company may affect mainly its own shareholders, who should be on their guard, the collapse of a bank has consequences on the health and stability of the entire payment system as well as on the development of the economy. If depositors lose confidence in the system, they will withdraw their deposits, which will not only destabilize the financial system but also reduce the availability of finance for development.

Secondly, the interests of depositors must be safeguarded. However, investment depositors also need greater protection than shareholders in non-banking organizations. This is due to the fundamental importance of investment deposits to banking activities. Such power of protection would come from deposits on demand/at sight. Therefore it is necessary to adopt certain procedures to prevent arbitrage in investment decisions, mismanagement and excessive exposure to risk, and to manage in a prudent manner any risks that are taken. Banks also need to establish adequate reserves to avoid excessive erosion of their investment deposits.

Third, it is also necessary to ensure the faithful compliance of banks with the precepts of Shariah.

Fourth, it is imperative to seek the acceptance of Islamic banks on the interbank market of the international financial system. This can take place only if they also comply with international regulatory standards. Therefore, the differences between Islamic and conventional banking systems will not reduce the need for regulation and monitoring to ensure its effective implementation.

The call for regulation is not new. It was issued in 1981 by the governors of Central Banks and the monetary authorities of member countries of the Organization of Islamic Conference (OIC) in their comprehensive report, "Promotion, Regulation and Control of Islamic Banks", which they approved at their fourth meeting, held in Khartoum on the 7th and 8th of March that year. This shows the great importance of regulation and supervision in an Islamic financial system that is still in its infancy.

Without such legislation and control, Islamic banks would be unable to win people's trust in their strength and their prospects for future development. Any serious failure during this stage would discredit the system and be seriously detrimental to the Islamization movement. However, regulation should not be too strict, nor inconvenient to the point of damaging the profitability and development of Islamic banks and rendering them unable to compete with conventional banks. It is also necessary to determine what should be stipulated by law and what should be left to the discretion of management. A good understanding of what these two methods may or may not achieve would help the financial system to be more flexible and to grow in ways appropriate to the circumstances of each country.

The control model

Islamic banks are generally controlled by existing international systems for the control of conventional banks. In some countries, special laws have been enacted to facilitate the functioning of Islamic banking, while in others, such laws have not yet been introduced. The operations of Islamic banks in these countries take place within guidelines issued by their Central Banks.

With regard to Islamic banks operating in a classical economy, the question arises of whether these banks and other Islamic institutions must adapt to the instruments of classic financial control (credit ceilings, reserves etc.) In most countries, there is no specific legislation covering the activities of Islamic banks. The relationship between these banks and the Central Bank is defined by the law on banks and credit. In fact, it consists of "translating" the operations of conventional banks into operations that may be performed by Islamic banks, thus raising issues about the economic and legal classification of these operations. Deposits of Islamic investments are treated by the Central Bank as credit agreements, and as such their accounting in monetary statistics is allowed. All this makes the calculation of the credit:deposits ratio and the national rules of credit control applicable to them. However, these elements are not without effect on their performance. It is important to know how to apply internationally accepted standards to Islamic banks while also allowing them to work in accordance with Shariah and maintain good performance.

Capital adequacy being at the center of systemic safety, it is therefore also at the center of control concerns, and the application of this basic requirement will help the credibility and growth of Islamic banking worldwide. Given the special nature of the investment deposits, and the risks incurred by the assets, of Islamic banks, the application of international standards of capital adequacy has become a difficult task. The capital of the bank is an effective means of regulation, because capital requirements may be imposed uniformly upon all institutions within all jurisdictions. (Capital here generally refers to the contributions of shareholders.) The equity is supposed to cushion the risks taken by undertaking operations, and play a stabilizing role in the event of loss. Traditionally, the adequacy of capital in a bank is measured by the ratio of capital to assets. We believe that the implementation of international norms concerning capital adequacy for Islamic banks may be difficult because of the profit-sharing system; Islamic banks actually need more proper capital than their capitalist rivals.

In his study on the determinants of the performance of Islamic banks, Beshir (2000) treated regulation as one of the variables affecting the profitability of a commercial bank. If regulators reduce the burden on banks, they can take more risks. This allows them to make more profits. Beshir (2000) used the minimum reserves variable as a measure of the financial rules. The constraints of the reserve requirement do not contradict the principles of Islamic banks, as these reserves are paid by banks into an unrewarded account with the Central Bank. The amount of these reserves is calculated as a proportion of the amount of deposits at sight and on demand entrusted to the bank.

Like conventional banks, Islamic banking supervision is necessary and even desirable. Traditional regulations, however, are not always applicable to Islamic banks. Many economists believe that Islamic banks should not be subject to the requirement of minimum reserves because these reserves do not produce revenue for the bank. Still, all Islamic banks operate in an environment where these control measures are traditionally employed.

The guarantee of deposits

Governments use the mechanism of deposit insurance to achieve two objectives. The first is to ensure the stability of the country's banking system. The second is to protect depositors, as bank failures due to moral hazard problems and adverse selection are numerous worldwide.

If the control system is weak and the capital requirements inadequate, the likelihood of moral hazard and adverse selection increases. Moral hazard results from a wide margin of maneuver that the borrower has in the use of funds placed at his disposal. It may be advantageous for him to engage in certain operations, but bad for the lender.

The adverse selection of borrowers by lenders is due to the fact that lenders do not have any or enough information that accurately assesses risk, and so reflect high risk in the prices they put on debt.

The effect of guaranteeing deposits on conventional bank performance has been the subject of a great deal of research, which has shown that the guarantee given by the state for deposits reduces the remuneration to some degree. These results indicate that, with the guarantee of deposits, banks that appear to generally take more risks will not be forced to offer higher remunerations. Furthermore, for a given level of risk, the existence of a guarantee on deposits could lead banks to lend money on terms more favorable than they have done previously and in other circumstances, thus contributing to the deterioration of the net interest margin and the overall profitability. Even banks that are not themselves engaged in risky lending strategies may experience a drop in interest margins due to competition between banks.

2.3.2. The results of studies using the efficiency approach

Literature on the efficiency of banks identifies the different potential sources of inefficiency. These studies can be grouped into four categories:

- Studies in which parametric methods are used to measure the efficiency of the banking system of a single country
- Studies in which non-parametric methods are used to measure the efficiency of the banking system of a single country
- Studies in which parametric methods are used to measure the efficiency of the banking system in many countries
- Studies in which non-parametric methods are used to measure the efficiency of the banking system in several countries

In a study of 19 Korean private banks, it was shown that over the period from 1985 to 1995 the banks which showed strong asset growth, had fewer employees, took more deposits and had lower cost ratios were the more effective. This work has the originality of having focused on the efficiency of management and not on productive efficiency or the efficiency of scale.

The results of a study by Dietsch (1996) of 375 banks and savings banks in France from 1988 to 1992 show that, in the French banking sector for that period, economies of scale existed and the average X-efficiency was about 70-80%. These results can be considered evidence supporting the hypothesis of overcapacity in the banking sector in France. Another thing suggested by the results of this study is that there is a positive relationship between X-inefficiencies and risk taking.

A study of 21 Turkish banks over the period of 1989-1996 shows to the same effect that, although the order of banks when ranked by efficiency changes each year in Turkey, public banks retain their structural inefficiency every year.

By comparing Spanish and French commercial banks and savings banks over the period of 1988-1992, it can be seen that environmental conditions play an important role in determining the cost efficiency of banks. These environmental variables are population density, income per capita, the density of demand, the concentration of the banking sector in terms of the *Herfindhal index*, the capital ratio, the intermediation ratio and the number of branches per square kilometer.

Some empirical results of a study of the panel data of 136 banks in six European countries (Belgium, Germany, Luxembourg, France, the United Kingdom and Switzerland) for the period of 1994-1997 reveal that efficiency differed significantly depending on the size of the country, and that the average efficiency of large banks is much higher than that of small banks. Two other important results are presented in this study:

- The coverage of risk by proper funds is a source of inefficiency for large banking establishments
- There is a positive correlation between the collection of deposits and the efficiency of small establishments

The differences in efficiency between banks in different European countries is shown again in a study by Gattoufi (2000) on the cost efficiency of banking systems in many OECD countries for the periods 1985-1995 and 1990-1995, which shows that the Turkish and Portuguese banking systems are chronically inefficient in terms of cost. In contrast, France and the Scandinavian countries enjoy the highest level of cost efficiency among OECD countries for the 1985-1995 period. The results of a study by Weill (1998) carried out on mutual commercial banks and savings banks in fourteen OECD member countries, including ten members of the European Union, over the period of 1990-1994, show that an increase in the number of banks has a negative impact on the efficiency of banks. Therefore, increasing competition in the banking sector generates a reduction in banking efficiency.

PART III

CONVENTIONAL VERSUS ISLAMIC BANKS: THEORY AND EMPIRICAL RESULTS

What are the reasons for the recent growth in Islamic finance?

Why is it developing at such a remarkable pace?

What are the determinants of profitability in the Islamic banking sector over the last decade?

There are many things to which the rise in Islamic banking can be attributed. Firstly, there is the strong demand from a large number of immigrant and non-immigrant Muslims for Shariah-compliant financial services and transactions. Secondly, growing oil wealth has led to the demand for suitable investments soaring in the Gulf region. Thirdly, the increasing competitiveness of many products offered by Islamic banks has attracted a large number of Muslim and non-Muslim investors, and finally, there is the fact that Islamic banking has so far been spared from a serious financial crisis, and only experienced a few events that could be called small crises.

Chapter 7 provides an analysis of the growth and rise of smaller Islamic banks over the last decade.

CHAPTER FIVE

AN ANALYSIS OF THE GROWTH AND RISE OF SMALLER ISLAMIC BANKS IN LAST DECADE

OMAR MASOOD

Introduction

Since their inception more than three decades ago, the number of Islamic financial institutions worldwide has risen from one, in 1975, to over 300. They are concentrated in the Middle East and Southeast Asia, with Bahrain and Malaysia the biggest hubs, but are also appearing in Europe and the United States. Their total assets worldwide are estimated to exceed 250 billion U.S dollars, and are growing at an estimated 15% per year (although cross-border data remains scarce).

Few papers have been written on governance structures in Islamic bank, despite the rapid growth of Islamic banks since the mid-1970s and their increasing presence on world financial markets. There are over 200 financial institutions worldwide which adhere to Islamic banking and financing principles. These banks operate in more than 45 countries, encompassing most of the Muslim world along with Europe, North America and various offshore locations.

How has Islamic banking changed banking regulations and banking as a whole in the last decade?

This chapter answers this question, using econometric techniques to provide a cross-country empirical analysis of the rise of small Islamic banks.

Islamic banking represents a radical departure from conventional banking, and in terms of corporate governance, embodies a number of interesting features, since equity participation, risk and profit-and-loss sharing arrangements form its basis.

Because of the ban on interest (Riba), an Islamic bank cannot charge a return fixed in advance, but instead shares in the yield resulting from the use of funds. The depositors also share in the profits according to a predetermined ratio as a reward for assuming risk.

This study adds to the available literature on the market structure of Islamic banking systems by using a larger sample of banks over a more significant amount of time than any previous study has done. We collected our dataset from 30 of the dominant banks in the Islamic banking sector over the period of 1998-2008.

We analyze the reasons for and factors in the rise and growth of small Islamic banks and Islamic financial institutions over the last decade. Previously published studies of the Islamic banking sector mainly concentrate on the rise of Islamic banking as a whole, and very little literature focuses on the significance and impact of smaller banks on Islamic finance.

This chapter is divided into five sections. Section 1 provides the literature review and is followed by section 2 which will give a brief overview of Islamic banking. Section 3 presents the methodology used in our research. Section 4 will give some empirical results.

Section 1. Survey of the Literature

Choong and Liu (2006) claim that Islamic banking as practiced in Malaysia deviates from the PLS paradigm, and in practice is not very different from conventional banking. They suggest that for purposes of financial sector analysis, Islamic banks should therefore be treated similarly to their conventional counterparts. A large proportion of the available literature contains comparisons of the instruments used in Islamic and conventional banking, and discusses the regulatory and supervisory challenges of Islamic banking (e.g., Sundararajan and Errico, 2002; World Bank and IMF, 2005; Ainley et al, 2007; Sole, 2007; Jobst, 2007).

A lot of literature examines risks in Islamic financial institutions, but does so in theoretical terms instead of through the analysis of data, while empirical papers on Islamic banks tend to focus on issues related to efficiency (e.g., Yudistira, 2004; and Moktar, Abdullah, and Al-Habshi, 2006).

Hasan et al (2003) investigated the relative efficiency of the banking industry of Bahrain by using the panel data of 31 banks for the years 1999 and 2000. They employed non- parametric data analysis to estimate efficiency. They found that the dominant cause of inefficiency in Bahrain banks is technical rather than allocative. Hasan et al also examined the differences in efficiency measures between domestic and foreign banks, also in Bahrain. They found that the two categories of bank differ only in scale efficiency. Recent studies by Ozkan-Gunay (1996, 1998), Mahmud and Zaim (1998), Yildirim (1999), and Mercan and Yolalan (2000) concluded that liberalization has increased the efficiency of the banking sector. Mahmud and Zaim (1998) focused on private commercial banks, while Cingi and Tarim (2000) studied the efficiency of 21 commercial banks, some state-owned and some private, with a deposit share in the banking sector of more than 1%.

Favero and Papi (1995) found that their results were not sensitive to reclassifying deposits as an output rather than an input. Heffernan (2005) also indicates that deposits may be treated either as inputs or as outputs. However, according to Brown and Skully (2004) deposits are considered output in most bank efficiency studies that apply the DEA technique. Berger et al (1993) argue that the chosen approach does have an impact on efficiency scores, but does not necessitate major modifications in their rankings.

Research on Islamic financial institutions in 28 countries by Khan and Ahmed (2001) found that credit risk is highest in Musharaka (3.69 from a possible score of 5) followed by Mudaraba (3.25). Their findings highlight the fact that bankers perceive profit-and-loss sharing (PLS) modes of financing to involve higher risk. Mark-up risk was found to be highest in product-deferred Istisna'a contracts (3.57). Sundararajan and Errico (2002) believe that while the use of PLS financing may shift the direct credit risk of Islamic banks onto their investment depositors, they may also increase the overall degree of risk of the asset side of their balance sheets since the assets financed this way are uncollateralized. Their analysis led them to the opinion that in theory, the ratio of riskier assets to total assets will typically be higher in an Islamic bank than in a conventional bank.

Samad and Hasan's (1999) study on Malaysian Islamic banking reveals that the performance of Bank Islam's riskier assets between 1984 and 1997, measured by Debt-Equity Ratio (DER), Debt to Total Assets (DTAR) and Earning Multiplier (EM) increased over those years. DER and EM are significantly related to profitability. In comparison with two conventional banks, Bank Pertanian and Perwira Affin Bank, Bank Islam's risk indicators were lower. The reason for the low risks in Islamic banks is that they invest much more in government securities than conventional banks.

Berger and Mester (1997) argue that profit efficiency is a superior measure of performance to cost efficiency, since profit efficiency accounts for errors on the output side, i.e. revenues, as well as on the input side, i.e. costs. They further argue that a bank may be more successful in minimizing costs than another firm but still make less profit than that firm if they do not make good choices regarding their combination of outputs.

Hasan and Marton (2001) noted that non-US studies found foreign banks, for example, Hungarian banks, to be more efficient than domestic banks. Similar results were found by Zaim (1995) and Isik and Hassan (2002) for Turkish banks. However, Sathye (2001) claims that foreign banks have no significant advantage.

Al-Jarrah and Molyneux (2003) included in their study banks in Bahrain, Egypt, Sudan and Saudi Arabia, and found that Islamic banks were the most efficient in their sample group. They observed that this was due to the cost of funds being lower for Islamic banks than it is for other financial institutions. Hussein et al (2004) found that Islamic banks outperform their conventional counterparts; more specifically, that at their very best, Islamic banks would be able to make 75% profit whereas conventional banks would be able to make 66%. They also suggested that this difference in profit efficiency, which appears to be between Islamic and conventional banks as a whole, is actually due to the difference in performance of just the commercial banks included in each.

Islam has a high regard for efficiency, but very little literature has focused on that aspect of Islamic banking; the bulk of published production efficiency studies have been conducted on conventional banks.

Section 2. Islamic Banking: An Overview

Islamic banking came into existence in communities of people that had to obey a different set of rules – those of the Koran – and who wanted access to modes of financing that also obeyed these rules. The profit-and-loss, P/L, sharing principle, that banks put into practice in order to meet these expectations imply a different relationship between bank and customer than exists under interest-based borrowing and lending rules. Islamic organizations must serve God. They must develop a distinctive corporate culture, the main purpose of which is to create a collective morality and spirituality which, when combined with the production of goods and services, sustains the growth and advancement of the Islamic way of life. (Janachi, 1995) Interest-free banking is based on the Islamic legal concepts of *shirkah* (partnership) and Mudaraba (profit-sharing). An Islamic bank is defined as a financial intermediary, mobilizing the public's savings and advancing capital to entrepreneurs on a Mudaraba basis.

More than two thirds of Islamic financial business currently takes place in the Middle East. The GCC countries, with the exception of Oman, are all major markets for Islamic finance. Bahrain is regarded as the hub of Islamic finance. Other major non-GCC markets for Islamic finance include Egypt, Malaysia, Turkey, Indonesia and Pakistan. Malaysia operates a dual banking system, promoted by the government, which allows conventional financial institutions, investment banks, commercial banks and finance companies to launch separate Islamic banking divisions, competing alongside the two Islamic banks, Bank Islam Malaysia and Bank Muamalat Malaysia. Bank Negara Malaysia (the Central Bank) has its own Shariah Advisory Board which sets the rules for the entire Islamic banking sector, ensuring the uniformity of products and services.

Over 150 Islamic financial institutions now operate in over 40 countries around the world, including commercial banks, investment banks, investment companies for leasing and insurance companies.

The Islamic financial system employs the concept of participation in all enterprises, utilizing the funds, at risk, on a profit-and-loss sharing basis. This by no means implies that investments with financial institutions are necessarily speculative. This can be avoided with a careful investment policy, diversification of risk and prudent management by Islamic financial institutions. It is possible for investment in Islamic financial institutions to provide profit in proportion to the risk assumed whilst satisfying the demands of participants from the conventional environment and still following the guidelines of Shariah.

Islamic banks around the world have devised many financial products based on the risk and profit sharing principles of Islam. For day to day banking activities, a number of financial instruments have been developed that both follow Islamic doctrine and provide acceptable financial returns for investors. Broadly speaking, the areas in which Islamic banks are the most active are trade and commodity finance, property and leasing. Almost every Islamic bank has a committee of religious advisers whose opinion on the acceptability of new instruments and services is sought and who have to provide a religious opinion of the bank's activities for end of year accounts.

Central to the framework of corporate governance for Islamic banks is the Shariah Supervisory Board (SSB). The SSB is vital for two reasons: first, those who deal with an Islamic bank require assurance that it is acting within Islamic law. Should the SSB report that the management of the bank has violated Shariah, it would quickly lose the confidence of the majority of its investors and clients; second, some Islamic scholars argue that strict adherence to Islamic religious principles will act as a counter to the incentive problems outlined above. Their argument is that the Islamic moral code will prevent Muslims from behaving in ways which are ethically unsound, so minimizing the transaction costs arising from incentive issues. In effect, Islamic religious ideology acts as its own incentive mechanism in reducing the inefficiency that can arise from asymmetric information and moral hazards.

An investment account operates under the Mudaraba al-mutlaqa principle, in which the Mudareb (active partner) must have absolute freedom in the management of the invested capital. The conditions of this account differ from those of a savings account by virtue of a) a higher fixed minimum amount, b) a longer duration of deposits, and most importantly c) the possibility that the depositor may lose some of or all his funds in the event of the bank making losses.

Special investment accounts also operate under the Mudaraba principle, and are generally targeted at larger investors and institutions. The difference between these accounts and normal investment accounts is that special investment accounts are related to a specified project, and the investors invest directly in a project of their choice that is being carried out by the bank.

If the paying and receiving of interest is prohibited, how do Islamic banks operate?

It is necessary to distinguish between the expressions "rate of interest" and "rate of return". Whereas Islam clearly forbids the former, it not only permits, but rather encourages, trade. In the interest-free system supported by adherents to Muslim principles, people are able to earn a return on their money only by subjecting themselves to the risk involved in profit sharing. As the use of interest rates in financial transactions is prohibited, Islamic banks are expected to undertake operations only on the basis of profit and loss sharing (PLS) arrangements or other acceptable modes of financing. Mudaraba and Musharaka are the two profit sharing arrangements preferred under Islamic law.

Mudaraba refers to a contract between at least two parties whereby one party, the financier *(sahib al-mal),* entrusts funds to another party, the entrepreneur (Mudareb), who is undertaking an activity or venture. This type of contract is different from Musharaka, under which there is also profit sharing, but all parties have the right to participate in managerial decisions. In Mudaraba, the financier is not allowed a role in the management of the enterprise. Mudaraba, on the other hand, is also a PLS contract where the return to lenders is a specified share in the profit/loss outcome of the project, but while they have a stake in that project, they have no voice.

Under Musharaka, the entrepreneur adds some funds of his own to those supplied by the investors, thereby exposing him or herself to the risk of capital loss. Profits and losses are shared according to predetermined proportions, but these proportions need not coincide with the ratio of financing input. The bank sometimes participates in the execution of the projects in which it has subscribed, for example, by providing managerial expertise.

Section 3. Methodology

3.1 Estimation of Bank stability

In this paper we use the z-score as the measure of bank risk. The z-score has lately become a popular measure of bank robustness. However, very few published studies have used this methodology to measure it; some that have are: Boyd and Runkle (1993), Maechler, Mitra, and Worrell (2005) and Martin Čihák and Heiko Hesse (2008). The z-score can be summarized as $z \equiv (k+\mu)/\sigma$, where k is equity capital and reserves as a percentage of assets, μ is average return as a percentage of assets, and σ is standard deviation of return on assets as a proxy for return volatility. The z-score measures the number of standard deviations by which a return realization has to fall in order to deplete equity, under the assumption that the bank's returns are normal. A high z-score corresponds to a low upper limit of insolvency risk; a higher z-score therefore implies a lower probability of insolvency risk.

The z-score applies equally to banks that use a high risk/high return strategy and those that use a low risk/low return strategy, provided that those strategies lead to the same risk-adjusted returns. If an institution chooses to have lower risk-adjusted returns, it can still have the same z-score, or higher, if it has higher capitalization. In this sense, the z-score provides an objective measure of soundness.

A large portion of an Islamic bank's financial liabilities consists of investment accounts that can be viewed as a form of equity investment, generally based on Mudaraba. Investment accounts are offered in different forms, and often have a pre-agreed period of maturity. The profits and returns are distributed between the depositors and the bank according to a pre-determined ratio, e.g. 80% to the depositors and 20% to the bank (Iqbal and Mirakhor, 2007).

3.2 Regression analysis

Using the regression of the z-score as a function of a number of variables, we can test the stability of Islamic banks of any size. We approximate commonly used panel data with the form:

$$z_{i,j,t} = \alpha + \beta B_{i,j,t-1} + \gamma I_{j,t-1} + \sum \delta_s T_s + \sum \phi_s T_s I_{j,t-1} + \sum \varphi_s B_{i,j,t-1} T_s + \varpi M_{j,t-1} + \sum \lambda_j C_j + \sum \pi_t D_t + \varepsilon_{i,j,t}$$

Where the dependent variable is the z-score $z_{i,j,t}$ (for bank *i* in country *j* at time t), $B_{i,j,t-1}$ is a vector of bank-specific variables and $I_{j,t-1}$ contains time-dependent industry-specific variables; T_s $I_{j,t-1}$ are the types of bank and the interaction between the types and some of the industry-specific variables; $M_{j,t}$, C_j and tD_t are vectors of macroeconomic variables, country and yearly dummy variables respectively; finally, $\varepsilon_{i,j,t}$ is the residual.

A negative result from the interaction of the Islamic banks' market share with the Islamic bank dummy would indicate that a higher share held by Islamic banks reduces those banks' soundness (reduces their z-scores). We want to examine the Islamic banks' impact on other banks and the hypothesis that the presence of Islamic banks lowers systemic stability; hence we calculated the market share of Islamic banks, in assets, for each year and examined its interaction with an Islamic banking dummy.

This regression includes a number of other control variables which take into account differences in size, asset composition, and cost efficiency between banks. We include the bank's asset size in billions of U.S. dollars, loans over assets, and the cost: income ratio. To compensate for differences in the structures of the banks' income, we also calculate a measure of income diversity. This enables us to determine the degree to which banks diversify from traditional lending activities into other activities. For Islamic banks, net interest income is generally defined as the sum of the positive and negative income flows associated with PLS arrangements. We also measure differences of business orientation in the banks, and instigate interaction between the income diversity variable and the Islamic bank dummy. Controlling these variables is important, because each one varies with each Islamic bank.

To account for cross-country variation in financial stability, caused by differences in market concentration, we include the *Herfindahl index*, defined as the sum of the squared market shares (in terms of total assets) of all major Islamic banks. The value of the index can be anywhere from 0 to 10,000. The macroeconomic and bank-specific variables, the *Herfindahl index*, and the Islamic banks' market share and their interaction with the Islamic and commercial bank dummies are lagged to capture any past effects these variables may have had on the risks of the individual banks. We also test the robustness of the lagged effects by restricting the explanatory variables to contemporaneous effects.

We test our regression analysis using the pooled ordinary least squares (OLS) technique. To test the sensitivity of the results with respect to the estimation method, we also estimate fixed effects and median least squares regressions. We also assess the robustness of the results with respect to the selected sample; more specifically, we estimate the regressions separately for sub-samples of large Islamic banks. We categorize those Islamic banks with total assets worth more than two billion U.S. dollars as large, and all others as small.

The complete list of all the variables used for the regression analysis is given in Table 1.

Table 1: Description of individual variables used in regression analysis

Variable	**Description**
Z-score	Defined as $z \equiv (k+\mu)/\sigma$, where k is equity capital as a percentage of assets, μ is average return as a percentage of assets, and σ is standard deviation of return on assets as a proxy for return volatility. Measures the number of standard deviations a return realization has to fall by in order to deplete equity, under the assumption of normality of banks' returns
Total assets	The total assets of the bank in USD
Loans_assets	Ratio of loans to assets (percent).
Exp_inc	Ratio of total expenditure to total income
Income Diversity	$1 - \left\lvert \frac{\text{Net operating income} - \text{other operating income}}{\text{Total operating income}} \right\rvert$
Islamic Bank Dummy	Equals 1 for large Islamic banks; 0 otherwise
Market Share	The share of the bank amongst various dominant Islamic banks in the dataset
Herfindahl Index	Sum of squared market shares of banks in the dataset

Source: Čihák and Hesse (2008)

3.3. Data

The data used in this paper was collected from 30 dominant Islamic banks functioning in different countries around the world during the period of 1998-2008. The Islamic banks whose data was collected are: ABC Islamic Bank (E.C.); Abu Dhabi Islamic Bank; Al Baraka Bank (South Africa); Al Baraka Islamic Bank B.S.C. (E.C.); Al Rajhi Bank; Albaraka Turk Participation Bank; Arcapita Bank B.S.C.; Bahrain Islamic Bank B.S.C.; Bank Al-Jazira; Bank Asya; Bank Islam Malaysia Berhad; Bank Muamalat; Boubyan Bank; CIMB Islamic Bank Berhad; Faisal Islamic Bank of Egypt; Faysal Bank (Pakistan); Hong Leong Islamic Bank; International Islamic; Islamic Bank Bangladesh Limited; Islamic Bank of Britain; Islamic International Arab Bank; Jordan Islamic Bank for Finance and Investment; Kuwait Finance House; Kuwait Turk Participation Bank; Meezan Bank; Qatar Islamic Bank; RHB Islamic Bank; Sharjah Islamic Bank; Tadhamon International Islamic Bank and Turkish Finance Participation Bank.

The pooled data was put together by combining the datasets from all the banks. The regression analysis was performed on this pooled data and the obtained results are detailed in the next section. The mean square and double accounting techniques were also used on the dataset when required.

Section 4. Empirical Analysis

A summary of statistics from the data sample (our chosen Islamic banks over the period of 1998-2008) is displayed in Table 2.

Table 2: Summarized statistics from the data sample

Large Islamic banks Small Islamic banks		
Z-score	10.68**	29.21**
Z-score excl. outliers	09.53	15.52
Loans/assets	0.79*	0.66*
Income diversity	0.41	0.39

** and * denote significance at 1% and 5 % respectively.

The 1st percentile of the distribution of the income diversity variable is excluded. The z-score without the outliers excludes the 1st and 99th percentile of its distribution.

The z-score without outliers excludes the 1st and 99th percentile of its distribution.

A basic analysis of the data suggests that smaller Islamic banks are more stable than larger ones, as a higher z-score indicates higher stability. A one-to-one comparison of means suggests that in both cases the difference is significant at the 1% level. The table also illustrates that the treatment of outliers is important. Furthermore, even with the outliers taken into account, we found that the smaller Islamic banks have higher z-scores. The larger Islamic banks have, on average, higher loan to asset ratios than the smaller ones, reflecting the fact that Islamic banking prohibits investment in non-lending operations such as regular bonds or T-bills.

We then turn to the regression analysis. The results of our tests are shown in Tables 3 and 4. Table 3 shows the results of the OLS estimation while Table 4 shows the results of a robust estimation technique which assigns smaller weightings to observations with large residuals, thereby making the estimation less sensitive to outliers.

Table 3: Regression Results: Ordinary Least Squares (Dependent variable – z-score)

Variable	All banks	Large banks	Small banks
Islamic dummy	-1.563 (0.151)	-13.771(0.011)	5.929 (0.007)
Loan/assets	-2.503 (0.284)**	-2.003 (0.332)**	-3.475 (0.023)**
Exp_inc	-0.029 (0.007)**	-1.153 (0.636)**	-2.969 (0.449)
Assets	0.192 (0.001)	0.281 (0.003)	-2.112 (0.011)
Income diversity	3.487 (0.474)**	17.734 (0.001)*	-4.873 (0.295)**
Market share		-0.575 (0.064)	0.011 (0.717)
Herfindahl Index	-0.001 (0.006)*	-0.005 (0.001)*	-0.001 (0.013)*
R-square	0.177	0.295	0.198
Constant	64.872	88.981	29.326

p-values are in parentheses.
** and * denote significance at 1% and 5% respectively.

The regression results also show that smaller Islamic banks are more stable than larger ones. We observe that for larger Islamic banks, the Islamic dummy is negative, while it is positive for smaller banks. Moreover, we found that z-scores tend to increase along with bank size for large Islamic banks, but decrease with increases in size for small banks.

Our results show that the larger banks have greater income diversity than the smaller banks. This suggests that they do not rely as much on income-bearing assets. Similarly, higher expenditure to income ratios have a consistently negative link to z-scores; this is consistently significant but only for the larger banks.

Table 4: Regression Results: Robust estimation (Dependent variable – z-score)

Variable	All banks	Large banks	Small banks
Islamic dummy	-0.22 (0.431)	-6.256(0.048)	1.235 (0.019)
Loan/assets	-5.727 (0.004)**	-12.026 (0.002)**	-3.292 (0.051)**
Exp_inc	-0.039 (0.009)**	-0.112 (0.001)**	-0.229 (0.009)
Assets	0.082 (0.239)	0.155 (0.047)	-4.571 (0.020)
Income diversity	-1.635 (0.128)**	-2.946 (0.038)*	0.321 (0.295)**
Market share		-0.368 (0.027)	0.019 (0.545)
Herfindahl Index	-0.001 (0.104)*	-0.003 (0.153)*	-0.001(0.262)*
R-square	0.272	0.259	0.181
Constant	55.783	45.357	16.399

p-values are in parentheses.
** and * denote significance at 1% and 5% respectively.

We found that the *Herfindahl Index* has a negative impact on Islamic banks. Our findings are therefore in agreement with previous studies by Schaeck, Čihák, and Wolfe (2006) and Čihák and Hesse (2008), who also found higher concentration to be associated with lower stability.

The robust regression results confirm our earlier findings, which tell us that small Islamic banks are more stable than larger ones, as the Islamic dummy is again negative for large banks but positive for smaller banks.

The difference in the income diversity results of the large banks and those of the small is important because there are significant differences in these variables between Islamic banks. We observe that the smaller Islamic banks show a higher degree of diversification than the larger banks.

Moreover, we observe that the expenditure to income ratio is smaller for small Islamic banks than it is for larger Islamic banks in both the OLS regression results and the robust regression results. This is a major factor in explaining the rise and growth of smaller Islamic banks and Islamic finance in the last decade, even after the prohibition of investment in non-lending operations such as regular bonds or T-bills.

The robust regression for the *Herfindahl Index* shows results similar to those of the OLS regression, as it is still negative, and significant for both the smaller and the larger Islamic banks. We conducted several additional checks to test the robustness of our results; we also tested for the robustness of the lagged effects by restricting the explanatory variables to contemporaneous effects, again finding no substantive change in the main results.

Conclusion

This paper investigates the factors responsible for the rise and growth of smaller Islamic banks that has taken place in the last decade. Using the regression of the z-score as a function of a number of variables, we tested the stability of smaller and larger Islamic banks. We then carried out a regression analysis using the pooled ordinary least squares (OLS) technique. Further to this, we also assessed the robustness of the results gained from the selected sample included in our pooled dataset for the period of 1998-2008.

Our results show higher z-scores for smaller Islamic banks; hence we conclude that smaller Islamic banks have been more stable than larger Islamic banks over the last decade, as higher z-scores imply higher stability. We found that, even with the outliers taken into account, smaller Islamic banks have higher z-scores. The large Islamic banks have on average higher loan to asset ratios than the smaller Islamic banks, reflecting the fact that Islamic banking prohibits investment in non-lending operations such as regular bonds or T-bills. We also observed that z-scores tend to increase as bank size increases for large Islamic banks, but decrease as size increases for the smaller ones.

The OLS regression results obtained confirmed our previous finding, i.e. that small Islamic banks are more stable than large Islamic banks. Our findings suggest that larger banks have greater income diversity than the smaller ones. We also found that expenditure to income ratios were negative and significant for larger Islamic banks. Furthermore, the *Herfindahl Index* was found to have a negative impact on Islamic banks.

Our robust regression results prove that the smaller Islamic banks have a higher degree of diversification than the larger ones, which is also responsible for their growth. We found significantly lower expenditure to income ratio values for smaller banks than for larger banks, which can be regarded as one of the paramount factors responsible for the growth and rise of smaller Islamic banks.

References

Abreu M. and V. Mendes. 2002. "Commercial bank interest margins and profitability: Evidence from E.U countries", *Porto Working paper series*.

Afanasieff T., P.Lhacer and M. Nakane. (2002). "The determinants of bank interest spreads in Brazil", *Banco Central di Brazil Working Papers*.

Allen, Franklin, and Douglas Gale, 2004, "Competition and Financial Stability," *Journal of Money, Credit and Banking*, Vol. 36, No. 3, pp. 453–80.

Archer, Simon, and Rifaat Abdel Karim (eds.), 2002, "Islamic Finance: Growth and Innovation," (London: Euromoney Books).

Aggarwal, R.K. and Yousef T. (2000), "Islamic Banks and Investment Financing", *Journal of Money, Credit and Banking*, Vol. 32, No.1 93-120.

Boyd, John H., and David E. Runkle, 1993, "Size and Performance of Banking Firms," *Journal of Monetary Economics*, Vol. 31, pp. 47–67.

Berger, A., D. Hanweck and D. Humphrey, 1987, "Competitive viability in banking: Scale, scope and product mix economies", *Journal of Monetary Economics*, Vol.20: 501-20.

Berger, A.N. and Humphrey, D. (1997) "Efficiency of Financial Institutions: International Survey and Directions for Future Research", *European Journal of Operational Research*, 98, 175-212.

Buser, S., A. Chen, and E. Kane. 1981. "Federal deposit insurance, regulatory policy, and optimal bank capital", *Journal of Finance*, Vol. 35: 51-60.

Choudhry, Nurun, and Abbas Mirakhor, 1997, "Indirect Instruments of Monetary Control in an Islamic Financial System," Islamic Economic Studies, Vol. 4, No. 2, pp. 27–66.

Ertugrul, A. and F. Selcuk (2001), "A brief account of the Turkish economy", *Russian and East European Finance and Trade* Vol. 37, 6-28.

El-Hawary, Dhalia, Wafik Grais, and Zamir Iqbal, 2004, "Regulating Islamic Financial Institutions: The Nature of the Regulated," World Bank Working Paper 3227 (Washington: World Bank).

Hesse, Heiko and Martin Čihák, 2007, "Islamic banks and financial stability," IMF Working Paper No. 08/16 (International Monetary Fund).

Isik, I. and Hassan M.K. (2002), "Technical, scale and allocative efficiencies of the Turkish banking industry", *Journal of Banking and Finance*, 26, 719-766.

Iqbal, Munawar (April 2001) "Islamic and Conventional banking in the nineties: A comparative study", *Islamic Economic Studies*, Vol. 8, No 2, 1-27.

Iqbal, Munawar, and David T. Llewellyn (eds.), 2002, "Islamic Banking and Finance: NewPerspective on Profit-Sharing and Risk," (Cheltenham, United Kingdom: Edward Elgar Publishing).

International Organization of Securities Commissions, 2004, Islamic Capital Market: Fact Finding Report. Report of the Islamic Capital Market Task Force of the International Organization of Securities Commissions (Madrid).

Guru B., J. Staunton and Balashanmugam. 2002. "Determinants of commercial bank profitability in Malaysia", *University Multimedia working papers*.

Keeley M. and G. Zimmerman. 1985. "Competition for money market deposit accounts", *Federal Reserve Bank of San Francisco Economic Review, Vol. 1:5-27.*

Meeusen, W., and van den Broeck (1977), "Efficiency Estimation From Cobb-Douglas Production Functions With Composed Error", *International Econometric Review*, 18, 435-444.

Maechler, Andrea, Srobona Mitra, and DeLisle Worrell, 2005, "*Exploring Financial Risks and Vulnerabilities in New and Potential EU Member States*," Second Annual DG ECFIN Research Conference: "Financial Stability and the Convergence Process in Europe," October 6–7, 2005.

Mishkin, Frederic S., 1999, "Financial Consolidation: Dangers and Opportunities," *Journal of Banking and Finance*, Vol. 23, pp. 675–91.

Moktar, Hamim S., Naziruddin Abdullah, and Syed M. Al-Habshi, 2006, "Efficiency of Islamic Banks in Malaysia: A Stochastic Frontier Approach," *Journal of Economic Cooperation among Islamic Countries*, Vol. 27, No. 2, pp. 37–70.

Naughton, S.A.J. and M.A. Tahir, 1988, "Islamic Banking and Financial Development," *Journal of Islamic Banking and Finance*, Vol. 5, No. 2.

Tartisma Tebligleri Serisi, 2000/1 Molyneux P. and J. Thornton. 1992. "The determinants of European bank profitability", Journal of Banking and Finance, Vol. 16: 1173-1178.

Rogers, K.E. (1998). Non-traditional activities and the efficiency of US commercial Banks, *Journal of Banking and Finance*, 22(4): 467-482.

Street, James O., Raymond J. Carroll, and David Ruppert, 1988, "A Note on Computing Robust Regression Estimates via Iteratively Reweighted Least Squares," *The American Statistician*, Vol. 42, pp. 151–154.

Shaffer S. 1985. "Competition, economies of scale, and diversity of firm sizes", *Applied Economics*, Vol.17: 467-76.

Smirlock M. 1985. "Evidence of the (Non)Relationship Between Concentration and Profitability in Banking," *Journal of Money, Credit, and Banking*, Vol.17: 69-82.

Street, James O., Raymond J. Carroll, and David Ruppert, 1988, "A Note on Computing Robust Regression Estimates via Iteratively Reweighted Least Squares," *The American Statistician*, Vol. 42, pp. 151–154.

Yildirim, C. (1999), "Evaluation of the performance of Turkish commercial Banks: A non-parametric approach in conjunction with financial ratio analyses", International Conferences in Economics III, METU.

Yudistira, Donsyah, 2004, "Efficiency in Islamic Banking: An Empirical Analysis of Eighteen Banks," *Islamic Economic Studies*, Vol. 12, No. 1, pp. 1–19.

Yolalan, R. (1996), "Turk bankacilik sektoru icin goreli mali performans olcumu", *TBB Bankacilar Dergisi*, Sayi 19.

Zaim, O. (1995), "The effect of financial liberalization on the efficiency of Turkish commercial banks", Economic Research Forum for the Arab Countries, Workshop on Financial Market Development.

PART IV

INTEREST RATES, PROFITABILITY AND THE CAPITAL STRUCTURE OF ISLAMIC INSTITUTIONS

Islamic finance has failed to capture the interest of Western writers and has developed in isolation from its Western counterpart. The Koran, the Islamic holy book, permits trade but forbids usury, and particularly interest. This fundamental principle is the main thing that differentiates the Western banking system from the Islamic system.

Islamic banks are involved in the process of implementing government monetary policy in addition to their important role in the mobilization and allocation of resources. There is a strong relationship between the deposits in an Islamic bank and its rate of profit, and also between the interest rate applied by conventional banks and deposits in Islamic banks. It is important to review and assess the present state of Islamic banking, both its theoretical and practical aspects.

The theory of Islamic banking is based on the principle of forbidding interest and usury. Islamic teachings provide a different system of organization for banks. Incidentally, the practice of interest has been condemned by many thinkers, for example Aristotle, who described it as a "birth of money from money".

This part includes three chapters.

Chapter 6 deals with recent findings regarding interest rates and profitability in Islamic banking.

Chapter 7 studies the results of recent studies on the performance of Islamic banks.

Chapter 8 deals with short- and long-term financing and the capital structure of Islamic institutions.

CHAPTER SIX

INTEREST RATES, PROFITABILITY AND ISLAMIC BANKING: RECENT FINDINGS

MONDHER BELLALAH AND OMAR MASOOD

In Islam, interest is prohibited because it is an augmentation of capital without effort; a creation of false value. An increase in income must result from investment, labor or some other activity. There are many arguments for the prohibition of interest in Islam. The first of these is simply that interest rates are morally unacceptable. The second is that abstinence from consuming does not justify the receiving of rewards. The third is that there is no risk to justify making extra gain from capital lending if the loan is guaranteed. The creditor/debtor relationship is redefined by Islam, with the creditor or provider of funds becoming a partner in the project, assuming the risk of the activity with the entrepreneur and sharing the profit in pre-agreed proportion (and not, like in conventional banks, at a fixed return).

The incremental creation of wealth justifies the sharing of the profits between the borrower of the money and the lender, but not a fixed return.

The new Islamic banking system is currently developing rapidly. The system is important due to the growth of investment in Islamic banks and the consideration given to it by governments. However, little importance is placed by Islamic banks upon the application of modern finance theories, although Islamic economic principles are characterized by the application of managerial techniques and models originally developed in the conventional financial framework.

Islamic banks operate on a set of principles based on Islamic law (Shariah). Instead of charging a fixed interest rate, Islamic banks use the profit and loss sharing principle (PLS) as an important part of two financing contracts: Musharaka and Mudaraba.

The effect of PLS on the commercial loan market, where interest-free Islamic banks operate side by side with conventional banks, has been studied by several authors.

Some Islamic countries have Islamized their entire financial systems, for example Iran, Pakistan and Sudan. However, there are also numerous Islamic banks in Egypt, Bahrain and Turkey.

The most important principle in Islamic law is the prohibition of interest or usury. Khan (1983, 1987) claimed that there was no difference between interest and usury. Both of them involve the return of some kind of benefit, as described by Aryan (1990). Hassan (1993) considered Islamic banks an entirely different type of institution from conventional banks. Islamic banking has shown a real boom during the beginning of the 21st century, with an increasing number of Islamic banks as well as Islamic windows of conventional banks, and exponential growth of its geographical footprint. The top 20 banks in the Gulf (GCC) countries have all seen their assets grow. The diversification of market players in Islamic banking has resulted in a growth in geographical reach and also the emergence of new financial centers of Islamic banking, aside from the already existing ones, such as Dubai, Bahrain and Kuala Lumpur. The emergence of a broader range of retail products and services has significantly contributed to making Islamic banking as competitive as conventional banking.

This chapter is organized as follows:

Section 1 presents the foundations of Islamic finance and banking.

Section 2 presents Islamic business contracts and introduces the theory behind Islamic banks.

Section 1. Islamic finance and banking and interest rates

The treatment of interest rates, or Riba, in Western literature

Instead of interest based products, Islamic banks use profit and loss sharing (PLS) financial instruments. The prohibition of interest is not unique to Islamic literature, having also been a feature of religious and non-religious literature for many decades. Historically, interest was opposed on the grounds of the social divisions that come with it, as verified by historical evidence of loans being given to the powerful without interest. Lending on interest is a blameworthy action, but is obviously sometimes necessary. Some authors have recognized the sharing of risks as an economic brotherhood. Christianity teaches its followers to "love thine enemies", which is in keeping with the prohibition of interest. Brunner (1937) believed that interest encourages a "parasitical existence". Aristotle considered money to be no more than a medium of exchange which holds no inherent value. Since the recent financial crisis in 2008, others have blamed interest for creating instability and economic fluctuation. The justification of interest is based on the principle that "time is money", but Islam sees it as unjustified to offer financial gain based on a factor of time alone.

1. Interest rates and the business cycle

There is a strong relationship between interest rates and the instability of an economy caused by inflation, unemployment, negative growth etc. The difference between market and natural interest rates is that the former is determined by monetary forces on the loanable funds market, e.g. money supply growth and bank credit creation, and the latter is determined by the profitability of investments.

In the long run, natural interest rates will outperform market rates because the former are based on a just value of reward which is not artificially inflated. Two economists captured well the role of the interest rate as the basis of the business cycle. Wicksell (1935) assumed full employment in his model. Hayek (1939) examined the cumulative process in terms of fluctuations in employment over the duration of the cycle, and his conclusion was in contrast to Wicksell's. The monetary theories of both of these authors were supported by the financial instability hypothesis, which argues that interest rates create instability.

Keynes (1931) criticized the role of interest rates and bank credit in the cyclical process. Klein (1965) argued that investment increases when the natural rate of interest exceeds the market rate and vice-versa, and that the divergence of the two rates is responsible for price movements. The Treatise of Money (1931) was no more than an attempt to spell out an appropriate banking policy which could maintain a monetary equilibrium. Minsky (1963, 1977, 1985) and Greenwald and Stiglitz (1988 a, 1988 b, 1990) developed few theories that assign interest a major part cyclical fluctuations.

There is a tendency in Western economic literature, which is not as common in work by Islamic scholars, which blames interest rates and associated bank credit expansion and contraction for many of the economic evils of our time.

Keynes (1936) explained how real people behave in the real world. Neoclassical macroeconomics had stipulated that a rational individual operates only for his own interest and not for the community, so in a modern economy, everyone acts in their own self-interest. According to Islamic economic theory, however, people and governments should act as parts of a perfect Islamic community, as described in the Koran. However, in reality, Muslims do not always behave in this ideal manner. It is necessary, therefore, for Western economists to understand the behavior of Muslims in the real world and search to reconcile Islamic theory with actual practice. It is also interesting for Islamic scholars to ascertain the actual behavior of Muslims involved in Islamic finance and to learn lessons from Western theory in order to make the most of the differences between the perfect Islamic system and the current views of Muslims around the world.

2. The interest rate and Islamic banking

Principles underlying the Islamic banking system

Usury is forbidden by the Koran because the main objective of Islam regarding financial matters is to achieve an equitable distribution of profits between entrepreneurs and investors. Indeed, it is unjust to guarantee a return on capital or a loan in a situation in which the lender is not making any effort. This has led to the implementation of PLS by Islamic banks. The equitable distribution of the returns and risks associated with investment is a principle applied in all Islamic economic institutions.

The business operations of Islamic banks

- There are commissions or fixed charges for services and business operations.
- The Islamic bank acquires funds by offering interest-free current accounts, as in the Western banking system, or on a profit sharing basis.

The unique feature of Islamic banks is that investors share in bank's profits and losses, rather than obtaining a fixed level of interest as they do in the Western banking system. Account holders share in the outcomes of banks at a profit and loss sharing ratio which depends whether the investment has been short- or long-term.

Long-term deposits usually have a higher profit and loss sharing ratio because of their greater risk. To obtain a profit share, depositors must not withdraw their funds for at least the contracted period. PLS exposes the bank to a high liquidity risk if losses occur. For this reason account holders have to give notice before withdrawals.

Funds can be used for profitable projects, such as investments in trade and loans on a profit sharing basis, or non-profitable projects such as holding of cash reserves and the provision of interest-free loans to customers and entrepreneurs.

3. Profitability in Islamic banking: A survey of the literature

The interest-free banking concept was established by the Mit Ghamer savings bank in the Nile delta in Egypt in 1963 and since then, many Islamic institutions have been created throughout the world, not just in Muslim and Arabic countries but also elsewhere, e.g. Islamic Banking System International Holding in Luxembourg (1978) and Dar al Mal al Islam in Switzerland (1981).

Despite the existence of conventional banks in Islamic countries, some of these countries continue to encourage the interest-free operations of Islamic banks.

Conventional banking studies are concentrated on the exploration of factors affecting the profitability of banks. Brucker (1970) noted that a higher concentration led to a higher interest on business loans and a higher profitability. Short (1979) found that there was evidence suggesting that concentration could lead to a higher profitability through oligopolistic rent. Concentration is measured by the percentage of assets or deposits held by the largest banks in the market. Revell (1980) showed that high inflation led to higher profit margins. Smirlock (1985) found that market share also had a positive effect on bank profitability. Haron and Guan (1997) established a relationship between profitability, interest rate and market share in Islamic banks.

A dual banking system is a system in which interest-free banks (Islamic banks) operate side by side with conventional banks. Islamic banking is based on using the PLS principle in a partnership (Musharaka) or a joint investment without participation in management (Mudaraba), and also on the mark-up principle through resale contracts (Murabaha) and leasing contracts (Ijara). Meanwhile conventional banks operate on interest.

In Islamic banks, there is no conflict between general banking operations and Islamic principles. Banking activities include foreign exchange transactions, domestic and international transfers, letters of credit and availing safe custody (Metwally 1993). Moreover, Islamic banks operate on the principle of no interest, or PLS, and use an agreed profit sharing ratio. Thus they can truly be said to share the risk with the borrower.

Khan (1986) showed that interest-free banks exhibit a much higher degree of stability than conventional banks, even though they operate under the PLS principle, which is characterized by high risk and variable returns.

Deposits in Islamic banks are considered shares and are rewarded with dividends in the profits. A strong financial position (in terms of total liabilities) encourages the bank to diversify its investment projects, to minimize the risk and maximize the profits. This may attract more depositors and expand activities further. Bashir, Darrat and Suliman (1993) studied equity capital, profit sharing contracts and investment.

4. The foundations of Islamic banking

Islamic law or Shariah and business principles

Islamic law or Shariah regarding business is based on four principles.

The first principle is that of profit and loss sharing (PLS). The second is that of fixed charges. The third is based on free of charge services, and the final principle is based on making agreements suitable to the nature of Islamic operations. There are two agreements that come under the PLS principle, namely: Mudaraba, or profit sharing, and Musharaka, or participatory financing.

The first principle, Mudaraba: this can be defined as an agreement between two parties, a supplier (provider of funds) and a user of funds (entrepreneur), under which the supplier provides funds to the user to finance a project in a pre-agreed way. The user then returns to the supplier the supplied amount and a proportion of any profit (pre-agreed share profit). In case of loss resulting from the financed activity, the supplier will bear all the losses and the user loses only his time and effort.

The second principle, Musharaka: this is a joint venture agreement between two or more parties who each participate in the project by providing a part of the capital and also participate in the management of the venture. All parties agree through negotiation on the ratio of participation in the financing of the project. In the case of profit, the partners share it in pre-agreed proportions, however, in the case of loss all parties bear a part of that loss in proportion to their share in the financing.

The third principle, free of charge financing: within the framework of the free of charge principle, Qard Hassan is an arrangement whereby the borrower returns to the lender only the original amount of the loan and no more.

Among the principles within the fixed charges category are:

- Murabaha (cost-plus financing)
- Bai-mua'jjal (deferred payment sale)
- Ijara (leasing)

The other principles

Other principles include Wadiah (trusteeship) and *Rahn* (pledges).

In the case of savings and investment deposits, Islamic banks offer facilities based on Mudaraba. Depositors have no prior knowledge of the rewards they will receive except the profit sharing ratio agreed in their contracts. The more that the ratio is to the bank's advantage, the less profit the user will get and vice-versa.

The PLS principle is applied through:

- The Musharaka, where both parties contribute to the capital and agree to share the net profit in pre-determined proportions.
- The Mudaraba, where the bank provides the capital and the borrower takes full responsibility for the management of the enterprise. Under this contract, the partner gets a proportion of the net profits, and in case of loss resulting from circumstances beyond the user's control, the bank bears all the losses and the borrower loses only his time and effort.
- The mark-up principle, applied through many activities. The most common is the Murabaha, which is a resale contract where the client wishes to purchase a commodity and the bank buys it and resells it to him at a price which covers the purchase price and includes a profit margin agreed by the two parties.

Another contract applying the mark-up principle is the leasing (Ijara) contract under which the bank purchases an asset and rents it to a client who has need of it. After that, if the client wishes to purchase it, rent is taken as payment installments until the asset is fully owned by the borrower.

Section 2. Islamic business contracts and the theory of the Islamic firm

1. Basic Shariah principles, or *Fikh al Muamalat*, of Islamic business contracts

The main objective of Islamic economics is that of achieving social and economic justice and guaranteeing an equitable distribution of income and wealth. The goal of Islam is the application of ethical concepts such as brotherhood and justice in order to create well-being, or *Falah,* for the entire Muslim community. For this reason, Islamic banks have developed specific investment products that are in keeping with Islamic principles.

1.1. Forbidden elements in contracts

Islam prohibits all sources of unjustified enrichment. There are three forbidden elements in the contract: Riba, Gharar and Maisir.

Riba

Riba is interest. It is forbidden in Islam because it is an enrichment of a lender without effort being made by that lender, whose money is in the first place not a commodity in itself, only a tool for transactions.

According to Shariah, there are two types of Riba: *Riba an nasiah* and *Riba al fadl.*

- Riba an nasiah is used as recompense for the deferred payment of a loan. It makes no difference whether the return is at a fixed or variable rate, an amount to be paid in advance or on maturity, or a gift or service to be received as a condition of the loan.
- Riba al fadl is related to the exchange of goods against themselves in unequal proportion. That is, goods should be exchanged on the spot and be equal and alike.

Shariah aims to establish an economic system free from exploitation and injustice. Interest is therefore forbidden in Islam in order to help create equality between the provider of funds and the entrepreneur. In Islam it is seen as unjust to guarantee a positive return for the financier without his sharing in the effort or the risk while the entrepreneur, in spite of his hard work, is guaranteed no such return.

Gharar or dubiousness in contract

A dubious contract is a contract over which there may be doubt. It is either uncertain, unclear or unconfirmed. Thus it is forbidden by Islam, because one or more parties may because of that doubt ignore the clauses of the contract.

There are many types of Gharar which are prohibited by Islam, some of which are as follows: selling goods that the seller cannot deliver; selling goods for an unspecified price; selling goods without description; selling goods without fixing the price; making a contract regarding an uncertain event; selling goods with a false description and selling goods without allowing the purchaser to examine them.

To avoid Gharar, contracts should specify the goods or object of sale and its characteristics, including quality, quantity and date of delivery.

Maisir or gambling

Gambling means playing a game of chance to win money, and generally it creates a certain level of expectation. Gambling is a risky undertaking which is prohibited by Islam and takes several forms, such as:

Muzabana: defined as an exchange of fresh fruits, the properties of which are estimated when they are still on the tree, for dry ones which are measured and fixed.

Muhakala: the sale of grains still growing in exchange for an equal quantity of already gathered grains.

Mulamasah: a contract in which the buyer or seller touches a piece of commodity (clothing.)

Basic Shariah principles in business contracts

A contract should specify the conditions of a business partnership between a principal and an agent.

Business capital should be in the form of money. If a commodity or property is used, it should be converted into monetary terms and treated as the contribution of the partner.

The terms of a contract should be specified to avoid dispute during the conduct of business or when the partners share out the profits.

In a partnership, the relationship between the parties is that of a principal and an agent, for example in the case of Mudaraba contracts.

Capital and labor are responsible for creating profits.

The rights and duties of the partners depend on the nature of the business and are governed by custom, convention and practicality.

Rights are concomitant to responsibilities. The partners may not claim any fixed return for their effort except a share in the profit.

In a joint business, productivity is measured relative to invested capital, but it is labor that actually creates the profit. The proportion of profit received does not necessarily have to be proportional to the share of capital invested.

Loss is incurred when the capital fails to grow or diminishes. Loss in capital is borne in capital and in proportion with the shares held by each partner in the capital.

Profit comes with liability. Consequently, only a partner who is ready to bear liability may share in profit. Profits are concomitant to risk, and no partner will take any share above his or her exclusive right. Losses arising from wilful negligence must be borne by the partner responsible for it. The liability of each partner depends on the nature of the partnership.

The definition and nature of the different classifications of Islamic business contracts

Islamic business contracts can be classified into three categories:

Business contracts on the basis of direct financial accommodation following the PLS principle, such as Musharaka and Mudaraba.

Business contracts on the basis of indirect financial accommodation, which are based on the mark-up principle and the lease and advance purchase principle.

Business contracts in other forms, such as direct investment and finance with a development charge.

A. Direct financial accommodation

Mudaraba is based on the PLS principle, which consists of sharing profit between the two parties in the contract in predetermined proportions, and in the case of loss resulting from the activity, the supplier of the funds bears all the losses and the entrepreneur loses only his time and effort.

Mudaraba can be restricted or unrestricted. In restricted Mudaraba, the owner of capital specifies to the entrepreneur the type of commodities to use, the time and the place of trade, and so on. However, in unrestricted Mudaraba, the user of funds is free in his choices regarding the trade.

There are also other variations on the Mudaraba contract:

Non-contractual Mudaraba (Mudaraba *Mutlaq*) and contractual Mudaraba (Mudaraba *Muqaiadah*).

Single Mudaraba (one entrepreneur and one financier) or compound Mudaraba (there are more than one Mudareb, or entrepreneurs, and more than one providers of the funds).

Limited-term Mudaraba, where profits are accounted for at the time the work is terminated, or continuous Mudaraba, where profits are accounted for periodically.

Commingled Mudaraba, in which there are two providers of funds, the Mudareb and the financier, but only the Mudareb can participate in the work, or non-commingled Mudaraba, in which there is only one financier.

Conditions of Mudaraba

Before the activity starts, the user of funds is considered a trustee of the capital of the owner, but after the activity has started he is considered a proxy for the owner of the capital. The two parties become partners.

The capital should be in the form of money and its amount must be clearly defined. It should also be delivered to the entrepreneur in full to enable him to trade freely with it.

Profits are distributed in pre-agreed proportions and stand as a guarantee for the capital, which means the entrepreneur gains profit only if he refunds at least the total amount of the original loan.

There are some activities that the entrepreneur is not allowed to do without the approval or permission of the owner of capital, e.g. to establish a new company or sign a new Mudaraba contract with other parties. As for cancelling a Mudaraba contract, Shariah scholars agree that it may be cancelled by either of the two partners at any time. In this event capital should be liquidated.

B. Profit and loss sharing principles: Musharaka (long-term)

In a Musharaka contract, two or more parties contribute to the capital as well as the management of the business. Profit may be divided by the pre-agreed ratio between the parties. Losses, however, will be shared in the exact proportion of the capital invested by each party.

Musharaka can be classified as either non-contractual Musharaka or contractual Musharaka. Non-contractual Musharaka is further divided into voluntary partnerships and involuntary partnerships.

Contractual Musharaka is divided into:

Shirkat al Inan: Unequal partnership contracts, where any party can participate in any proportion.

Shirkat al Mufawada: An equal partnership contracts where capital, profit and loss are all shared equally.

Shirkat al wujuh: A good-will based partnership.

Shirkat al Abdan: A partnership which is formed on the basis of labor, skill and management.

Permanent Musharaka: A continuing Musharaka contract.

Muzara'a: A contract between an owner of a piece of agricultural land and a farmer.

Musaqat: A variant of Muzara'a.

It is believed in traditional finance that a debt contract (Mudaraba) is superior to an equity contract (Musharaka) when there is asymmetry of information.

An Islamic bank is not only a company, but also a moral trustee of deposits. An Islamic bank is likely to be more liquid and solvent when compared to a conventional bank.

An Islamic bank has the objective of avoiding interest in all transactions and replacing it with Shariah-compliant interest-free products, such as Musharaka (joint venture profit sharing) and Mudaraba (trust profit sharing).

Interest is forbidden by Islam. Muslims, through Islamic transactions, can follow this rule while also earning profit. Islamic banks expect a minimum level of failure, so the supply of loans will increase over time.

Indirect financial accommodation

The mark-up principle or Murabaha:

Murabaha is a contract under which a party wishing to buy a commodity requests that another party purchase this commodity and sell it to him at cost plus a declared profit.

The lease principle or Ijara:

This contract involves purchasing an asset and loaning it out on a rent-payment basis. The lessee becomes the owner of the asset at the end of the agreed period.

Advance purchase principle:

Bai Salam: An advance payment, or forward buying contract.

Salam: The sale of a commodity to be delivered at a future date.

Istisna'a (progressive financing): A contract for the acquisition of goods or services where the price is paid in installments as the job progresses.

Comparative economic features of Islamic business contracts:

Bai-Salam and Murabaha are debt-based modes of finance. However, in Mudaraba and Musharaka, the entrepreneur pays his debt back using the PLS principle to share the profit that he can only make in the first place with the use of financing. In Murabaha and Ijara the provider of the funds has some control over the user's activities. However, in Mudaraba and Bai-Salam, the financier has no control over the user's actions and does not participate in management. In Mudaraba, the owner of the capital bears all losses incurred, but in Musharaka he bears financial loss only in proportion to the capital he has contributed to the total invested amount.

2. Agency problems in Islamic contracts and their Implications

Islamic contracts based on the PLS system can face many problems resulting from costly monitoring and asymmetric information.

The bank suffers from the limitations of having only ex ante information about project quality. Borrowers choose PLS financing to enjoy high returns and an artificially low cost of capital.

PLS banks will attract entrepreneurs despite the riskiness of their projects, and borrowers will inflate the profit expectations they declare in order to be quoted a lower profit sharing ratio by the bank (Nienhaus 1983). The borrower then reduces his declared profit at a later stage in the process. Therefore Islamic banks also bear monitoring costs to help assess the quality of the entrepreneur in question and find a more realistic profit expectation. This ex post information asymmetry opens up Islamic banks to problems of moral hazard. The excessive dead-weight costs resulting from collecting information reduces the competitiveness of Islamic banks against conventional banks (Goodhart, 1987).

Solutions to agency problems in Islamic banking

* The PLS banking system itself can help resolve agency problems because the rewards that result from cooperation induce parties to be more honest.
* Muslims' belief in the afterlife and in the blessing that is a reward from Allah for honesty encourages them to be honest. Moreover, honest entrepreneurs force dishonest ones out of the market. Thus there is also a financial incentive for being honest (Bashir 1990).

The theory of the firm: Competence based, evolution and reward sharing

There are several firm theories which have been developed by economists; competence based, evolutionary and reward sharing.

Coase (1937) emphasized the cost of making and monitoring transactions. Williamson (1975, 1985) made a distinction between markets and hierarchies, and introduced the concept of "transaction cost" economics, so called because of its emphasis on the costs of formulating and monitoring contracts.

Adam Smith (1776) argued that the division of labor within a firm means that employees can improve their skills in practical ways. Marx (1876) believed that the process of production is a dynamic one. However, nowadays the firm is seen less as an organization and more as a set of cost and revenue curves. Knight (1921) saw the firm as a means of coping with uncertainty by assembling units of organization.

3. The nature and characteristics of the Islamic theory of the firm

The main objective of Muslims is to create welfare as described in Islamic law (Shariah). The process of production in an Islamic firm should therefore be governed by the ethical principles of Shariah:

- Maximization of utility by the Islamic community.
- Prohibition of causing detriment to others.
- Primacy of social benefit over private benefit.

Any firm has to maximize its profit as well as its welfare (Falah) in the hereafter.

An Islamic firm is bound by ethical values, and the most important of these is the principle of economic trusteeship which suggests that the main object of an Islamic firm should not be profit maximization, and that it is important to do good in order to please god.

Finally, a separate analysis must be applied to corporate Islamic finance because of the prohibition of interest in financial transactions.

Conclusion

An ongoing agreement should be established between Western and Islamic researchers because Western theories include many similar conclusions about interest relating to its prohibition and its effect on the business cycle. It is interesting for Islamic scholars to explore the wealth of supportive arguments to be found in Western literature in order to be able to encourage Western researchers to focus more on the Islamic paradigm for their studies.

- The commercial loans market within a dual banking system requires a different demand-supply model, because the modes of operation of the two types of bank are completely different.
- The commercial loans market is cleared through changes in the price of loanable funds. The price has a negative effect on the demand for, and a positive effect on the supply of, commercial loans.
- The supply of commercial loans is influenced by the interest rate applied by conventional banks.
- Borrowing in a dual banking system is affected by the forward level of activity.
- The demand for funds from Islamic banks is influenced by the interest rates of conventional banks in a dual banking system. However, the PLS rates of Islamic banks have no impact on borrowing from conventional banks.
- Deposits have a greater influence on the supply of loans offered by Islamic banks than on those offered by conventional banks.

References

Aryan, H. (1990), "Iran: the impact of Islamization on the financial system", in R. Wilson (ed), Islamic financial markets, Routledge, pp. 155-170.

Brucker, E. (1970), "A Microeconomic Approach to banking competition", Journal of finance, vol. 25, December, pp. 1133-41.

Brunner, E. (1937) The Divine Imperative (translated by O.Wyon), London: Lutterworth press.

Bashir, A.F. Darrat and M.O. Suliman, Equity capital, profit sharing contracts, and investment: theory and evidence, Journal of Business and Accounting, 20, (5), September 1993, 0306 686 X.

Friedman, M (1957), A Theory of Consumption Function, Princeton university press, Princeton, N.J.

Galbraith, J.K. 1967 "The new industrial state". Boston: Houghton Mifflin.

Greenwald, B.C. and Stiglitz, J.E. (1988 a) "imperfect information, finance constraints and business fluctuations", in M. Kohn and S.-C. Tsiang (eds), finance constraints, expectations and macro-economics, Oxford: Clarendon press, 103-140.

Greenwald, B.C. and Stiglitz, J.E. (1988 b) "Money, imperfect information and economic fluctuations", in M. Kohn and S.C. Tsiang (eds), finance constraints, expectations and Macroeconomics, Oxford: Clarendon press, 141-165.

Greenwald, B.C. and Stiglitz, J.E. (1990) "Macroeconomic models with equity and credit rationing", in R.G. Hubbard (ed.), Asymmetric information, corporate finance and investment, Chicago: university of Chicago press, 15-42.

Hayek, F. Von (1939) Profit and Interest and Investment.

Hassan, N.A (1993), "Measurement of financial performance of Islamic banks vis-à-vis western type commercial bank: some conceptual differences", paper presented at international conference in Islamic banking, November, Sydney.

Keynes, J.M. (1936), The General Theory of Employment, Interest and money, Macmillan, London.

Klein, L. (1965) The Keynesian revolution, London: Macmillan.

Khan, M.F. (1983) "Islamic banking as practiced now in the world", in A. Ziauddian, M. Iqbal and M.F. Khan (eds), Money and banking in Islam (institute of policy studies), pp. 259-284.

Khan, M (1986), "Islamic interest-free banking: A theoretical analysis IMF, staff papers, vol. 33 (March 1986), pp. 1-27.

Metwally, M.M. (1997), "Differences between the financial characteristics of interest- free banks and conventional banks". European Business Review, vol. 97, No 2, pp 92-98.

Modigliani, F. (1977), "The monetarist controversy or, should we forsake stabilization policies?" American Economic Review, March, pp. 1-19.

Minsky, H.P. (1963) "Can 'it' happen again?" in D. Carson (ed.), Banking and monetary studies, Homewood, Illinois: R.D. Irwin, 101-111.

—. (1977) "Of systematic fragility", in E.I. Altmaq and A.W. Sametz (eds), financial crises – institutions and markets in a fragile environment, New York: John Wiley & Sons.

Nienhaus, Volker (1983), "Profitability of Islamic banks competing with interest banks", Journal of Research in Islamic Economics, Vol. 1. No. 1 (Summer), pp. 37-47.

Revell, J.R.S (1980), costs and margins in banking: an international survey, organization for economic co-operation and development.

Short, Brock. K. (1979). The relation between commercial bank profit rate and banking concentration in Canada, Western Europe and Japan". Journal of Banking and Finance 3: 209-219.

Short, B.K. (1979), "the relation between commercial bank profit rate and banking concentration in Canada, western Europe and Japan", Journal of Banking and Finance, vol.3, pp. 209-219.

Smirlock, M. (1985), "Evidence on the (non)relationship between concentration and profitability in banking", Journal of Money, Credit and Loaning, vol. 17, No.1, (February), pp. 69- 83.

CHAPTER SEVEN

ISLAMIC BANKING AND THE PERFORMANCE OF ISLAMIC BANKS

MONDHER BELLALAH

The practice of interest is condemned by many thinkers, for example Aristotle, who described it as a "birth of money from money". Under Judaism, it is forbidden to demand any interest on a loan. In Christianity, the saying attributed to Christ, "lend freely, hoping nothing thereby" is taken by many researchers as a condemnation of interest. However, the church gradually changed its doctrine about interest, and after the reformation, it began allowing it. In Islam, the Koran forbids interest in all its forms, but due to the influence of Western colonial domination and the decline in the importance of religion, the practice of charging interest began to emerge in Muslim societies. The development of the financial system could have taken a different course, and it is possible that there could have been in actual operation an alternative system, free of interest but still suitable to the needs of modern society.

There are two different approaches to the adoption of Islamic banking practices. Private initiative Islamic banks co-existed with conventional banks for a long time, but many governments have opted for the economy-wide Islamization of banking.

The performance of an Islamic bank for a simple example, the Bank Islam Malaysia Berhard or BIMB), is judged on its profitability, liquidity, risk, solvency and community involvement.

Financial ratios are used to measure these and thereby measure performance.

It is important to evaluate a bank's performance. Depositors, bank managers and regulators use the evaluation of a bank's performance as a sign of the overall financial situation of that bank. The evaluation of BIMB's performance is based on two hypotheses. The first states that liquidity ratios are expected to be higher in the earlier years of a bank's existence than they are in later years due to a learning curve. The second states that Islamic financial modes of lending are expected to grow more the longer the bank has been in existence.

It is very important for the prosperity of any organization that its performance is evaluated. The changing goals and objectives of commercial banks affect the process of evaluation.

To measure the efficiency of Islamic banking, a banking efficiency model and its criteria have been taken into consideration. The criteria used to test efficiency are measures expressed as ratios. To measure and analyze the performance of the Islamic banking system in Bangladesh, operating within a wider conventional banking system, five efficiency test criteria are used.

This chapter is organized as follows: section 1 presents the foundations of conventional interest rates and rates of profit sharing on funds deposited within the Islamic banking system; sections 2 and 3 study the performance of Islamic banks.

Section 1. On the foundations of conventional interest rates and rates of profit sharing on funds deposited within the Islamic banking system

1. The foundations of conventional interest rates

According to the classic economic approach, interest on savings is a banking function that continues to become more and more important to consumers, who wish to maximize their resources while acting within the limits of acceptable consumer behavior. Keynes (1936) argued that a structural change in the interest rate could modify the subjective tendency to save. Friedman (1957) found that the main variable determining the average likelihood of a consumer opening an account with a bank is the interest rate offered by that bank. Wright (1967), Taylor (1971), Darby (1972) and Blinder (1975) all focused on the inverse relationship between interest rate and usage of financial products. Modigliani (1977) concluded that the interest rate's effects on demand are substantial. It is acknowledged by conventional banks that depositors must be rewarded and different types of deposit must carry different amounts of return. Therefore, assuming that the customers of Islamic banks have the same attitude as those of conventional banks, managers of Islamic banks must provide them with a reward that is the equivalent of a conventional bank's interest rate.

Metwally (1997) confirmed that conventional and Islamic banks offer their depositors similar returns. However, there are other factors that dictate the economic behavior of Muslims in addition to monetary rewards. Muslims believe in the afterlife and in the day of judgment. Thus decisions made by Muslims are based not only on immediate rewards but also on potential rewards in the afterlife and blessings from Allah.

In Islam, wealth is a gift from Allah and it is considered a tool to help achieve an objective, one which may be used for good and evil. Interest is forbidden in Islam because it creates wealth without any effort being made, so it cannot be considered a reward and therefore should not be paid out by Islamic banks. Islam defines success as obedience to Allah and not the accumulation of wealth. Applying this principle to the relationship between banks and consumers means that consumers should accept the low profits they receive from Islamic banks. Islamic bank customers are not guided by motives of profit-making, because wealth is a bounty from Allah and he can provide it to everyone. Similarly, losses are also caused by Allah.

2. Market structure and the determinants of performance in Islamic banks

It is also important to examine the relationship between market structure and the performance of banks, both conventional and Islamic. Nienhaus (1983) found a relationship between profitability and market structure. He shows that the profit and loss sharing (PLS) ratio is equivalent to the interest rate offered by conventional banks. Khan (1983) indicated that in the long run, PLS rates will be higher than interest rates and will not necessarily remain the equivalent of the market rate, as was claimed by Nienhaus (1983). However, neither of these two authors' claims have been verified empirically.

2.1. External determinants of profitability In Islamic Banking

There are two kinds of determinants of conventional bank profitability; internal and external. Internal variables are those controlled by the bank, such as use of funds, capital and liquidity management. External variables, on the other hand, are not controllable by the bank and include regulation, competitiveness, market share, concentration and inflation.

Competitiveness: Competitiveness can be considered a determinant of bank profitability.

Regulation: Regulation provides banks with a stable and healthy financing system.

Concentration: Concentration is the number and the size of firms in the market, and has emerged as a variable used for measuring performance from the Structure-Conduct-Performance (SCP) theory, which is based on the proposition that market concentration promotes accord between firms.

Market share: As a result of efficiency, the market share of the bank will be increased and thus promote profitability due to increasing the power of the bank in controlling market prices.

Ownership: The ownership of a bank has a strong impact on its profitability.

Scarcity of capital: Short (1979) found that scarcity of capital can be used to measure the economic performance of all industries. Capital scarcity has a significant positive relationship with profitability, according to both Short (1979) and Bourke (1989).

Money supply: Bourke (1989) also noted that market development can increase profits.

Inflation: Revell (1980) believed that inflation can be another factor affecting the bank's profitability.

Economies of scales and bank size: Economies of scales can be defined as the reduction in cost per unit of product that occurs as production becomes larger. As a result, large banks will earn higher rates of profit. However, the effect of economies of scale has not yet been entirely covered by scholars of banking.

2.2. Determinants of Islamic bank profitability: Some empirtical results

There are two kinds of determinants of profitability in the banking system: controllable, or internal to the bank, e.g. income statement management, and uncontrollable, or external to the bank, e.g. competition, regulation and market share.

Edwards (1977) found that salary expenditure in banking increases with monopoly on power. Hannan (1979) and Hannan and Mavinga (1980) also showed that the more control of power a bank has, the larger the number of people that bank employs.

Smirlock and Marshall (1983) argued against these findings by showing that this theory was subject to breakdowns in other markets.

Risk aversion theory was derived from a hypothesis established by Galbraith (1967) and states that the avoidance of uncertainty by large firms varies in direct correlation with the degree of market power possessed by them. Firms with more power may be more risk averse.

Heggest (1973) found that having a higher level of market domination may make banks choose a safer portfolio than other competitive banks. He also found that risk was an important determinant of a bank's profits, and that banks with more power tend to be involved in less risky activities.

Short (1979) introduced additional variables: relationship with the government, growth of assets, the discount rate and long-term government bond rates, all of which have significant relationships with profitability (excepting the growth of assets).

Revell (1980) pointed out a relationship between inflation, bank costs and profit margins gained through interest, asset prices.

Bourke (1989) concluded that concentration was positively related to profitability.

Molyneux and Thornton (1992) supported the expense-preference theory.

Section 2. Islamic banking: State of art

1. The theory of Islamic banking

There was nothing that could be called a prototype of modern banks in the early history of Islam. The attitude of Islam to innovation is that it allows anything which is useful to human society and respectful the principles of the Koran and the Sunnah. Sunnah is the speech of the prophet Mohammed. This means that the use of interest is not acceptable. Thus there is a dilemma regarding the reconciliation of Islamic principles with modern finance. The solution is to run economies without interest, even in modern societies, by replacing interest based banking with interest-free banking. Islam may forbid interest, but it does allow trade and profit. For this reason it is permitted to use PLS for the purposes of financial intermediation.

We will review the main contributions to the theory of Islamic banking under the following broad headings:

- The concept and models of Islamic banking
- The viability of Islamic banking
- The socio-economic consequences of Islamic banking

1.1. The foundations, basic concepts and models of Islamic banking

Even though banks did not exist in the early Islamic period, scholars of that time, in search of a new form of financial intermediation, wrote about the two forms of profit and loss sharing known as Mudaraba and Musharaka, still used today, and showing that they were already being used in the pre-Islamic period. In Mudaraba, one party provides the capital and the other manages the business. Profit is shared at a pre-agreed ratio and loss is borne by the provider of capital, assuming there has been no violation of agreement.

In Musharaka, partners pool their capital to undertake business. They can participate in management but do not necessarily do so. Profit is distributed among the partners at a pre-agreed ratio while loss is borne by each partner in proportion to their respective capital contributions.

Musharaka and Mudaraba are compatible with the principles of Islam. They represent two methods of financing used in modern finance in Islamic banks.

The contract of Mudaraba sets out the relationship between depositors and the bank and between the bank and the parties to whom finance is provided.

Earlier Islamic banking models identify three sources of funds: Mudaraba financing, Musharaka financing, and purchase of ordinary shares in commercial and industrial companies, Qard al hasanah.

The rules regarding the sharing of profits between banks and holders of deposits used in Mudaraba, and also between the banks and the users of bank funds under PLS arrangements, are also governed by Shariah principles.

Profit sharing arrangements between these two broad groups of providers of capital were originally envisaged along the following lines:

- Profit earned by the bank is divided into two parts of agreed proportions. One part is kept by the bank and the other part is given to the holders of Mudaraba deposits.
- Under a Musharaka contract, in the case of loss, that loss will be shared between the two parties in strict proportion to the capital contributed by each party.
- There is limitation to the amount of loss that can be borne by Mudaraba deposit holders based on the amounts of their deposits.

Islamic banking models are based on the principle of sharing profit and loss between the user and the provider of funds in proportions settled in advance.

The PLS principle is the most important feature of Islamic finance. However, different points of views have developed regarding the operations of Islamic banks. For example, some commentators believe:

- There is a difference between demand or safe keeping deposits and Mudaraba deposits.
- Islamic banks should not resort to credit creation.
- An Islamic bank should be a decentralized chain of institutions that has the features of not just a local bank, but also a cooperative society and a social service organization.

Others are against larger sized banks because they believe they have the potential to seize too much power, or believe that, since Islamic banks do not pay rewards for deposits, some of the money they save this way should be used for the financial needs of the government.

The replacement of conventional banks by Islamic banks does not constitute the replacement of interest by interest-free modes of financing; the real substitute for interest in an Islamic financial system is the profit and loss sharing system.

Interest is forbidden by Islam because of the inequitable system it encourages whereby the provider of capital funds is assured a fixed return, and all the risk is borne by the user of these capital funds.

The main objectives of Islamic banks are the realization of an equitable pattern of income distribution and the generation of maximum employment opportunities. The Central Bank plays a leading role in the development of new financial instruments, which include participation term certificates, specific investment certificates and leasing certificates.

In an interest-free economy, the Central Bank will have no use for the traditional monetary policy instrument of changes in the bank rate. Open market operations in the traditional sense of the term will also lose their relevance in an interest-free framework.

The Central Bank will be able to use measures of selective control, like restricting the use of bank resources to certain purposes and setting mandatory targets for financial assistance to be provided by banks to stated causes.

Regarding open market operations, various different opinions have been expressed:

- There should be no government securities market in an interest free-economy.
- Open market operations should not be favored when dealing with shares in private concerns, for many reasons:
    - The Central Bank should buy and sell the stocks of private sector companies.
    - The issuance of variable divided securities by the Central Bank, in which such operations could be conducted, should be related to their profit.

1.2.The viability of Islamic banking

The more important misgivings are:

- The commitment to share in losses leads to higher risk of failure and insolvency.
- Islamic banks will experience frequent defaults and losses of their earnings on account of the ability of their clients to conceal genuine income amounts, which will undermine their stability.
- Islamic banks cannot perform all banking functions while sticking to their interest-free principles in a world which is dominated by interest based transactions, so they do have to deal with conventional banks.

Default can be based on several factors:

- The nature of the party to whom finance is provided.
- The purpose for which finance is provided.
- The type of supervision exercised by the banks over the end-use of funds.

1.3. The socio-economic consequences of Islamic banking

Effects on savings and investment

PLS principal leads to an adverse effect on savings (i.e. increases uncertainty about the rate of return), but that increased risk is compensated for by generally higher returns.

Impact on the rate and pattern of growth

The expected favorable effect of PLS based banking on investment levels would bring a pronounced tendency toward growth to the economy. Innovation and experimentation always contribute to growth.

Impact of allocative efficiency

The PLS system would be more efficient in allocating resources than the conventional interest based system. This produces better allocation than a system which is based on productivity and rates of return.

The interest rate is not an appropriate discount factor under conditions of uncertainty, even in interest based economies.

Under uncertain conditions, the rate of return on equity is the proper discount rate.

The acceptance of uncertainty and risk implies that the party in question deserves cash flows discounted, not by a riskless interest rate, but by the true opportunity cost of venture capital.

Consequences for the stability of the banking system

In the interest based system, the nominal value of deposit liabilities is fixed, but there is no assurance on the assets side that all loans and advances will be recovered. The banking system can suffer a loss of confidence in its processes, caused by banking crises and shocks.

In the PLS based system, the nominal value of investment deposits is not guaranteed, and shocks to the values of assets are absorbed by investment deposits. This minimizes the risk of bank failures and enhances the stability of the banking system.

Effects on the stability of the economic system

The interest based system is faced with many potential disturbances, however, a PLS based system is characterized by its stability.

If business concerns are beginning to incur losses, banks reduce the assistance they are providing and call in loans, as a result of which some firms have to close down. This leads to a reduction in demand, which leads to an increase in unemployment, and the infection spreads. Islamic banks bear a part of losses and this decreases business collapses; they can therefore be said to be promoters of stability.

2. The practice of Islamic banking

2.1. Practices of Islamic banking: Individual entities

Islamic banks are successful in mobilizing large amounts of funds. Deposits in almost all Islamic banks are growing at a rapid pace. Between 1980 and 1986 the relative growth of Islamic banks was better, in most cases, than that of other banks. This tendency has been exhibited again since the global financial crisis of 2008. Islamic banks have also had problems in recovering their dues during certain periods, however, these institutions recovered by 1985 and showed good profits. The objectives of Islamic banks are:

- The achievement of a pattern of growth
- The eradication of poverty
- Equitable distribution of income and wealth
- The creation of opportunities for gainful employment

2.2. Islamic banking in Pakistan

The Central Bank in Pakistan has issued a directive specifying twelve modes of financing. These are broadly classified into three groups: loan financing, trade related modes of financing and investment modes of financing. Loan financing takes the form of either Qard al hasanah, free of any interest, or loans with a service charge which may not exceed a certain proportion of the cost of the operation. There are 41 trade-related modes of financing, including the following: purchases by banks and subsequent sales to clients at a mark-up in price on a deferred payment basis; purchase of trade bills; purchase of movable or immovable property by banks from their clients with buy-back agreements; leasing; higher purchase and financing or development of property on the basis of a development charge.

Investment modes of financing include the following:

Musharaka, equity participation, purchase of shares, purchase of participation-term certificates, Mudaraba certificates and rent sharing (Murabaha).

Since 1979, many an effort has been made to eliminate interest from the financial sector in Pakistan, but nothing has so far been done to eliminate it from government transactions.

2.3. Profitability of Islamic banking in Iran

The holders of current and savings accounts are rewarded by incentives. They are guaranteed the safety of their deposited amounts as well as:

- The granting of prizes in cash or kind
- Reduction in or exemption from service charges
- Priority use of banking facilities.

The holders of term investment deposits are entitled to receive a variable return depending on the profitability of the projects in which these funds are invested.

Banks are obliged to set aside a proportion of their resources for the granting of Qard al hasanah to help achieve their socio-economic objectives. Banks are authorized to extend financial assistance to productive ventures on a profit and loss sharing basis in accordance with the principles of Mudaraba and Musharaka.

2.4. Profitability of Islamic banking in Sudan

Equity participation and PLS are regarded as the chief distinguishing features of Islamic banking and finance in Sudan.

Section 3. The performance of Islamic banks: A case study using financial analysis; The case of Malaysia

The performance of the Bank Islam Malaysia Berhard (BIMB) is measured through profitability, liquidity, risk, solvency and community involvement. Financial ratios are used to measure each of these. To measure the performance of banks, we use accounting ratios. Bank regulators use financial ratios to help them in evaluating a bank's performance.

Samad (1999) used financial ratios for evaluating the performance of banks. These ratios are grouped into four categories: profitability, liquidity, risk and solvency, and commitment to the domestic and Muslim communities.

1. Profitability ratios

Profitability can be measured using the following ratios:

Return on asset (ROA) = profit after tax: total asset

This ratio is an indicator of managerial efficiency, and represents the net earning per unit of a given asset. A higher ratio shows a higher ability and a higher performance.

Return of equity (ROE) = profit after tax: equity capital

This ratio measures the net earning per dollar of equity capital. A higher ratio indicates a higher managerial performance.

Profit expense ratio (PER) = profit: total expense

This ratio measures the profit associated with a unit of expense. A higher PER indicates a higher cost efficiency and a higher profit per unit of expense.

2. Liquidity ratios

There are many different ratios which can be used to measure liquidity:

Cash deposit ratio (CDR) = cash: deposits

This ratio measures the amount of debt in comparison to equity capital. A higher CDR indicates that a bank is relatively more liquid than a bank which has a lower CDR.

Loan deposit ratio (LDR) = loan: deposits

The higher the loan deposit ratio, the higher the ability to bear financial stress by increasing loans.

Current ratio = current asset (CA): current liability (CL)

This ratio indicates how well the bank's management is able to meet current liabilities. A higher current ratio shows a higher liquidity of assets that can be used to pay back deposits.

Current asset ratio (CAR) = current asset: total asset

The higher the CAR, the higher the liquidity of the assets held by the bank.

3. Risk and solvency ratios

There are also several measures of risk and solvency:

Debt equity ratio (DER) =debt: equity capital

A lower DER ratio is a positive indicator for a bank.

Debt to total asset ratio (DTAR) = debt: total asset

This ratio indicates the financial strength of a bank, i.e. its ability to pay its debtors. A high DTAR shows that a bank is involved in more risky business.

Equity multiplier (EM) total assets: share capital

This ratio measures the amount of assets per dollar of equity capital. A higher EM indicates that the bank has borrowed more funds in the form of share capital to convert into assets.

Loan to deposit (LDR) = loans: deposit

This ratio measures liquidity as well as credit risk for a bank. A higher value indicates a higher potential illiquidity and insolvency.

4. Commitment to the economy and the Muslim community

Long term loan ratio (LTA) = long term loans: total loans

A high LTA indicates a bank's commitment to supporting long term development projects.

Government bond investment (GBD) = deposits invested in government bonds: total deposits

A higher GBD indicates high liquidity and low risk.

Mudaraba-Musharaka ratio (MM/L) = Mudaraba and Musharaka combined: total loans

A higher ratio of MM/L shows a greater commitment to community development.

Section 4. The performance of Islamic banks: A case study of performance, problems and prospects; The case of Bangladesh

To measure and analyze the performance of the Islamic banking system in Bangladesh, operating within conventional banking, five efficiency test criteria are used.

1. Productive efficiency of the Islamic banks

Several criteria have been developed to measure performance:

1.1. Investment opportunity utilization test

The utilization of funds by Islamic banks is not optimal due to competition, a difficult economic climate and most importantly, the behavioral and decision-making differences between conventional and Islamic banks.

1.2. Profit maximization test

Project efficiency test

The following elements can be used:

a) Project selection criteria
b) Pre-financing appraisal of projects
c) Post financing supervision
d) Built-in mechanical linkage of the bank to its financed projects

Islamic banks use mostly trade modes. Thus they have little relevance to project financing.

1.3. Loan recovery test:

The analysis of the Central Bank showed that the amount of bad debt owed to Islamic banks is growing.

Test of elasticity in loan financing

The loan financing system in Islamic banking is characterized by a lack of elasticity in meeting loan demands. This problem also affects interbank borrowing. There are two criteria for measuring operational efficiency in Islamic banks: per employee administrative cost (PEAC) and administrative cost to loanable fund ratio (ACLFR).

2. Problems and challenges of Islamic banking

2.1. The nature of the problems and challenges

The principal characteristic of the Islamic system in Bangladesh is interest-free banking. This causes some problems at micro- and macro-operational levels.

2.2. Problems related to the macro-operations of Islamic banks

- Liquidity and capital
- Valuation of bank assets
- Financial stability
- The ownership of banks

- Lack of capital market and interest-free financial instruments
- Insufficient legal protection
- Controlling and supervision by the Central Bank on the basis of Islamic Shariah
- Lack of unified Shariah ruling
- Absence of Islamic interbank money market
- New banking regulations
- Accounting principles and procedures
- Shortage of support and link institutions
- Shortage of skilled and trained manpower in Islamic Shariah banking
- Lack of co-operation among the Islamic banks
- Lack of familiarity in the international financial and non-financial sectors with Islamic products and procedures
- Severe competition in the financial sector
- Economic slowdown and the political situation of the country
- The inadequate track record of Islamic banking
- Absence of infrastructure for international Islamic trade financing
- Default culture of borrowers
- Short-term asset concentration in the Islamic banks
- Lack of courses and papers on Islamic economics, banking and finance at educational institutions
- Lack of uniform operating procedure throughout Islamic banking
- Lack of specialized Islamic banks and non-bank financial institutions
- Lack of a consortium or syndicate of Islamic banks
- Lack of harmonization on Islamic financial practices
- Lack of inter-country studies on the practical operations of Islamic banking
- Lack of secondary securitization market
- Lack of coordinated research work on Islamic economics, banking and finance
- Lack of Apex training institutes for Islamic banking

3. Problems related to the micro-operations of Islamic banks

- Increased cost of information
- Lack of control over cost of funds
- Mark-up financing and corrupted mark-ups
- Excessive resorting to the Mudaraba mode of financing

- Utilization of interest rates for fixing the profit margin in Bai modes
- Financial social concerns
- Lack of positive response to the requirement of government financing
- Failure of Islamic banks to finance high return projects
- Sacrifice of allocative efficiency
- Loss of distributive efficiency
- Depression of profits
- Lack of fully-fledged Shariah auditing
- Fraud: forgery and corruption in Islamic banks
- Relatively small budget for research and development
- Working environment
- Issuing of letters of guarantee (LGs)
- Small budget for research and development
- Lack of a Shariah manual or guidelines
- Islamic investment risk analysis and measurement methodology
- Non-exemption from stamp duty for banks when purchasing property
- Lack of cooperation between Islamic banks and Islamic NGOs for extending microcredit
- Lack of establishment of links with other training institutes and Shariah supervisory bodies
- Lack of commitment by management to work strictly within Shariah guidelines

These are some of the immediate problems from which Islamic banks in several countries, and in particular in Bangladesh, suffer. However, a lot of operational work has affirmed that Islamic banks possess high quality and strength.

4. The future of Islamic banking in Bangladesh

The need for re-organization of the whole financing system

Faced with problems of structure, Bangladeshi banks may have to challenge themselves to develop new features for their promotion and survival.

A new philosophy for Islamic banks

There is a big difference between the ideal and the actual practice of Islamic banking in Bangladesh. However, these banks are working towards a just society, free from exploitation.

Future policy and strategy

Islamic banks in Bangladesh should demonstrate the use of practices guided by profitability criteria and show that they are able to ensure efficient allocation of resources and provide true market signals through PLS. They should also further publicize the impact of their operations on the distribution of income between the bank, depositors and entrepreneurs. They also need to establish a field of academic research dedicated to Islamic banking.

Striving for distributional efficiency

Islamic banks have to promote their distributional efficiency and profitability, and most importantly, they have to be converted into profit and loss sharing banks by investing more money in PLS contracts.

The promotion of allocative efficiency

Islamic banks should allocate a large portion of their investible funds to social priority sectors like agriculture, and export-led industries like garment manufacture. Then, when the allocation of remaining investible funds is determined among investment financing sectors, profitability should be the criterion for allocation.

Modern banking policies and practices

Competition between just Islamic banks, and between all banks including the conventional, pushes them to adapt their operations and get in line with modern business practices through improvement and expansion of their relationships with other banks in the sector.

Government and Central Bank responsibilities

The government should have an active role in the development of Islamic banking in Bangladesh, and it should write legislation that creates a favorable environment for them to operate in.

Interbank cooperation and prospective planning

To realize sustained growth and development, Islamic banks should help each other and adopt a plan for the prospective Islamization of the banking system in Bangladesh. Thus it is vital to participate in the work of a research academy and have access to a training institute with modern tools. Results of working with such institutions are reported by Sarker (1999).

Conclusion

The effects of various determinants on profitability for conventional banks and Islamic banks are very similar. This similarity is explained by the fact that Islamic banks operate in the same environment as conventional banks, and use the same techniques in managing assets and liabilities. Moreover, Islamic banks' fixed profit sharing system and mark-up ratios have their equivalent in conventional banks in the form of interest rates.

Risk aversion theory is supported by empirical studies on Islamic banks, but the efficient structure theory and expense preference theory are not supported.

Islamic banks try to avoid risky partnerships by applying the mark-up principle in their financing activities.

The incorrectness of the efficient structure theory obliges Islamic banks to increase their efficiency because they are faced with stiff competition from the conventional banks which operate side by side with them.

The disproving of expense preference theory shows that an increase in salary expenses has no relation to the increase of total income; even if that were not the case, Islamic banks must recruit more Muslim bankers to guarantee the continuing support of the Muslim community and to expand their activities.

A pattern of banking so different from the conventional one has attracted the attention of the entire world. This system, based on Shariah principles, aims for the achievement of prosperity and general good will for and within the Islamic community as a whole. There is a positive relationship between the deposits in the Islamic bank in Malaysia and returns given on those deposits. In reality, depositors are motived by profit and not only by the potential blessings and rewards from Allah on which most of the theoretical research up until now have focused.

References

Blinder, A.S. (1975), "Distribution effects and the aggregate consumption function", Journal of Political Economy, June, pp. 447-475.

Bourke, Philip (1989), "Concentration and other determinants of bank profitability in Europe, North America and Australia", Journal of Banking and Finance 13: 65-67.

Darby, M.R. (1972), "The allocation of transitory income among consumers' assets" American Economic Review, December, p.p. 928-941.

Friedman, M. (1957), A theory of consumption function, Princeton university press, Princeton, N.J.

Edward, Franklin R. (1977), "Managerial objectives in regulated industries: expense preference behavior in banking", Journal of Political Economy 85 (February): 147-162.

Gabraith, J.K. (1967), "The new industrial state". Boston: Houghton Mifflin.

Hannan, Timothy H. (1979), Expense-preference behavior in banking: a re-examination." Journal of Political Economy 87(4): 891-895.

Hannan, Timothy H. & Mavinga, E. (1980), "Expense preference behavior and managerial control: the case of banking firms." Bell Journal of Economics 11 (Autumn): 667-682.

Heggested, Arnold A. (1977). "Market structure, risk and profitability in commercial banking, Journal of Finance 32 (September): 1207-1216.

Keynes, J.M. (1936), The general theory of employment. Interest and money, Macmillan, London.

Khan, M. Fahim (1983), "Comments on Volker Nienhaus: profitability of Islamic banks competing with interest banks", Journal of Research in Islamic Economics, vol.1, No 2 (winter), pp. 73-78.

Metwally, M.M. (1997), "Differences between the financial characteristics of interest-free banks and conventional banks." European Business Review, vol. 97, No 2, pp. 92-98.

Modigliani, F. (1977), "the monetarist controversy or, should we forsake stabilization policies?" American Economic Review, March, pp. 1-19.

Molyneux, Philip & John (1992), "Determinants of European bank profitability: A note." Journal of Banking and Finance 16: 1173-1178.

Nienhaus, Volker (1983), "Profitability of Islamic banks competing with interest banks", Journal of Research in Islamic economics, Vol. 1. No. 1 (Summer), pp. 37-47.

Revell, J.R.S. (1980), Costs and margins in banking: an international survey, organization for economic co-operation and development.

Samad.A &Hassan.K (1999), "The performance of Malaysian Islamic banks during 1984-1997: an exploratory study." International Journal of Islamic Financial Services vol.1 No.3 Oct-Dec 1999 pp.3-11.

Sarker M.A.A. (1999), "Islamic banking in Bangladesh: performance, problems and prospects", International Journal of Islamic Financial Services vol.1 No.3 Oct-Dec 1999 pp. 12-28.

Short, Brock. K. (1979), The relationship between commercial bank profit rate and banking concentration in Canada, western Europe and Japan." Journal of Banking and Finance 3: 209-219.

Smirlock, Michael & Marshall, William. (1983), "Monopoly power and expense preference behavior theory and evidence to the contrary," Bell Journal of Economics 14(1): 166-178.

Sudin, H. (1997), "Determinants of Islamic bank profitability: some evidence," Journal Pengurusan 16 (1997) 33-46.

—. (1996), "Competition and other external determinants of the profitability of Islamic banks," Islamic Economic Studies vol.4. No 1 December 1996.

Sudin, H. & Norafifah, A. (2000), "The effects of conventional interest rates and rate of profit on funds deposited with the Islamic banking system in Malaysia", International Journal of Islamic Financial Services vol.1 No.4 Jan-Mar 2000 pp. 3-9.

Taylor, L.D. (1971), "Saving out of different types of income", Brooking Papers on Economic Activity, No. 2, pp. 384-415.

Wright, C. (1967), "Some evidence on the interest of consumption". American Economic Review, September, pp. 850-854.

CHAPTER EIGHT

SHORT- AND LONG-TERM FINANCING AND THE CAPITAL STRUCTURE OF ISLAMIC INSTITUTIONS

MONDHER BELLALAH AND OMAR MASOOD

Liquidity can be defined as the ease with which an asset can be converted into cash without loss of value. A bank manager tries to maximize a bank's returns by investing in liquid assets; the bank needs liquidity to meet the mismatch between the maturity dates of assets and liabilities. There are two basic principles of Islamic finance: profit and loss sharing (PLS) and deferred sale (mark-up). Studies of these two principles show that the benefits inherent to PLS are more significant than those of mark-up, but over very short periods of time, the mark-up principle is the primary basis of an Islamic bank's operations.

The mark-up principle is consistent with the traditions of conventional banks, and also dominates the operations of Islamic banks. In the PLS model of Islamic banking developed by Siddiqi (1967, 1983 a and 1983 b), the Islamic economy was visualized as an entirely debt-free economy.

The mark-up principle is a form of debt financing used by Islamic banks. It returns to the user choices about debt and equity. PLS does not allow retention and re-investment of profits in the enterprise, however, the mark-up principle does, and this is another reason why it is often preferable.

The application of *Bay'al inah* and *Bay'al dayn* to Malaysian Islamic bonds has been found unacceptable by the majority of Islamic researchers. *Muquarada* and Musharaka principles have been found to be the best alternatives to interest-bearing financial instruments.

Islamic banks have a unique capital structure, using funds collected via deposit in investment accounts based on the PLS principle. Conventional banks, meanwhile, use a debt financing system which is based on interest. Modigliani and Miller (1958) characterized the capital structure debate in terms of the debt-equity environment and searched for the optimal capital structure. They assumed that funds can only be raised through debt and equity. However, this fails to explain the cost of capital and the market value of Islamic banks. There is a structure of capital (PLS between banks and their clients) entirely unique to Islamic banks. The augmentation of investment accounts implies an augmentation of the market value of the bank, but the weight average cost of capital (WACC) of the bank remains constant.

This chapter is organized as follows:

Section 1 presents short-term Islamic instruments for managing liquidity. Section 2 explains debt financing with respect to Islamic finance. Section 3 describes bonds and debt instruments, including the use of Bay'al-inah and Bay'al-dayn in Malaysian Islamic banks. Section 4 studies the capital structure of, and the cost of capital to, Islamic banks.

Section 1. Short-term Islamic instruments for managing liquidity

1. The problem of liquidity management in Islamic Banking

Islamic interest-free banks, or *Lariba* banks, support opportunity costs by holding cash to insure against damaging runs. They also suffer from two serious handicaps:

- lack of access to the safety net provided by the Central Banks to cover the risk of a run.
- lack of access to government guarantees of security; they can only hold cash. Thus they pay more seignorage to the government than interest-based (Riba) banks holding treasury bills.

Shariah or Islamic law has established principles for managing a bank's activity:

- Refusal to use interest.
- Accepting interest only with the purpose of using it in charitable activities.
- Investing in precious metals and "cash and carry" forward contracts.

- Replacing interest with terms of service and interest-free facilities. Therefore it is the duty of Islamic Lariba bankers to promote profitable Islamic Lariba products in order to minimize their losses as compared with those of their Riba counterparts.

Islamic Shariah guidelines relating to liquidity management

Money is a tool of exchange and does not reproduce. Economic profit is instead created by investing in activities.

Shares in companies and partnerships can be bought or sold for investing purposes but not for speculative ones.

The owner of the funds should be informed if the entrepreneur uses the money for a purpose other than what they have specifically agreed.

An Islamic Lariba bank accumulates deposits and reinvests them to generate productive economic activities, job opportunities and credit which enhance economic growth.

As regards contracts, there are some restrictions that must be respected. For example, a contract should be registered and should specify price, delivery terms, default penalties to be applied, the ramifications of a breach of contract, etc. The object of a contract must be a *halal* business (i.e. a business not forbidden by Islam). Buying and selling should be genuine, not artificial or simulated. All parties should be qualified and capable.

There are also restrictions on the transactions carried out using Islamic banks' financial instruments:

Money is only a tool used for transactions; it has no inherent value.

Value per share must be approved by all parties in the business.

Cash transactions should be settled as per the relevant contract. Titles and cash should be transferred immediately after the mutual agreement taking place.

It is possible to purchase shares which have debt on their balance sheet, however, this debt should not be dominant.

A share can be transferred from one party to another without being directly handled by either if both delegate someone to act on their behalf.

Liquidation and/or conversion of shares: the owner of capital can terminate the contract whenever he wishes, unless otherwise stipulated in the contract.

2. Designing Islamic short-term liquidity financial instruments

Riba-based debt securities are generally in the form of short-term instruments such as commercial papers, certificates of deposit (CDS), banker's acceptances (BA), municipal and government loans and treasury bills.

- Commercial papers are notes of short maturity issued by highly rated firms and are entitled to an interest rate (which can be below the general rate of the bank). These papers are forbidden in Islam because they are based on interest charges.
- Certificates of deposit (CDs) have a maturity of between one month and several years. They are not used in the Lariba banking system because they are also based on paying interest.
- Banker's acceptances (BA) are short-term loans granted to importers and exporters by their banks, and consist of credit commitments made by customers before goods are delivered (commercial drafts). They are a mode of discounting prices and are not accepted by Islamic Lariba laws (Shariah).
- Municipal and government loans are short-term loans to finance municipalities and government agencies' short-term capital needs.
- Treasury bills are short-term debt securities created by the government.

To compete with Riba liquidity instruments, Islamic Lariba bankers have to:

- Create new instruments to meet the needs of the Lariba market.
- Promote and manufacture these new products.
- Make the products comparable to their Riba counterparts.

For example, CDs in Riba bank are replaced by SPIN CDs (Specific Investor CDs). A SPIN CD is a specific portfolio, for example of automobile lease (Ijara), which provides an expected rate of return. This can create more liquidity to finance more projects in Lariba ways. It is also important to create a Lariba market with new instruments, market makers, sales forces and brokers in order to compete with Riba banks.

Some money market funds use futures, options and derivatives to increase income, but share value always stays at US $1.

Riba money market funds in the USA are the most diversified market in the world. So the question is: can Muslim bankers promote and develop Lariba money market mutual funds into a similarly important market in the USA? The answer is yes, because many products can be manufactured in this market, such as oil, gas, petroleum, food items and capital goods.

3. The need for specialization in Lariba Islamic banking services

In the past, Lariba Islamic banks have offered their customers many services:

Direct investment and deal making investment companies: Direct investment and deal making investment companies created instability in the Lariba system during the 20th century. The damage taken by the Islamic banking system then has propagated through three generations in Islamic countries.

Retail Lariba banks: Retail Lariba banks provide regular banking services, for example, financing small businesses in the community, construction financing, short-term financing, leasing automobiles, etc. Their products can be packaged and used as the basis of Lariba short-term instruments.

Wholesale Lariba banks: Wholesale Lariba banks serve medium and large size institutions, as well as high net worth savers/investors, and should provide sufficient liquidity for smaller retail Lariba banks.

Mega Lariba regional banks: Mega Lariba regional banks should provide liquidity to wholesale banks.

Lariba investment banking institutions: Lariba investment banking institutions invest in activities using interest-free methods such as organizing direct, interest-free investment deals, arranging for the issue of Islamic bonds and making public Musharaka deals.

These institutions play an important role in developing the money market mutual fund when it comes to knowing the capital market and the short-term instruments available on the market.

Lariba brokerage institutions: Lariba brokerage institutions identify and assemble available short-term instruments. Moreover, they market the instruments and products provided by investment bankers. With the system of Lariba banking involving all kinds of products and services, Islamic banks can attract Muslim as well as non-Muslim customers.

Section 2. Debt financing and Islamic finance: Demand for and supply of mark-up and PLS funds in Islamic banking: Some alternatives

1. The dichotomy between theory and practice in Islamic banking: an overview of the consequences:

1.1. The diversity of Islamic modes of financing

The Koran provides basic guidelines for establishing just and efficient contractual relationships between Muslims. Trust is an important value in Islam and the prophet Muhammad (PBUH) was a perfectly trustworthy person in all his transactions. There is a diversity of contracts in Islam, and the most important are:

- Contracts of exchange, which are based on deferred payment.
- contracts of partnership, which are based on sharing the outcome of a transaction or enterprise.
- Leasing contracts, which are based on the utilization of the benefits of assets.

1.2. Overview of consequences

Islamic economic preferences: The Council of Islamic Ideology (1981), Siddiqi (1988) and Khan (1992) showed that the PLS principle is very distinct from interest-based financing. Indeed, PLS is often synonymous with Islamic financing.

Homoud (1976) believed that the mark-up is the most Islamic substitute possible for interest. There are many financing needs where no profit is expected which can be fulfilled using this principle.

Homoud and Ismail (1989) argued that a mark-up based on a fixed price is different from a rate of return. Chapra (1985), and Kahf and Khan (1992) took a middling stance in this argument by integrating the above two views. Although the mark-up principle is more prone to violation of Shariah requirements than PLS, it is still the more regularly used in Islamic financial operations.

Stability of the banking system: Khan (1986) compared the characteristics of the balance sheets of Islamic PLS banks with those of traditional banks. The balance sheets of Islamic banks have no fixed liabilities, and deposits are treated as shares. Any shock on the assets side is automatically absorbed and adjusted for on the liability side. This can lead to a high level of stability in Islamic banks. Meanwhile, in conventional banks, when a crisis arises on the assets side, banks turn to liability management, and this leads to instability.

Bankruptcy is less likely to happen in Islamic banks, because PLS and mark-up operations are based on the solvency and trustworthiness of partners.

Demand side consideration: the firms' preferences of forms of finance

Preferences of Infant firms for PLS

Infant firms prefer to avoid risk. They prefer the PLS mode of finance, because they are relatively lacking in financial resources. These firms gradually take a larger and larger share of a project's risks.

Moreover, it is important for infant enterprises to diminish PLS contracts over time for many reasons. First, the role of Islamic banks is to generate more projects to work toward the elimination of poverty. Second, diminishing PLS can reduce foreign control over local projects. It can diminish the commercial risks and promote foreign investment. If the financier's ownership is not terminable, despite a need for funds, demand for PLS cannot be generated.

Implications of the different forms of funding

Infant firms need capital and funds with risk-spreading characteristics. Thus, they choose to use the PLS mode of finance. However, growing firms need to acquire assets, so they will not be so attracted by PLS, and will usually choose instead the mark-up mode.

PLS does not allow the retention of profits and their re-investment in the growth of the firm.

Section 3. Bonds and debt Instruments: The application of Bay'al-inah and Bay'al-dayn in Malaysian Islamic bonds; an Islamic analysis

1. Islamic Bond markets: bonds in Malaysia

To explain the role of Bay'al dayn in an Islamic bond market, we will describe the three steps of the process of its use:

- Securitization: The creation of the Bay'al-inah assets.
- Bond issues: The issuing of the debt certificate (*Shahdah al-dayn*).
- Trading of debt certificates: The buying and selling of debt certificates on the secondary market using the Bay'al dayn contract.

1.1 The first step: The creation of a Bay'al inah underlying asset

In Islamic law, an object for sale must have a value, and when this object is an asset assuring a bond, the bond itself is transformed into an object of the same value and can be traded on the primary and secondary markets.

Bay'al inah asset securitization is the process of a financier buying an asset from an issuer and selling it back to the same party at a credit price. The issuer will receive the money in cash while the financier will be paid a contracted amount through bond issue at a later date. The difference between the credit price and the cash becomes the profit of the financier. The underlying asset can be a factory, equipment, stock, building, properties etc.

Table 1: Selected Islamic Debt Securities (IPDS) in Malaysia: underlying assets

Issuer	Instrument	Underlying asset
Hicom holding BHD	Guaranteed Murabaha Note issuance facility	Mixture of halal share (including unquoted shares)
Amanah international finance Snd Bhd	Guaranteed Murabaha Note issuance facility	A list including buildings and properties
KFC Holdings	Al-Bai-Bithaman ajil Islamic debt securities	Restaurants, breeder, farm and hatchery
Petronas Dagangan Bhd	Redeemable Islamic debt securities	Gas processing line and pipeline

Source: Rating Agency Malaysia (1998)

1.2. The second step: The issue of an Islamic debt certificate (Shahdah al dayn)

An issuing company will sell debt certificates or bonds which are supported by assets (BBA or al Murabaha assets) to investors. If the first stage involves an Ijara contract, then the debt certificate is called the *Sukuk al Ijara*, and if an Istisna'a contract is used, we call it *Sukuk al Istisna'a*. There are bond issues with coupons (Islamic coupon bonds) and those with none (Islamic zero coupons).

1.2.1. Islamic coupon bond

A coupon represents a proportion of the profit of the Islamic bond, in both al-Murabaha note issuance facilities (MUNIF) which have short- and medium-terms, and al-Bai-Bithaman ajil Islamic debt securities (ABBA) which are issued on a long-term basis, as shown in the table below:

Issuer	Instrument	Tenure
Houlon corporation	Al-Bai-Bithaman ajil Islamic debt securities	7 years
Teleda Sdn Bhd	Guaranteed Murabaha Notes Issuance Facility	5 years
Moccis trading Sdn Bhd	Guaranteed Murabaha Notes Issuance Facility	5 years

Source: Rating Agency Malaysia, (1998)

There are two types of certificates issued by both MUNIF and ABBA.

The first type, the primary note, represents the capital component. The second type, the coupon note, represents a proportion of profit.

1.2.2. Al Murabaha note issuance facility (MUNIF)

The Shahdah al-dayn is a debt certificate which includes both primary and secondary notes.

1.2.3. Islamic zero coupon bonds

With this kind of bond, there is no coupon, but there is a difference between par value and discount value.

1.2.4. *Khazanah* Islamic benchmark bonds

Khazanah bonds are guaranteed by the government and must meet the insurance needs of the Khazanah Nasional Berhal (KNB) as pertaining to its assets.

Although the Khazanah is an Islamic benchmark, bonds are sold at a discount. The discount price is determined through the process of bidding. While the buy back price at par value is set by the issuer, secondary trading will mean the rights over the debt are sold to a third party.

1.2.5. The Third Step: The trading of discounted debt certificates Bay'al dayn

Once bonds have been securitized, they are considered an article of trade and can be sold by investors to the issuers, or to a third party if a secondary market for Islamic bank products exists.

The trading of debt certificates is called Bay'al dayn and is permitted by the Malaysian government.

2. Islamic securities in the Middle East

Of the instruments available for financing projects in the Middle East, largely dominant are Murabaha and al-Ijara, as shown in Table 3 below:

Table 3: Selected project finance deals and transactions in the Muslim world

Country	Project	Mode of financing
Bahrain	Purchasing construction material for Pakistan's Lahore-Islamabad Highway	Syndicated Murabaha
Kuwait	Purchase of capital equipment for the production of medium density fibre-board	Ijara (lease finance)
Malaysia	Financing of Tenaga National's current expenditure	Bai-Bithaman ajil bay al-dayn (debt trading)
Bahrain	Water and power development authority	Syndicated Murabaha
Egypt	Alexandria National Iron & Steel company	Ijara (lease finance)
Pakistan	Equity capital investment in al-meezan investment bank	Musharaka

Source: Islamic banker, various issues

3. Bay'al inah and Islamic securitization process

3.1. Bay'al inah

When a lender or borrower secures any benefit, whether in the form of money or otherwise, this is usury; the prophet Muhammad (SAW) said "every loan entailing benefit is usury".

3.1.1. The meaning of Bay'al inah

Bay'al inah is a transaction of *Nasi'ah* (delay). The debtor sells an object to the creditor for cash (which is payable immediately) and then buys the same object back for a greater amount at a future date. Thus the transaction amounts to a loan. The difference between the two prices represents the interest.

3.1.2. Islamic debt discounting

It is possible for a creditor to settle a debt before maturity and accept the reduction in the amount he receives. This is called *Dha'wa Ta'ajjal* and is encouraged by the prophet (SAW).

In the case of a Khazanah Islamic bond, the debtor sells the bond at a discount to the creditor; this process is entirely separate from Dha'wa Ta'ajjal. In the same fashion, secondary trading can take place between debtors and a third party who is not the creditor. However, in the case of bond issuance, the discounting mechanism takes place during the initial public issue of zero coupon bonds.

4. Muqarada bonds: An alternative to Islamic debt bonds

A Muqarada bond is an Islamic bond that does not provide interest, and its value varies with the market value of the asset it is linked to and the expected interest rate.

4.1. The salient features of Muqarada bonds

The Muqarada bond is a financial instrument which serves to raise capital. The unit price of the bond is determined by the number issued. It is referred to as a Muqarada Sukuk Bond (MSB) and has three main characteristics:

- MSBs represent common ownership, and entitle their holders to shares in the project for the financing purposes of which the bonds have been issued.
- The contract is based on the official notice of bond sale, which specifies the amount of debt and the proportion and distribution of profits.
- On their expiry dates, MSBs can be converted to shares, sold or traded.

4.2. The Muqarada bond: an illustration

A hypothetical Mudareb (entrepreneur) is given a contract with the value of RM 100 million to build a university. The cost of the project is RM 60 million (which another company intends to raise using Muqarada bonds), the value of the unit is RM 1.00 and there are 60 million units.

The profit expected is 40 million, which will be shared between the entrepreneur and the financier at percentages of 50:50.

If the value of the project at maturity is RM 100 million, 40 million will be divided in two: 20 million to the investor and 20 million to the financier. However, if the project has a value of 30 million, the investor will lose his profit while the financier bears the loss of the 30 million. In conclusion, the sale of Muqarada bonds to investors is free from any discounting mechanism, and when investors wish to dispose of Muqarada bonds before their maturity they do so on the basis of the project's performance, meaning that the bonds can be sold at an amount below or above face value.

Section 4. The capital structure and the cost of capital of Islamic banks

1. The capital structure of a prototype of an Islamic bank

Islamic banks cannot accept the payment of interest on loans, and do not pay fixed charges to their depositors; instead they have a unique capital structure based on lending funds under the PLS principle.

1.1. Sources of funds

- Shareholders' equity (shares and reserves)
- Current accounts (the equivalent of checking accounts in conventional banks)
- Investment accounts (equity funds which do not constitute a financial risk to the bank)
- Savings accounts

1.2. Uses of funds

Islamic banks use eight financial instruments:

Musharaka (joint venture) and Mudaraba (trust finding) are based on the PLS principle, while Murabaha, Salam, Ijara, *Ijara muntahia bittamleek,* Istisna'a and Bai Bithaman ajil are all based on the mark-up principle (sales for immediate payment and deferred delivery at cost plus negotiated margin).

There are two methods of deferred sale: Istisna'a and Bai Bithaman ajil. The Istisna'a is a sales contract whereby one party must manufacture the subject of the contract and sell it to the other party, not actually delivering the goods until a specified future time. Bai Bithaman ajil, on the other hand, while still involving the sale of goods, also involves the payment being deferred.

1.3. Profit sharing methods

Islamic banks use two profit sharing methods: the pooling method and the separation method, both of which will be explained in an appendix.

2. Are modern capital structure theories relevant for Islamic Banks?

2.1. The traditional school and MM propositions revisited

The cost of capital, the cost of debt and the weighted average cost of capital are represented by the expressions below:

Ke = (DV1/P0) + g
Kd = I/Pd
With:
g: growth rate
P0: share price
DV1: dividend at first year
Ke: shares cost
Kd: debt cost
I: annual interest paid per unit of bank liabilities
Pd: current ex interest face value of each unit of bank liabilities
K0 = WACC = Ke (Q/Q+D) + Kd (D/ Q+D)
With:
Q: the amount of capital
D: the amount of debt

The classical theory of capital structure argues that an increase in debt financing leads to an increase in WACC and a decrease in the value of the bank if debts exceed optimal levels. However, Modigliani and Miller came up with a different theory, arguing that WACC and market value remain constant whatever the structure of capital. Both of these theories are based on the dual mode of finance, i.e. equity and debt.

2.2. The case of Islamic banks

Funds deposited in these accounts are not guaranteed a predetermined fixed return, nor do they constitute a liability. An increase in investment account financing does not pose a financial risk. There is no justification for an increase in the rate of return, because the probability of bankruptcy does not change, so WACC in an Islamic bank should not increase with increases in investment account financing. Holders of investment accounts face the same risk as shareholders and receive the same returns, but this risk is higher than that borne by depositors in a conventional bank.

In most Islamic banks, holders are not allowed to withdraw their funds until the aggregate portfolio investment is liquidated so they bear their share of profits and losses.

Islamic banks cannot use a promised or predetermined rate as the cost to them of investment account financing, because it is expressly prohibited by Shariah.

Due to the equal risk that shareholders and holders of investment accounts take on, they can also expect the same rate of return from investing their funds in a portfolio of projects (ex-ante).

Referring to a valuation model, the cost of investment account financing would seem to be equivalent to the rate used by the market in capitalizing the estimated future dividends of a bank.

Tomkins and Karim (1987) have estimated the cost of capital to an Islamic firm using the following formula:

$Re = i + \beta\ (Rm - i)$

With:

Re = required equity yield

Rm = expected market portfolio return

i: the risk-free interest rate

The capital cost of an Islamic bank: $Re = \beta\ Rm$ (reflecting the business risk and not the financial risk).

3. Modelling the capital structure of an Islamic bank

Proposition 1

If an increase in investment accounts financing yields positive income, it will increase the Islamic bank's market value without a supplementary financial risk, so the market value of an Islamic bank is not independent of its capital structure.

The cost of equity to an Islamic bank is given by:

Ke = (DV1/P0) + g + e1
Where:
e1: is a shock variable

The cost of investment accounts financing is given by:

Ki = (Fe/DEi) + gf + e2
Where:
Ki = the cost of investment accounts
Fe = expected profit earnings from Islamic bank investment
gf = the expected growth rate of profit generated by investment accounts each year based on backward looking expectations
e2 = a random shock term conditioned by the investment climate.

Given that an equal risk is supported by each holder of an investment account and shareholder, (Fe/DEi) = (DV1/P0).

Thus the WACC is given by:

K0 = Ke (Q/Q+DE) + Kd (DE/ Q+DE) + e3
e3 = shock parameter incorporating e1 and e2

Proposition 2

Given the similar risk taken on by shareholders and depositors of funds, an increase in investment account financing will make the WACC of an Islamic bank constant.

Proposition 3

Given the contractual relationship between shareholders and holders of investment accounts, if an increase in investment accounts financing yields positive income, it will increase the rate of return on equity at no extra financial risk.

Proposition 4

Increasing investment account financing and reducing equity by the same amount makes the level of earnings and the Mudareb's share constant. The rate of return, before the Mudareb share is accounted for, for both shareholders and investment account holders will remain constant. However, after the Mudareb share is taken into account, the shareholders' rate of return will continue to increase while that of investment account holders can decrease or remain constant in the swapping process. Thus the WACC remains always constant, and there is no optimal capital structure, because while the bank can increase its market value, it cannot decrease its costs as the financial risk remains constant.

Regarding the imperfection of financial markets in regions where Islamic banks are located, and the fact that Islamic banking regulatory mechanisms are not well established, it is important for Islamic banks to set up a capital structure as mixed as possible to resolve any agency problems.

Finally, Islamic bank capital structure theory refers to both the constant WACC of Modigliani and Miller and the non-constant market value of traditional capital structure theory. Islamic bank theory is derived from the contractual relationship between an Islamic bank and its clients.

Conclusion

The goal of this chapter is to identify ways to improve the interaction between Lariba banking and the rest of the international financial and monetary system, and its standing as an alternative within the global system. Lariba banking should be regarded as complementary to Riba banking, and a system which has the potential to provide stability to the world's financial system.

The Islamic system was not established to replace the existing conventional banking system. It provides new instruments which can be used as an alternative and added to the range of products available for investors to choose from.

The Lariba system is not simply an interest-free banking system, but also a system which has an objective of improving social conditions and creating productive economic activities and community affluence.

The rate of profit of an Islamic bank is different from an interest rate, and is justified in the eyes of Islamic law as it is based on the PLS principle which involves sharing the profits resulting from investment activities. Finally, we always say "Allah knows best" and we ask him for support and guidance.

This chapter has the objective of showing that the generally accepted concept of financial risk is not adequate for explaining the capital structure of an Islamic bank; also, that under certain assumptions, the increase in investment account financing increases the return of shareholders without any extra risk and increases the market value of an Islamic bank, while the WACC remains constant.

Appendix

Should investment account holders share in all types of revenues and expenses of the bank, or should these account holders only participate in the revenues and expenses pertaining to their investments?

- In the pooling method, all contributors of funds share in all revenues and expenses except those generated by subsidiaries or the remuneration of the bank's directors and external auditors' fees.
- In the separation method, there is a distinction between the revenues and expenses of investment operations from those of the other banking services. Investment account holders only share in the revenues and expenses related to their investment.

Finally, the ratio of PLS is a direct result of the proportion of funds from each source multiplied by the weightings of liquidity requirements and any days outstanding.

References

Aryan, H. (1990), "Iran: the impact of Islamization of financial system", in R. Wilson (ed), Islamic financial markets, Routledge, pp. 155-170.

Brucker, E. (1970), "A Microeconomic Approach to banking competition", Journal of finance, vol. 25, December, pp. 1133-41.

Bourke, Philip (1989), "Concentration and other determinants of bank profitability in Europe, North America and Australia", Journal of Banking and Finance 13: 65-67.

Brunner, E. (1937), The Divine Imperative (translated by O.Wyon), London: Lutterworth press.

Blinder, A.S. (1975), "Distribution effects and the aggregate consumption function", Journal of Political Economy, June, pp. 447-475.

Bashir, A.F. Darrat and M.O. Suliman, Equity capital, profit sharing contracts, and investment: theory and evidence, Journal of Business and Accounting, 20, (5), September 1993, 0306 686 X.

Bourke, Philip (1989), "Concentration and other determinants of bank profitability in Europe, North America and Australia", Journal of Banking and Finance 13: 65-67.

Chapra, M. Umar, (1985), "Towards a Just Monetary System," Leicester: the Islamic Foundation.

Council of Islamic Ideology Pakistan (1981), "A report on the elimination of Riba economy".

Darby, M.R. (1972), "The allocation of transitory income among consumer's assets" American Economic Review, December, p.p. 928-941.

Friedman, M. (1957), A Theory of Consumption Function, Princeton university press, Princeton, N.J.

Edward, Franklin R. (1977), "Managerial objectives in regulated industries: expense preference behavior in banking", Journal of Political Economy 85 (February): 147-162.

Gabraith, J.K. (1967), "The new industrial state". Boston: Houghton Mifflin.

Greenwald, B.C. and Stiglitz, J.E. (1988 a), "Imperfect information, finance constraints and business fluctuations", in M. Kohn and S.C. Tsiang (eds), Finance Constraints, Expectations and Macro-economics, Oxford: Clarendon press, 103-140.

Greenwald, B.C. and Stiglitz, J.E. (1988 b) "Money, imperfect information and economic fluctuations", in M. Kohn and S.C. Tsiang (eds), "Finance Constraints, Expectations and Macro-economics, Oxford: Clarendon press, 141-165.

Greenwald, B.C. and Stiglitz, J.E. (1990) "Macroeconomic models with equity and credit rationing", in R.G. Hubbard (ed.), Asymmetric Information, Corporate Finance and Investment, Chicago: University of Chicago press, 15-42.

Homoud, Sami Hasan, (1985), "Islamic banking", London: Arabian information, translation of Arabic book published in 1975.

Hannan, Timothy H. (1979), "Expense-preference behavior in banking: a re-examination," Journal of Political Economy 87(4): 891-895.

Hannan, Timothy H, and Mavinga, E. (1980), "Expense preference behavior and managerial control: the case of banking firms." Bell Journal of Economics 11 (Autumn): 667-682.

Heggested, Arnold A. (1977), "Market structure, risk and profitability in commercial banking", Journal of Finance 32 (September): 1207-1216.

Hassan, N.A (1993), "Measurement of financial performance of Islamic banks vis-à-vis western type commercial bank: some conceptual differences", paper presented at International Conference in Islamic banking, November, Sydney.

Ismail, Abdul Halim (1989), "Al Qur'an on deferred contracts of exchange", Kuala Lumpur, Malaysia, Prime Minister's secretariat, mimeographed.

Keynes, J.M. (1936), the general theory of employment. Interest and money, Macmillan, London.

Klein, L. (1965) The Keynesian revolution, London: Macmillan.

Khan, M.F. (1983) "Islamic banking as practiced now in the world", in A. Ziauddian, M. Iqbal and M.F. Khan (eds), Money and banking in Islam (institute of policy studies), pp. 259-284.

Khan, M (1986), "Islamic interest-free banking: A theoretical analysis IMF, staff papers, vol. 33 (March 1986), pp. 1-27.

Khan, M. Fahim (1983), "comments on Volker Nienhaus: profitability of Islamic banks competing with interest banks", Journal of Research in Islamic Economics, vol.1, No 2 (winter), pp. 73-78.

Khan, M.S (1987), "Islamic interest-free banking: A theoretical analysis", in K. Moshin and A mirakhor (eds), Theoretical Studies in Islamic banking and finance (institute for research and Islamic studies), pp. 15-35.

Kahf, Monzer and Khan, Tariqullah, (1992), "Principles of Islamic financing: A survey", Jeddah: IRTI.

Khan, M. Fahim, (1992), "PLS System: Firms' behavior and taxation", first Draft, Jeddah: IRTI.

—. (1992), "Human resource mobilization through the profit-loss-sharing-based financial system" Jeddah: IRTI.

Metwally, M.M (1993), Essays on Islamic economics, Calcutta academic publishers.

Modigliani, F. and Miller. M.H, "The cost of capital, corporation finance and the theory of investment", Amer. Econ. Rev 53 (3) (1958) 261-297.

Metwally, M.M. (1997), "Differences between the financial characteristics of interest- free banks and conventional banks". European business review, vol. 97, No 2, pp 92-98.

Modigliani, F. (1977), "The monetarist controversy or, should we forsake stabilization policies?" American Economic Review, March, pp. 1-19.

Molyneux, Philip & John (1992), "Determinants of European bank profitability: A note", Journal of Banking and Finance 16: 1173-1178.

Minsky, H.P. (1963), "Can 'it' happen again?" in D. Carson (ed.), Banking and Monetary Studies, Homewood, Illinois: R.D. Irwin, 101-111.

—. (1977), "Of systematic fragility", in E.I. Altmaq and A.W. Sametz (eds), financial crises – institutions and markets in a fragile environment, New York: John Wiley & Sons.

—. (1985), "The financial instability hypothesis: A restatement", In P. Arestis and T. Skouras (eds), Post-Keynesian economic thought, Brighton: Wheatsheaf Books, 24-55.

Nienhaus, Volker (1983), "Profitability of Islamic banks competing with interest banks", Journal of Research in Islamic economics, Vol. 1. No. 1 (Summer), pp. 37-47.

Revell, J.R.S. (1980), Costs and Margins in Banking: an International Survey, Organization for Economic Co-operation and Development.

Short, Brock. K. (1979), The relationship between commercial bank profit rate and banking concentration in Canada, western Europe and Japan", Journal of Banking and Finance 3: 209-219.

Smirlock, M. (1985), "Evidence on the (non) relationship between concentration and profitability in banking", Journal of Money, Credit and Loaning, vol. 17, No.1, (February), pp. 69- 83.

Smirlock, Michael & Marshall, William (1983), "Monopoly power and expense preference behavior theory and evidence to the contrary", the Bell Journal of Economics 14(1): 166-178.

Siddiqi, M.N. (1967), "Banking without interest (Urdu)", Lahore: Islamic publications.

—. (1988), "Islamic banking: theory and practice", in Mohammed Ariff, ed., Banking in Southeast Asia, Singapore: Institute of Southeast Asian studies, pp. 34-67.

Sabi, Manijeh (1996), "Comparative analysis of foreign and domestic bank operation in Hungary", Journal of Comparative Economics, vol.22, pages (179-188).

Samad, Abdus (1999), "Comparative efficiency of the Islamic bank Malaysia vis à vis conventional banks", Journal of Economics and Management, vol.7, No.1.

Tomkins. C and Karim. R.A, "The Shariah and its applications for Islamic financial analyses: an opportunity to study interactions among society, bank, and accounting", The Amer, J. Islamic Social Sciences 4 (1) (1987) 101-115.

Taylor, L.D. (1971), "Saving out of different types of income", Brooking papers on economic activity, No. 2, pp. 384-415.

Von Hayek, F. (1939), Profit and Interest and Investment.

Wright, C. (1967), "Some evidence on the interest of consumption", American Economic Review, September, pp. 850-854.

Waleed al-Sultan, A study of the commercial loans market in a dual banking system: a simultaneous equation model, The Middle East Business and Economic Review, vol.9, No.2 (1997).

Wicksell, K. (1935), "Lecture on political economy", London: Routledge and Kegan Paul.

PART V

ADVANCED RISK MANAGEMENT TECHNIQUES

CHAPTER NINE

ADVANCED RISK PROFILE ANALYSIS OF ISLAMIC EQUITY INVESTMENT: EVIDENCE FROM THE AMERICAN, ASIAN AND EUROPEAN MARKET

MONDHER BELLALAH AND ZEINEB CHAYEH

Abstract

As far as the management of assets and liabilities is concerned, the advanced analysis of the risk and return profile of Islamic financing and investment products constitutes one of the great challenges faced by Islamic financial institutions today. Due to the fact that by design, Islamic financial institutions should be keeping a large portion of their assets in equity investments, this paper discusses the dynamics of the specific risk profile inherent to Islamic equity investment based on investing in the Shariah-compliant stock market. We investigate three Islamic equity indexes, as classified by economic hubs (the Dow Jones Europe, Asia-Pacific and USA), and compare them with their conventional peers from 2003 to 2009. Our risk profile analysis is based on the estimations of two well-known advanced risk measures, namely the Value at Risk and the Expected Shortfall. Four VaR methodologies are performed: the Historical VaR, the Risk Metrics and GARCH conditional models of VaR and finally the Cornish Fisher VaR model. Assessments made using these models, based on the Kupiec test, lead us to be able to investigate the equity indexes' daily returns tail in more detail through the estimation of the General Pareto Distribution VaR and ES measures. The results of our advanced risk profile analysis show that Islamic equity indexes clearly display a risk profile's specific characteristics, based on region as well as time period. Drawing on the specific features of the Dow Jones Islamic index and its inherent features, the paper argues that Shariah screening, which alters the composition of Islamic indexes, can contribute to the shaping of a distinguished risk profile.

Introduction

By design, Islamic banks should be keeping a handsome portion of their assets in equity investments, in order to be consistent with the fundamental principle of Islamic finance that is profit and loss sharing. Islamic banks are supposed to hold equity in corporations and sit on their boards of directors. Nevertheless, any investment in equity based or profit and loss sharing partnerships exposes Islamic financial institutions to equity investment risks that are not applicable to conventional financial institutions. While Islamic economics and banking have been the basis for a fair amount of research and investigation, the existing academic literature on Islamic equity investment is still embryonic, despite its increasing growth and popularity. For the sake of enhancing the assets and liabilities management of Islamic banking and even insurance, the investigation of the risk profile of Islamic equity investment as one of the main Islamic theoretical investment products is of great interest. Thus this study aims to investigate the main risk features of Islamic equity investment. We focus on three markets, the American, European and Asian markets. Such investigations contribute to the enrichment of the debate on the portfolio diversification of Islamic financial institutions.

Moreover, the current global crisis, which began in the United States out of the subprime crisis, driven by an unethical attitude of greed and excessive speculation, has gradually engulfed the world. This financial crisis is based largely on the development of an environment where loan volume has considerably exceeded loan quality, meaning excessive risks are being taken. In fact, the nature of the debt-based interest delivery system that has developed in recent years, as well as poor and inadequate regulation and lax lending standards, have contributed largely to the enhancement of the gap between the real economy and the financial sphere.

While the biggest conventional financial institutions may drop into bankruptcy and accumulate huge losses leading them to the very edge of collapse, Islamic financial institutions seem able to find a safer path and to be spared the consequences of a global financial crisis (at least early on in the crisis, before it turns into a true economic crisis) in comparison to conventional financial institutions. However, while the Islamic banking system has been said to have been largely spared from the current financial crisis, in comparison to how conventional banking has fared, there is no evidence of how the Islamic capital market, and especially equity investment, has responded to the global crisis differently than the conventional one. Therefore, in order to fill the research gap that exists regarding Islamic compared with conventional equity investment behavior during the current global crisis, we divide the whole period under study into two sub-periods; a period before the current crisis, from 2003 to July 2007, and a period during the current crisis, from July 2007 to July 2009. The purpose of the analysis of these two sub-periods is not only to investigate the risk profile of Islamic equity investment relative to conventional equity investment under each period, but also to analyze relative changes in behavior profiles, and thus to investigate the extent of the stability and solidity of Islamic, in comparison to conventional, equity investment.

The risk profile analysis is based on the estimations of two well-known advanced risk measures, namely the Value at Risk and the Expected Shortfall.

Literature Review

As far as we know, the first study involving the risk profile assessment of Islamic equity investment is that carried out by A. Al-Zoubi and A. Maghyereh (2007). They contributed to the empirical risk profile assessment of Islamic equity investment through an estimation of the Value at Risk measure of the Dow Jones Islamic World index against its conventional counterpart, the Dow Jones World index. Based on a moving window of 500 days and a one day holding, three Value at Risk estimation models were performed (risk metrics, Student-t APARCH, and skewed Student-t APARCH). The period of study stretches over nine years, from 1996 to 2005. The authors found that the DJ Islamic index displayed a less risky profile than its conventional counterpart. According to the authors, this result is mainly due to the profit and loss sharing system (PLS), a basic principle of Islamic Finance. They argued that this principle was behind the less risky profile that characterizes Islamic equity investment. For them it was thanks to the Mudaraba contract that Islamic firms could provide lower contingent payoffs for shareholders in good states and higher contingent payoffs in bad states than non-Islamic ones. They assumed that investors in Islamic firms receive less volatile payoffs than investors in non-Islamic firms. After all, an Islamic bank is only able to provide an entrepreneur with funds if his or her project has a relatively low level of risk, since it will share any losses incurred. Based on the PLS mechanism, it is highly probable that the agency costs which emerge from interest conflict between a firm's managers and the lender or financer will be reduced since the latter is more involved in the monitoring of the financed project as he knows he will share in any profits and bear any losses. The financer becomes more interested in studying the soundness of the financed investment; this is also why overinvestment will be reduced to an optimal level.

The authors also argued that the PLS system contributes to the reduction of bankruptcy costs. Use of this mode of financing supports the Meyers and Majluf pecking order theory (1984), which stipulates that firms are more interested in issuing securities than in borrowing new debt in order to preserve liquidity and debt capacity for potential profitable projects or to decrease the potential for bankruptcy. With respect to the asset substitution problem that afflicts the relationship between debt holders and equity holders, the Musharaka and Mudaraba contracts, under which debt holders and shareholders must share both losses and profits, may push equity holders to avoid accepting a risky, negative net present value project in order to decrease the value of the debt at the expense of a small increase in equity value, because the two values are positively correlated.

As far as Islamic equity investment, and in particular the Islamic equity index, is concerned, these interpretations are not appropriate, and are far from being the real factors behind the less risky profile of Islamic equity investment as compared to its conventional counterpart. The authors have made clearly confused Islamic Equity Investment with Islamic Equity Finance vehicles based upon the PLS principle. The risk profile of Islamic equity indexes should be interpreted on the basis of an examination of the components or stocks that are included in them, which is how the Dow Jones is treated in this paper. In various references to the PLS principle they show their miscomprehension of what an Islamic equity investment actually is. It is possible that one of the companies included in an Islamic index utilizes an Islamic financial instrument in order to increase its equity capital, but that is not the case in the DJ Islamic index. In this paper we clarify this misunderstanding by defining the two aspects, and seek to give alternatives to the authors' interpretations and demonstrate how their work may better be understood.

The Theoretical Framework

The Value at Risk Measure

The Value at Risk is a useful downside risk measure. It refers to the maximum expected amount of loss over a given time period and at a given confidence level (1-α). It assesses the likelihood of losses that may be incurred as a result of adverse market movement.

Statistically, the VaR refers to the concept of a quantile:

$$\boldsymbol{VaR_\alpha} = \boldsymbol{Sup}\{\boldsymbol{q} \in \mathbb{R} : \boldsymbol{P}(\boldsymbol{r} < q) \leq \boldsymbol{\alpha}\} = \boldsymbol{Sup}\{\boldsymbol{q} \in \mathbb{R} : \boldsymbol{F_r}(\boldsymbol{q}) \leq \boldsymbol{\alpha}\}$$

For instance, if the VaR on an asset is €100 million per week with a 95% confidence level, there is a chance of 5% that the value of the asset will drop more than €100 million over any given week.

The VaR Methodologies Estimation

Empirical VaR

The empirical method is one of the traditional non-parametric VaR evaluation methodologies. It is based on the idea that the past is the best predictor of the future. It consists of identifying the appropriate quantile of the distribution historical returns.

Risk Metrics method

The Risk Metrics approach was developed in 1994 by JP Morgan Bank. It uses an Exponential Weighted Moving Average (EWMA) of volatility to forecast the time-varying risk. Formally, the variance forecast at time t is a weighted average of the previous forecast, using weight λ, and of the latest squared innovation, using weight $1 - \lambda$:

$$\boldsymbol{\sigma_t^2 = \lambda\sigma_{t-1}^2 + (1 - \lambda)\varepsilon_{t-1}^2}$$

The parameter λ is called the decay factor. The classical values defined by Risk Metrics are $\lambda = 0.94$ for one day volatility and $\lambda = 0.97$ for one month volatility. The effective number of days can be derived from the decay factor. 99.9% of the information is contained in the last log (0.001)/log λ days. For example, if we use $\boldsymbol{\lambda = 0.94}$, then 99.9% of the information is contained in the last 112 days. For $\boldsymbol{\lambda = 0.97}$, 99.9% of the information is contained in the last 227 days. Hence, the monthly $\lambda = 0.97$ EWMA is smoother than the daily $\lambda = 0.94$.

The Risk Metrics left tail Value at Risk for a long trading position is as follows:

$$\boldsymbol{VaR_t = \bar{R}_t + \sigma_t z_\alpha}$$

Conversely, the right tail VaR for a short trading position is defined as follows:

$$\boldsymbol{VaR_t = \bar{R}_t + \sigma_t z_{1-\alpha}}$$

Where z_α refers to the α normal quantile and $z_{1-\alpha} = -z_\alpha$.

GARCH VaR method

The GARCH model was introduced in the seminal works of Engle (1982) and Bollerslev (1986). This approach allows the conditional distribution of the return series to have a time related variance. The returns are assumed to be normally distributed, with a conditional mean and variance. The model can be represented with a set of equations:

$$\boldsymbol{r_t = \mu + z_t\sigma_t}$$

With z_t a residual IID standard variable:

$$\boldsymbol{E[z_t|I_{t-1}] = 0 \; E[{z_t}^2|I_{t-1}] = 1}$$
$$\boldsymbol{E[r_t|I_{t-1}] = \mu \; E[(r_t - \mu)^2|I_{t-1}] = Var[r_t|I_{t-1}] = {\sigma_t}^2}$$

Where I_{t-1} represents all the information available at time t-1. The standardized residuals are coherent with a standardized normal distribution; however, other assumptions can be made, including the Student distribution.

Finally, the conditional variance is defined as

$$\boldsymbol{\sigma_t^2 = a_0 + a_1 r_{t-1}^2 + a_2 r_{t-2}^2 + \cdots a_q r_{t-q}^2 + b_1\sigma_{t-1}^2 + b_2\sigma_{t-2}^2 + \cdots + b_p\sigma_{t-p}^2}$$

Most commonly used is the GARCH (1, 1) model:

$$\boldsymbol{\sigma_t^2 = a_0 + a_1 r_{t-1}^2 + b_1\sigma_{t-1}^2}$$

The expected value of variance at time $t+k$ is an autoregressive process:

$$\boldsymbol{E}\left[\boldsymbol{\sigma}_{t+k}^{2}\right] = \boldsymbol{a}_{0} + (\boldsymbol{a}_{1} + \boldsymbol{b}_{1})\boldsymbol{E}\left[\boldsymbol{\sigma}_{t+k-1}^{2}\right]$$

The parameter $\boldsymbol{\lambda} = \boldsymbol{a}_1 + \boldsymbol{b}_1$ can be interpreted as the mean reverting parameter; $\frac{\mathbf{1}}{\mathbf{1}-\boldsymbol{\lambda}}$ is the mean time taken to recover to previous levels after a shock.

The GARCH Value at Risk forecast for a long trading position is computed as follows:

$$\boldsymbol{VaR}_{t} = \overline{\boldsymbol{R}_{t}} + \boldsymbol{\sigma}_{t}\boldsymbol{z}_{\alpha}$$

Where z_α refers to the α normal quantile.

Cornish Fisher VaR

Under the normal hypothesis, both skewedness and excess kurtosis should be equal to zero. However, distribution returns always exhibit a strong negative skewedness and an excess of kurtosis. This is a very common stylized fact.

Zangari (1996), Campbell et al. (2001) and Favre and Galeano (2002) provided a modified VaR calculation that takes the higher moments (skewedness and kurtosis) of non-normal distributions into account through the use of the Cornish and Fisher (1937) model, better approximating the shape of the asymmetry and the tail shape of the distribution.

That modified VaR calculation is as follows:

$$\boldsymbol{z}_{cf} = \boldsymbol{z}_{0} + \frac{\mathbf{1}}{\mathbf{6}}\left(\boldsymbol{z}_{0}^{2} - \mathbf{1}\right)\boldsymbol{S} + \frac{\mathbf{1}}{\mathbf{24}}\left(\boldsymbol{z}_{0}^{3} - \mathbf{3}\boldsymbol{z}_{0}\right)\boldsymbol{K} - \frac{\mathbf{1}}{\mathbf{36}}(\mathbf{2}\boldsymbol{z}_{0}^{3} - \mathbf{5}\boldsymbol{z}_{0})\boldsymbol{S}^{2}$$

$$\boldsymbol{VaR}_{modifiedt} = \overline{\boldsymbol{R}}_{t} + \boldsymbol{\sigma}_{t}\boldsymbol{z}_{cf}$$

Where z_0 is the α quantile of the normal distribution: $\boldsymbol{N}(\boldsymbol{z}_0) = \boldsymbol{\alpha}$, S is the skewedness, K is the kurtosis of the return series and $\bar{R}$ is the mean return. Note that if the skewedness is null, the approximation is reduced to the simple calculation:

$$\boldsymbol{z}_{cf} = \boldsymbol{z}_{0} + \frac{\mathbf{1}}{\mathbf{24}}\left(\boldsymbol{z}_{0}^{3} - \mathbf{3}\boldsymbol{z}_{0}\right)\boldsymbol{K}$$

There are two methods of estimating the higher moments: a univariate estimate based on the historical returns of the whole portfolio, or a multivariate estimate of the moments for a more accurate representation of the portfolio's VaR. The Cornish Fisher VaR will give a larger loss estimate than traditional VaR when returns are negatively skewed or fat-tailed. Conversely, it will give a smaller loss estimate when returns are positively skewed or leptokurtic.

Extreme Value VaR

Among the semi-parametric VaR methods, the extreme value theory remains one of the most powerful and accurate frameworks. The evaluation of the Value at Risk based on the extreme value theory tends to take into account the non-normality of the financial returns series and to catch their heavy tails behavior. Two approaches exist in this framework: the Fisher-Tippett approach and the Peaks over Threshold (POT) approach.

The second approach, known also as the generalized Pareto approach, is the most common method of identifying the distribution of the series over a certain level.

Generalized Pareto distribution[1]

For a given threshold $\boldsymbol{u}$, the distribution of excess values of x over threshold u is defined by:

$$\boldsymbol{F_u(y) = \Pr\{X - u \le y | X > u\} = \frac{F(y+u) - F(u)}{1 - F(u)}}$$

This represents the probability that the value of x exceeds the threshold u by at most an amount y given that x exceeds the threshold $\boldsymbol{u}$. A theorem developed by Balkema and de Haan (1974), as well as Pickands (1975), shows that for a sufficiently high threshold $\boldsymbol{u}$, the distribution function of the excess may be approximated by the generalized Pareto distribution (GPD) such that, as the threshold increases, the excess distribution $F_u(y)$ converges with the GPD, which is:

$$\boldsymbol{G(x) = \begin{cases} 1 - \left(1 + \xi \frac{x}{\beta}\right)^{-1/\xi} & \text{if } \xi \neq 0 \\ 1 - e^{-x/\beta} & \text{if } \xi = 0 \end{cases}}$$

$\boldsymbol{\xi}$ is the shape parameter, $\boldsymbol{\beta}$ is the scale parameter

[1] Gencay et al (2002).

The GPD constitutes a family of known distributions depending on the ξ parameter which indicates the tail observation's weight:

If $\xi > 0$ then the GPD is an ordinary Pareto distribution. This particular case is the most relevant for financial time series analysis, since the financial returns series is a heavy-tailed one.

Either the probability-weighted moments method or the maximum likelihood method is used in order to estimate parameters of the GDP.

In this respect, the estimation of the ξ and β parameters is obtained through the maximization of the logarithm of the likelihood function:

$$L(\xi,\beta/X) = \left\{ \begin{cases} -n\log\beta - \left(\frac{1}{\xi}+1\right)\sum_{j=1}^{n} log\left(1+\frac{\xi}{\beta}x_j\right) & if\ \xi \neq 0 \\ -n\ log\beta - \frac{1}{\beta}\sum_{j=1}^{n} X_j & if\ \xi = 0 \end{cases} \right\}$$

GPD Value at Risk estimation

The GDP estimator of VaR for the left tail with threshold u is obtained as follows:

$$VaR_\alpha = \mu - \frac{\hat{\beta}}{\hat{\xi}}\left(\left(\frac{n}{N_\mu}(1-\alpha)\right)^{-\hat{\xi}} - 1\right) \qquad if\ \xi \neq 0$$

$$VaR_\alpha = \mu - \hat{\beta}LN\big(-n\,LN(1-\alpha)\big) \qquad if\ \xi = 0$$

Where N is the number of excess beyond the threshold u.

GPD Expected Shortfall Estimation

The Expected Shortfall is defined as the expected value of losses, assuming that the loss is larger than the VaR.

Statistically, it is defined as follows:

$$ES_\alpha(R) = E(R\ /\ R > VaR_\alpha = VaR_\alpha + e_r\ (VaR_\alpha\ (R))$$

e_r is the mean excess function defined as follows:

$$e_r = E(R - \mu/R > \mu)$$

Under the Generalized Pareto Distribution theory, the Expected Shortfall is estimated as follows:

$$ES_\alpha = \frac{VaR_\alpha(R)}{1-\hat{\xi}} + \frac{\hat{\beta}-\hat{\xi}\mu}{1-\hat{\xi}}$$

Backtesting VaR Methodologies

The Kupiec Test

One of the easiest means of back testing a VaR model is the Kupiec test. It tests whether the number of exceptions (N) is significantly higher than the expected value (p*T). If it is, then the VaR has been underestimated, and conversely, too few violations indicate that the VaR is overestimated.

The Kupiec test supposes that N is distributed as a binomial variable:

$$Prob(N) = \binom{T}{N} p^N (1-p)^{T-N}$$

Where:

$E(N) = p * T,$
$V(N) = T * p * (1 - p),$
$\hat{p}$ refers to the actual ratio (N/T).

The null hypothesis of the binominal test is ($p=p_0$) where p_0 is the p failure value. The test statistic follows asymptotically the $X^2(1)$ and is formally defined as follows:

$$LL_{PF} = 2LN(\hat{p}^N(1-\hat{p})^{T-N}) - 2LN(\widehat{p_0}^N(1-p_0)^{T-N})$$

Data and Distribution Analysis

We investigated the risk profile of the Dow Jones Islamic Europe, Asia Pacific and US equity indexes against the DJ conventional Europe, Asia Pacific and US equity indexes over the period from 2003 to 2009. The analysis of the day ahead VaR estimated plotting of the Islamic equity indexes against their counterparts leads to the detection of two trends (Figure 16) which interestingly, correspond to the two sub-periods which are analysed in the previous chapter; the first period is from 2003 to July 2007 and the second period refers to the time of the current crisis.

All computations and graphics made in this chapter are performed by R software.

The daily return of the equity index at date t is defined as the Naperian logarithm of the price equity index at date t divided by the price at date t-1, formally expressed as follows:

$$\boldsymbol{Rt = LN\ (Pt/Pt-1)}$$

Figures 1.a, 1.b, 1.c, 1.d, 1.e and 1.f present respectively the paths of the Dow Jones Islamic Asia Pacific total price equity index, the Dow Jones conventional Asia Pacific total price equity index, the Dow Jones Islamic US total price equity index, the Dow Jones conventional US total price equity index, the Dow Jones Islamic Europe total price equity index and finally the Dow Jones conventional Europe total price equity index.

We can observe in all these figures the strong fluctuations of the total price at the end of 2007, reflecting the state of panic and the lack of confidence in the equity markets. However, these fluctuations seem to be followed by a sharp decline at the beginning of 2008, when the consequences of the current financial crisis start to really be felt on the equity market.

Figures 2.a, 2.b, 2.c, 2.d, 2.e and 2.f show respectively the equity index daily returns evolution of the different equity indexes mentioned above. When looking at these figures we notice the volatility clustering phenomenon that is well known from the first half of 2007, when high volatility is followed by yet higher volatility.

Descriptive statistics of the DJ Islamic Europe, US and Asia Pacific equity indexes against their DJ conventional counterparts are presented in the following Table (Table 1).

Table 1: Descriptive statistics from 2003 to 2009

	Mean	Med	Max	Min	Std	Sk	Ku	J-B	P_v
DJIM_ASIA	1.12E-04	4.29E-04	4.21E-02	-4.21E-02	5.83E-03	-5.08E-01	9.81	3.39E+03	0.000
DJA	1.31E-04	3.72E-04	3.91E-02	-3.96E-02	5.81E-03	-4.49E-01	9.03	2.66E+03	0.000
DJIM_US	7.27E-05	2.09E-04	5.10E-02	-4.21E-02	5.64E-03	-3.83E-02	15.41	1.10E+04	0.000
DJUS	4.12E-05	2.43E-04	4.74E-02	-4.18E-02	5.98E-03	-2.97E-01	14.38	9.27E+03	0.000
DJIM_EU	7.69E-06	2.13E-04	4.99E-02	-4.31E-02	7.06E-03	8.75E-02	12.99	4.96E+03	0.000
DJE	-3.30E-05	1.97E-04	4.57E-02	-4.40E-02	7.11E-03	-6.88E-02	11.82	3.87E+03	0.000

Std refers to Standard deviation; Sk refers to skewedness; Ku refers to Kurtosis; J-B refers to Jarque Bera test; P_v refers to P-value Jarque Bera test.

We see also that the highest average daily return is realized by the Asia Pacific equity market, followed by the United States and Europe. This result is highly interesting and in my opinion can be largely explained by the Asia Pacific DJ equity indexes' country allocation (see Annex). In fact, most of the countries included in the Asia Pacific DJ equity indexes are emerging countries with high levels of growth as well as high inflation rates. These characteristics are far from being features of the Europe and US indexes. Moreover, it is amazing to find that the DJ conventional Europe displays a negative mean daily return; such a result necessitates a real investigation into the key economic features of developed European countries, as well as emerging countries. However, the impact of the latter, in our opinion, remains small, as the emerging countries represent only 20% of the Europe DJ indexes' country allocation. Therefore we cannot analyze these results without reference to the current period, during which the equity markets have seen a real drop. It seems that the DJ conventional Europe equity index negative mean daily return over the period of the current crisis was beyond the positive returns performed over the first period. In addition, with reference to the same table we can see that the Asia Pacific equity indexes have shown the lowest negative value of average returns during the current financial crisis.

We may also remark that the DJ Islamic equity indexes have exhibited the highest values of mean return. Besides this, they also seem to display the highest maximum value. In addition, the lowest minimum negative value of daily returns is shown by the Islamic equity indexes; the only exception to this is the DJ Islamic Europe index.

The Europe DJ equity indexes stand out as having the highest value of standard deviation, followed by the Asia Pacific and the United States.

The DJ Islamic Europe and U.S equity indexes seem to be less volatile than their respective conventional counterparts. This result is not true for the DJ Asia Pacific Islamic equity index, which appears to be more volatile than its DJ conventional counterpart.

These results, based on standard deviation, must be reported and analyzed with care. In fact, as indicated by Artzner (1997), volatility is far from being a coherent measure, as it does not meet the monotony axiom, nor the invariance translation axiom. In addition, such measure of risk is not valid for distributions with fat tails, the precise position of the greatest risk, as the calculations of such measures invariably require the exclusion of outliers.

The sample's skewedness shows that the daily returns have an asymmetrical distribution. The DJ equity indexes, with the exception of the DJ Islamic Europe equity index, appear all to have negative skewedness values, which indicates that the asymmetric tail extends more towards negative values than positive. The DJ Islamic Europe equity index seems to have a daily return distribution with an asymmetric tail that extends more towards positive values than negative ones.

According to the sample kurtosis estimates, the daily returns of the Islamic equity indexes, as well as their DJ conventional counterparts, are far from being normally distributed. In fact, the lowest kurtosis estimate is nine for the Asia Pacific equity indexes and the highest is about 15 for the US equity indexes. Based on the sample's kurtosis, it may be argued that the return distributions in all the equity indexes are fat tailed[2]. In order to confirm this statement, we also studied the Q-Q plots[3] of the DJ Islamic equity indexes and their peers' daily returns against normal distribution. We also performed the Jarque Bera normality test (see Table 1), the results of which indicate non-normality in the different equity indexes' daily returns. The graphic approach may provide an assessment of the fit between the equity indexes' empirical distribution and a theoretical normal distribution that is not simply reduced to a numerical summary.

Figures 3.a, 3.b, 3.c, 3.d, 3.e and 3.f set out the Q-Q plots of Islamic equity indexes and conventional indexes against normal distribution. There is evidence, shown by the previous figures, that both Islamic and conventional equity indexes' daily returns exhibit fat, asymmetric left tails. We observe that tails of the empirical distributions draw significantly away from the line of theoretical values of quantiles of normal distribution. This observation can be better appreciated when considered together with the backtesting day ahead VaR estimation models or analyzed based on the Q-Q plot exponential distribution approach.

These findings are similar to those obtained by taking a different graphic approach which allows adjustment of the empirical distribution (histogram) and the Gaussian Normal distribution (see Figures below 5.a, 5.b, 5.c, 5.e and 5.f). Thus, we can remark that the daily returns of our equity indexes present at the same time both central values higher than

---

[2] The normal distribution has a kurtosis of about 3.

[3] The Q-Q plot is a probability plot, which is a graphical method for comparing two probability distributions by plotting their quantiles against each other. If the two distributions being compared are similar, the points in the Q-Q plot will lie approximately on the line $y = x$. If the distributions are linearly related, the points in the Q-Q plot will lie approximately on a line, but not necessarily on the line $y = x$. Moreover, a Q-Q plot is used to compare the shapes of distributions, providing a graphic view of how properties such as location, scale, and skewedness are similar or different in the two distributions.

those of a normal distribution and also distribution tails thicker than those of the normal density function (distribution).

We can conclude from our earlier distribution analysis of the Islamic equity indexes and their conventional counterparts that our daily returns are far from having a normal distribution. These results are very interesting, especially when considered alongside a VaR approach estimation that takes account of leptokurtosis as well as the asymmetric features of the different equity indexes' daily returns distributions.

Empirical Methodology, Analysis and Results

Empirical Methodology

In order to estimate the Value at Risk of the Islamic DJ equity indexes and their DJ peers for the three economic regions (Asia Pacific, Europe and the USA) and thereafter perform a comparative risk profile analysis of them, we firstly considered four different approaches; the historical non-parametric VaR approach, the Risk Metrics and GARCH conditional parametric models with normal distribution, and finally the Cornish Fisher semi-parametric approach. Secondly, we used the extreme value framework for further analysis of tail behavior and subsequently to estimate the Expected Shortfall measure for each equity index.

Our methodology also consists of estimating daily VaR forecasts for the left tail of each model, for three different confidence levels (99%, 97.5% and 95%). We also adopt a moving window of 50 days and thus estimate the 1665 day ahead VaR. The moving window approach consists of placing a window between the first and 50th data points and then the model is estimated and the VaR forecast is obtained for the 51st day at a different p level. Next, the window is moved one period ahead, to between the second and 51st day, and updated return parameters are taken from this new sample.

Thus for the GARCH approach, the model parameters were updated every 50 trading days and we can assume a stability window of 50 days for them. We repeat the procedure until all days (except the last one) have been included in the estimation sample.

Furthermore, to assess the relative performance of each model at each different confidence level, we use proportion failure (PF) backtesting, or the Kupiec test (1995). The latter, as seen above, summarizes the relative performance through the application of a violation ratio. A violation occurs if the realized daily return is greater than the estimated VaR on a given day. The violation ratio is defined as the number of violations divided by the total of the estimated VaR. The number of exceptions follows binominal law and the proportion failure test involves comparing the theoretical p failure level, which is equal to one minus the confidence level value, to the violation ratio. This test is realized at the 5% critical level. If the P-value of the PF test is above the 5% critical level, then we accept the null hypothesis, which indicates that the model performs well; conversely, if the P-value of the PF test is below the 5% critical level, the null hypothesis is rejected and the model is not suitable for the VaR estimation.

Assessment Performance VaR models

Table 2 presents the number of exceptions and the PF test P-value for the different estimation models' VaR at the various confidence levels for the left tail. With respect to the left tail, daily VaR at a given confidence level refers to the maximum loss that an investor with a long position may bear on that day with the same confidence level, in other words, there is a one minus the confidence level of chance that the investor bears a loss that is beyond the VaR at that level of confidence.

In our empirical study, and following Giot and Laurent (2003)[4], we specify a failure rate f_l for left tails, a rate which is equal to the percentage of negative returns smaller than one day ahead VaR for buying or long positions.

With a single glance at Table 2 we can see that the number of exceptions is inversely related to the confidence level. The higher the confidence level, the lower the number of exceptions.

Results from Table 2 indicate that VaR estimation based on the historical and the Risk Metrics models perform the worst in modeling the DJ Islamic Asia Pacific, US and Europe equity indexes, as well as their conventional counterparts, as the PF test p-value for these two models is always above the 5% critical level, especially at the 99% and 97.5% confidence levels, and the number of exceptions is the lowest value.

---

[4] Giot, P. and Laurent, S. (2003).

Table 2: VaR estimation

Methodes	0.01	0.01	0.025	0.025	0.05	0.05
DJ_A Historique	58	5.06E-15	76	2.92E-06	111	6.58E-03
DJ_A RiskMetrics	33	5.59E-04	57	3.62E-02	94	3.46E-01
DJ_A Garch	28	1.43E-02	58	2.45E-02	95	2.93E-01
DJ_A Cornish Fisher	17	1.00E+00	48	4.38E-01	85	1.00E+00
DJIM_A Historique	57	1.76E-14	75	6.02E-06	121	1.99E-04
DJIM_A RiskMetrics	30	4.73E-03	60	1.06E-02	101	9.62E-02
DJIM_A Garch	24	1.12E-01	56	5.25E-02	94	3.46E-01
DJIM_A Cornish Fisher	10	8.83E-02	39	6.42E-01	85	1.00E+00
DJ_US Historique	50	6.63E-11	74	1.25E-05	113	3.88E-03
DJ_US RiskMetrics	33	5.59E-04	64	1.92E-03	101	9.62E-02
DJ_US Garch	31	2.14E-03	57	3.62E-02	102	7.60E-02
DJ_US Cornish Fisher	20	4.65E-01	46	5.88E-01	94	3.46E-01
DJIM_US Historique	55	2.03E-13	75	6.02E-06	117	8.72E-04
DJIM_US RiskMetrics	36	4.84E-05	64	1.92E-03	107	2.29E-02
DJIM_US Garch	28	1.43E-02	58	2.45E-02	102	7.60E-02
DJIM_US Cornish Fisher	19	6.26E-01	53	1.21E-01	93	4.06E-01
DJ_EU Historique	58	5.06E-15	87	1.52E-09	129	6.65E-06
DJ_EU RiskMetrics	34	2.30E-04	54	8.85E-02	92	4.71E-01
DJ_EU Garch	28	1.43E-02	53	1.21E-01	91	5.42E-01
DJ_EU Cornish Fisher	21	3.30E-01	51	2.15E-01	90	6.18E-01
DJIM_EU Historique	51	2.16E-11	89	3.25E-10	126	2.43E-05
DJIM_EU RiskMetrics	27	2.75E-02	59	1.62E-02	98	1.83E-01
DJIM_EU Garch	21	3.30E-01	40	7.57E-01	91	5.42E-01
DJIM_EU Cornish Fisher	15	7.15E-01	44	8.17E-01	94	3.46E-01
Average						
Historic	54.8	1.47E-11	79.3	4.57E-06	119.5	1.93E-03
RiskMetrics	32.2	5.61E-03	59.7	2.59E-02	98.8	2.03E-01
A Garch	26.7	8.13E-02	53.7	1.69E-01	95.8	3.13E-01
A Cornish Fisher	17.0	5.38E-01	46.8	4.70E-01	90.2	6.19E-01

The GARCH conditional model improves slightly on the performance of the previous two VaR models, although its performance is still not satisfactory. It appears that the Cornish Fisher VaR estimation improves further on the GARCH model based on normal distribution, at all confidence levels but even more so at the highest confidence level (99%) which shows the lowest number of exceptions and the highest p-value, which reaches in many cases 100%.

These results are not really surprising. In fact, the previous distribution analysis has already shown that our daily returns present fat left tails.

Empirical Results

Comparative Risk profile results based on the Cornish Fisher VaR

Table 3 sets out the estimations of average daily Cornish Fisher VaR left tail forecasts for the whole period under study, at a confidence level of 99%. We choose to present VaR estimation results only for this level of confidence for simplicity of reading, as the results of Cornish Fisher estimations for the different confidence levels all exhibit the same trend. Then, we present the results for the highest level of confidence.

As previously stated, the analysis of the day ahead VaR plots of the Dow Jones Islamic indexes set against those of their counterparts have permitted us to detect two different phases of VaR evolution (see Figures 6.a, 6.b and 6.c). From these we compute the average daily Cornish Fisher estimation VaR forecast for the periods of the start of 2003 to July 2007 and July 2007 to July 2009. The results of different sub-periods seem to suit being displayed visually.

When looking at Table 3, we find that the left tails of the Islamic equity indexes' VaR display characteristics specific to both time period and region. The DJ Islamic US equity index seems to be less risky than its conventional counterpart over the whole period. However, the Dow Jones Islamic Europe and Asia equity indexes seem to be riskier than their conventional peers. We also note that the variation in risk profile is more conspicuous for the Asia markets, with a difference of 0.051%.

The analysis of the risk profile for the two sub-periods shows that this trend seems not, in fact, to continue over the entire timeframe of the two sub-periods.

In fact, the Dow Jones Islamic Europe and US equity indexes appear to be less risky during the current crisis than their counterparts and vice-versa. However, the Dow Jones Islamic Asia Pacific seems to be riskier during the current crisis, having been less risky over the first period than its conventional peers.

These results mean that during the current financial crisis, a short position investor seems to bear less loss risk if he invests in the Islamic Europe or US equity market than if he invests in a conventional one, while the opposite is true of investing in the Islamic Asia pacific equity index.

We also remark on the equity investment in the Asia Pacific market looking to be a less risky investment during the current financial crisis than the US and European equity markets.

Moreover, we notice that although the US equity market looks to have been the less risky market before the current crisis, this trend seems to have been inversed by the crisis. In fact, during the current crisis, the US equity market, as well as the European one, appears to be the riskiest equity market.

Furthermore, even if we point out the obvious general increase in the VaR of the different indexes when comparing the period of the current crisis to our first sub-period, further study of the relative evolution of VaR left tail estimation has allowed us to detect a distinctive feature of the Islamic equity indexes (mainly the DJ Islamic US and Europe). In fact, we can notice easily from the same table (Table 3) that the relative evolution of the VaR left tail displays the lowest value within the Islamic equity indexes. Conversely, the DJ Islamic Asia Pacific equity index exhibits a higher VaR relative evolution value than its counterpart. We can therefore state that the US market underwent the greatest change in its risk profile dynamic, as its VaR variation displayed the highest value. This is not, in fact, a surprising result.

Table 3: VaR left tail Cornish Fisher 99% for all indexes

	Left Tail				
Dates	Global average	2003 - 2007 aver.	2007 - 2009 aver.	Evol VaR (ratio)	VaR abs. var.
DJ_E Cornish Fisher	-0.033110183	-0.0303114	-0.0527	1.739304656	74%
DJIM_EU Cornish Fisher	-0.033543825	-0.0312148	-0.0499	1.599230725	60%
Dates	Global average	2003 - 2007 aver.	2007 - 2009 aver.	Evol VaR (ratio)	VaR rel. var.
DJ_A Cornish Fisher	-0.0296434	-0.0243119	-0.0376	1.54773805	55%
DJIM_A Cornish Fisher	-0.0301532	-0.0238596	-0.0396	1.658857255	66%
Dates	Global average	2003 - 2007 aver.	2007 - 2009 aver.	Evol VaR (ratio)	VaR rel. var.
DJ_US Cornish Fisher	-0.026362475	-0.0166	-0.0409	2.458900737	146%
DJIM_US Cornish Fisher	-0.025993422	-0.0176	-0.0386	2.19391169	119%

GPD Framework

In order to endorse our previous results, and to better investigate the tail behavior of the DJ Islamic equity indexes against their conventional counterparts, we used the extreme value framework. We performed this investigation for both sub-periods. The analysis of the shape parameter was relevant mainly to the period of the current crisis, however, we also computed the GPD VaR for the other, non-crisis period in order to support our previous results and complete them by estimating the Excepted Shortfall measures for the indexes.

Tail estimation

The determination of the threshold value μ is a crucial step in estimating the parameters of the GPD. Threshold selection is a tough task. It is desirable to find a threshold that is high enough that the underlying theoretical development is valid, but low enough that there is sufficient data with which to make an accurate fit. That is, the selection of a threshold that is too low will give biased parameter estimates, but a threshold that is too high will result in a large variance in parameter estimates. Some useful and informative tools for threshold selection exist, more specifically, the hill plot, the mean excess function or mean residual life plot and another method involving the fitting of data to a GPD several times using a range of different thresholds. However, these graphic tools are able only to give a range of plausible threshold values, not one single precise value.

In order to make it short and simple, we first propose to fix the number of excesses at 100 and to verify if the threshold corresponding to this number falls within the range of plausible threshold values. We then use two graphical measures; the mean excess function plot and the mean residual life plot.

According to the mean excess function plot, the range of plausible thresholds starts at the point when the sample mean excess function starts displaying a positive slope. In fact, the estimated mean excess function is an upward linear function of μ. The idea of the mean residual life plot is to find the lowest threshold at the point where the plot is nearly linear, taking into account the 95% confidence bounds.

According to the two measures mentioned above, the threshold for each index (as presented in Table 4) is well within the range of plausible thresholds, among the lowest values. (See figures 7.a, 7.b, 7.c, 7.d, 7.e and 7.f, which present the mean excess function plot and the mean residual life plot for each index respectively.)

This analysis was performed on the periods before and during the current crisis. The threshold for each index for the left tail, presented in Table 5 for both periods, appears also to be within the range of plausible thresholds.[5]

[5] We do not report the figures in order to simplify this paper. Figures can be provided on request.

Table 4

Left Tail					
Index	Threshold	xi	beta	VaR	ES
DJ Europe	-1.82E-02	8.80E-02	1.44E-02	-4.38E-02	-6.40E-02
DJ Islamic Europe	-1.90E-02	1.82E-01	1.20E-02	-4.48E-02	-6.40E-02
DJ Asia	-2.02E-02	2.56E-01	8.39E-03	-3.83E-02	-5.66E-02
DJ Islamic Asia	-1.95E-02	2.20E-01	9.39E-03	-4.12E-02	-5.75E-02
DJ US	-1.74E-02	1.18E-01	1.35E-02	-4.55E-02	-6.25E-02
DJ Islamic US	-1.73E-02	2.49E-01	9.48E-03	-3.96E-02	-5.79E-02

Table 5

Left Tail					
Index	Threshold	xi	beta	VaR	ES
DJ Europe	8.78E-03	1.04E-01	5.10E-03	-2.11E-02	-2.90E-02
DJ Islamic Europe	9.69E-03	1.74E-01	4.39E-03	-2.15E-02	-2.98E-02
DJ Asia	1.10E-02	8.46E-02	6.49E-03	-2.53E-02	-3.57E-02
DJ Islamic Asia	1.17E-02	8.37E-02	5.73E-03	-2.61E-02	-3.35E-02
DJ US	9.65E-03	-1.36E-02	4.14E-03	-1.71E-02	-2.28E-02
DJ Islamic US	9.84E-03	-9.23E-02	4.95E-03	-1.90E-02	-2.36E-02

Table 6

Left Tail					
Index	Threshold	xi	beta	VaR	ES
DJ Europe	1.66E-02	1.46E-01	1.37E-02	-6.80E-02	-8.59E-02
DJ Islamic Europe	1.63E-02	1.07E-01	1.41E-02	-6.77E-02	-8.17E-02
DJ Asia	1.62E-02	1.14E-01	1.11E-02	-5.22E-02	-6.82E-02
DJ Islamic Asia	1.52E-02	7.44E-02	1.28E-02	-5.64E-02	-7.05E-02
DJ US	1.54E-02	3.81E-02	1.59E-02	-6.28E-02	-7.91E-02
DJ Islamic US	1.49E-02	1.25E-01	1.22E-02	-5.48E-02	-7.38E-02

GPD Parameter estimation

For a given threshold level, tail estimation involves the estimation of the parameters of the Generalized Pareto Distribution. The maximum likelihood estimates of the shape parameter ξ and scale parameter β at various threshold levels are displayed in Tables 4, 5 and 6 for the entire period covering the study, just the first period and just the current crisis period respectively for all indexes.

As regards the whole period of the study, we can see from Table 4 that the range of shape parameter values starts at 0.08 for the DJ conventional Europe equity index. As the shape parameter values are higher than 0 but lower than 0.5, we can ascertain as stated in the previous subsection (3.2) that the tail is exhibiting a Fréchet distribution with infinite variances.

However, for the first sub-period, the shape parameter looks to be lower, on average, than that of the entire study period. The range of the shape parameter is between -0.0923 (the DJ Islamic US equity index) and 0.256 (the DJ Islamic Europe index). The US equity market tail distribution seems to be a Weibull distribution, with a negative shape parameter that indicates a thin tail.

During the current financial crisis (see Table 6), it is interesting to note that the shape parameter records a big jump from its position during our first sub-period, especially for the conventional equity indexes and the Islamic US equity index. In addition, ξ for the Islamic equity indexes appears to be lower than that for the conventional equity indexes in the left tail. This again indicates the high level of risk associated with conventional equity investment during the financial crisis when compared with Islamic equity investment.

Over the same period, the ratio $(\boldsymbol{\xi\, right\, tail/\xi\, left\, tail})$[6] for Islamic equity is higher than that of the conventional equity indexes. Therefore the frequency of the occurrence of substantial loss equaling less than the same day's extreme gain is higher for Islamic indexes than their counterparts.

GPD VaR and Expected Shortfall estimation

This analysis, mainly focused on the period of the current financial crisis, has shown that Islamic equity indexes are less risky than their conventional counterparts. This sub-section is devoted to the current results of the GPD VaR and the Expected Shortfall (see Tables 4, 5 and 6).

At first glance, these tables show that the GPD VaR estimation results strongly support the previous Cornish Fisher VaR estimations for the indexes (the exception being the Asia Pacific equity indexes). However, we can also note that the Expected Shortfall results seem to alleviate this ambiguity and corroborate again our previous risk profile analysis and its interpretations based on the Cornish Fisher approach.

---

[6] This ratio was calculated based on results in the right tail.

Summary and Interpretations

To summarize the results for the left tails day ahead VaR that we have already detailed, we can state that the Islamic equity indexes display region- as well as a period-specific risk profiles. With reference to the current financial crisis, the Islamic Europe and US equity indexes look to be less risky than their conventional counterparts. We strongly believe that sector allocation largely underpins these results, as the sector most affected by the current crisis is the financial, which is nearly absent in the Islamic equity indexes (see sector allocation in Annex). Moreover, the low leverage, along with the large average market capitalization that characterize the firms included in the Islamic US and Europe equity indexes (See Table 1: Market Capitalization) helps support our risk profile analysis of the Islamic Europe and US equity indexes.

However, the Islamic Asia Pacific equity index seems to be exhibiting a higher risk profile than its conventional counterparts during the financial crisis. This result could be explained by the relatively small size, along with the low leverage, of the firms included in the Islamic Asia Pacific index. In fact, these features may indicate the low debt capacity and subsequently the high volatility, or even low profitability of these firms. The reverse trend observed in the first period is likely due to the fact that the firms included are of growth stock.

Moreover, although we have claimed that the financial crisis has strongly affected the different equity markets, as the VaR has considerably increased, the Asia Pacific market, by and large, looks to be the least risky market relative to the European and the US markets in a time of financial crisis. This is not really surprising, as the current financial crisis stemmed particularly from the United States, followed by Europe. For the emerging markets, and particularly the Asia Pacific market, the current crisis, which has become a real recession, has affected their real economies more than their financial systems, and has therefore affected their profitability. However, in the US and Europe, both the real economy and the financial sphere have experienced real dysfunction and huge losses.

Our results imply that Islamic investment can be used as a hedging instrument during any financial meltdown or economic slowdown.

Figures

USA

Figure 4.a

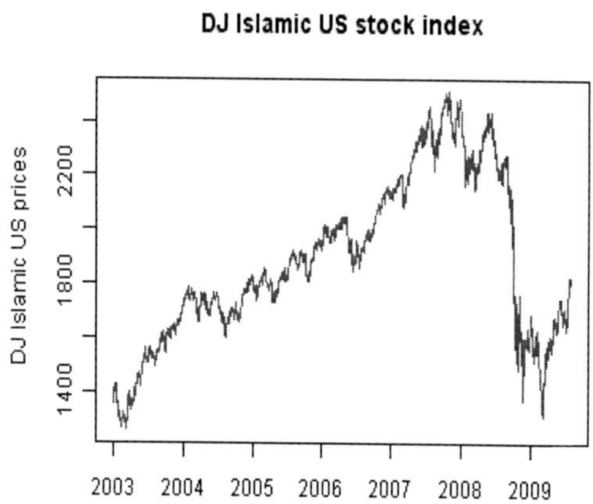

Figure 4.b

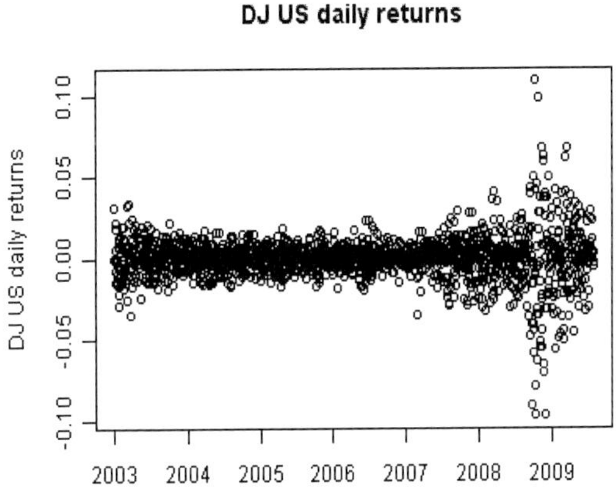

Figure 4.c

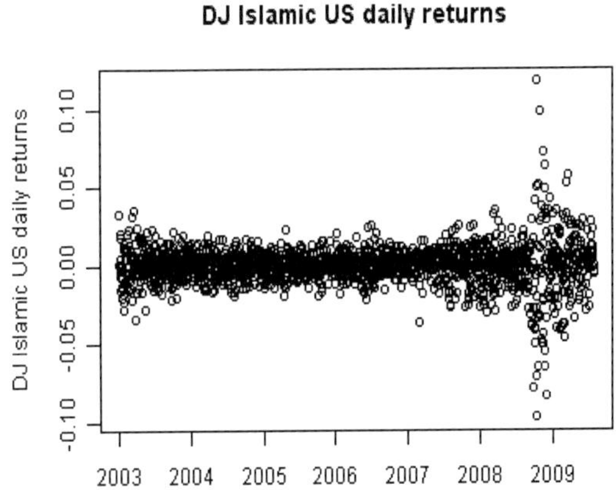

Figure 4.d

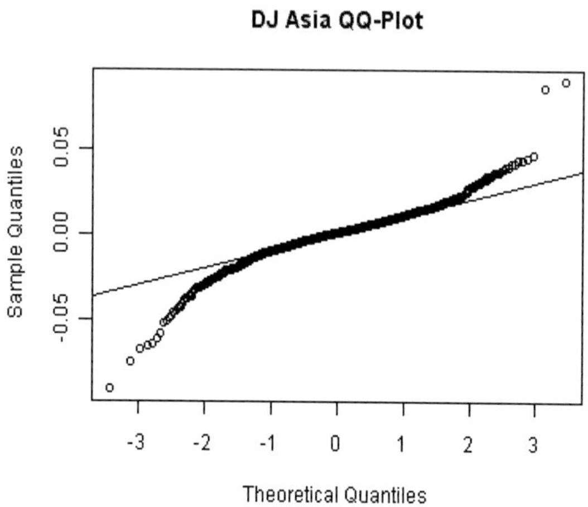

Figure 4.e

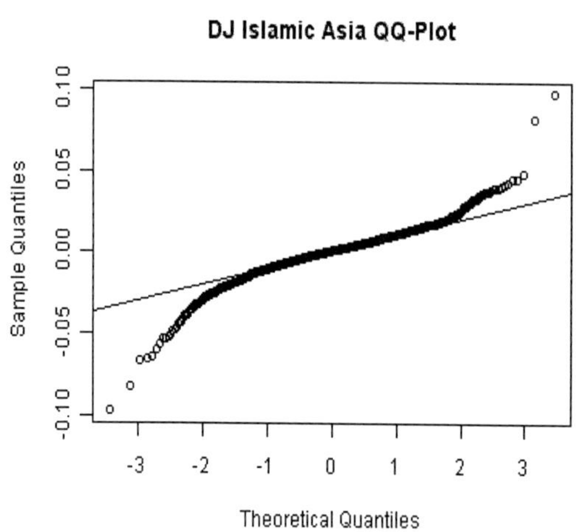

Figure 4.f

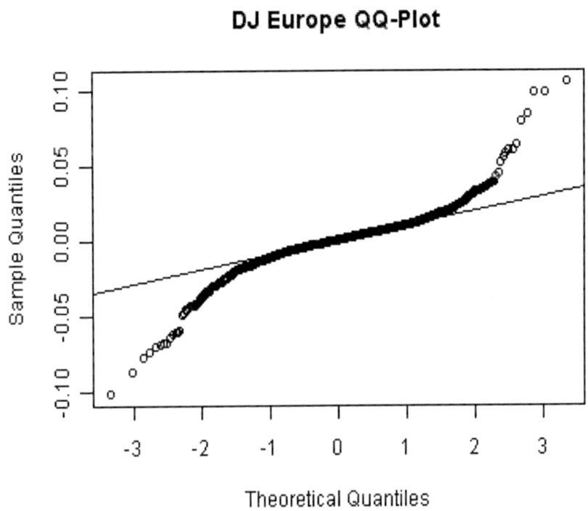

Figure 4.g

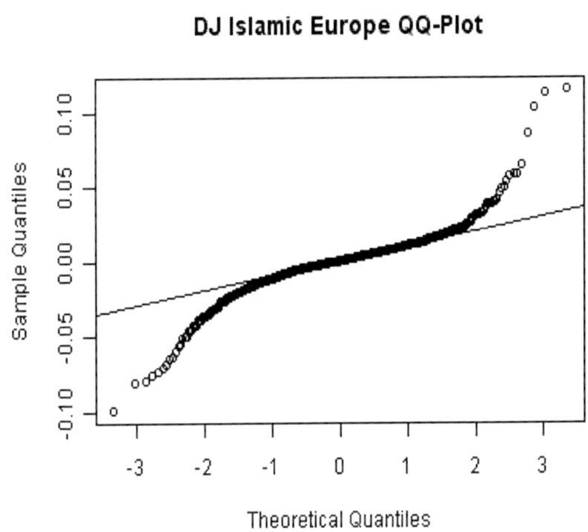

Figure 4.h

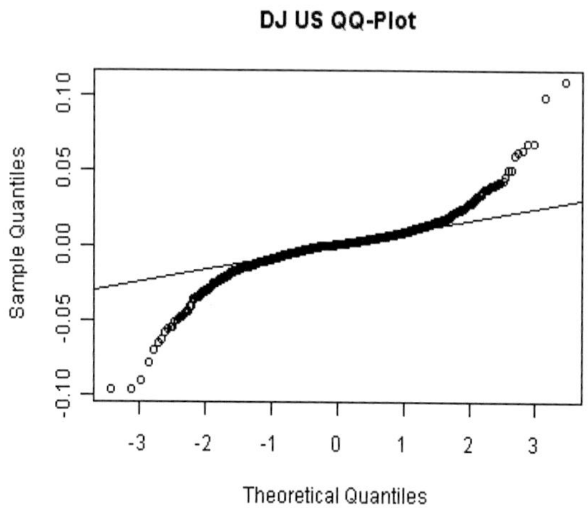

Figure 4.i

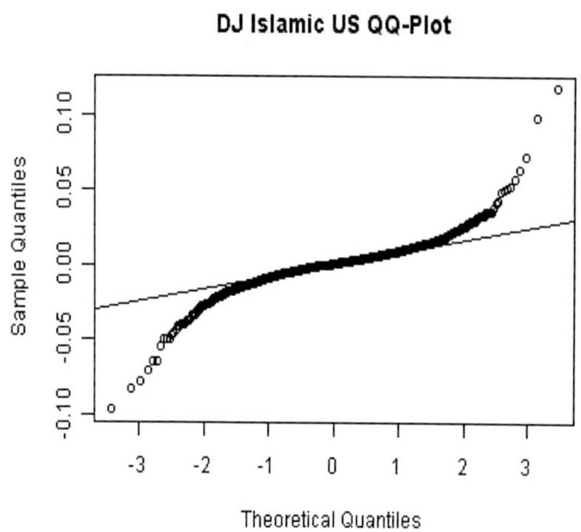

Figure 4.j

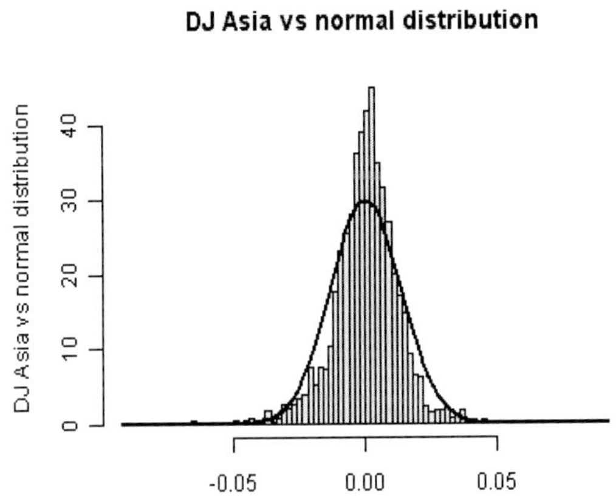

Figure 4.k

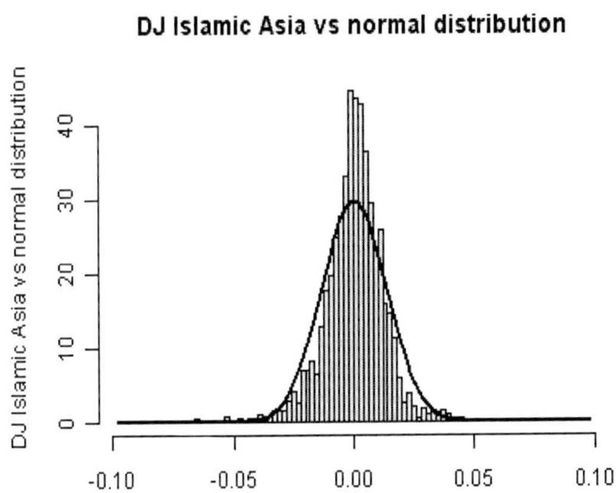

Figure 4.l

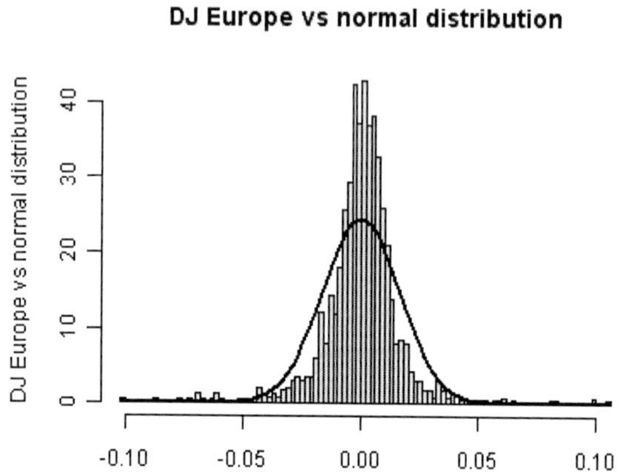

Figure 4.m

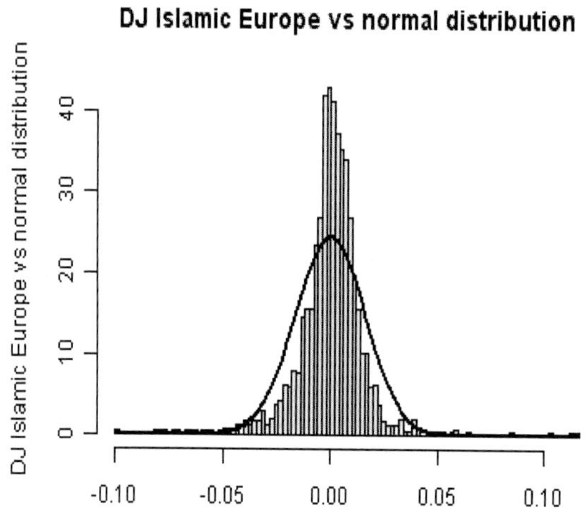

Figure 4.n

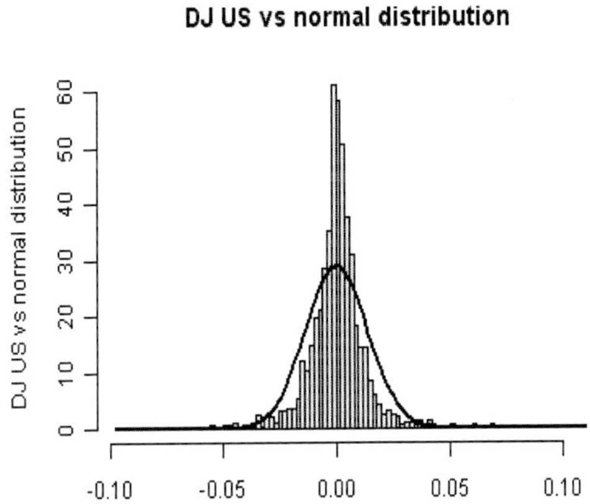

Figure 4.o

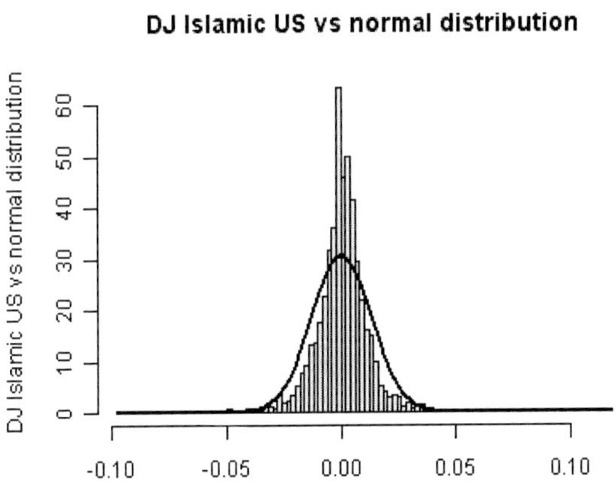

Figure 4.p

ASIA

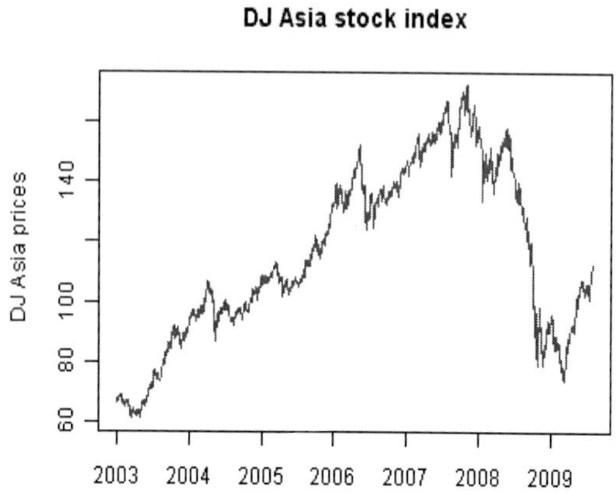

Figure 5.a

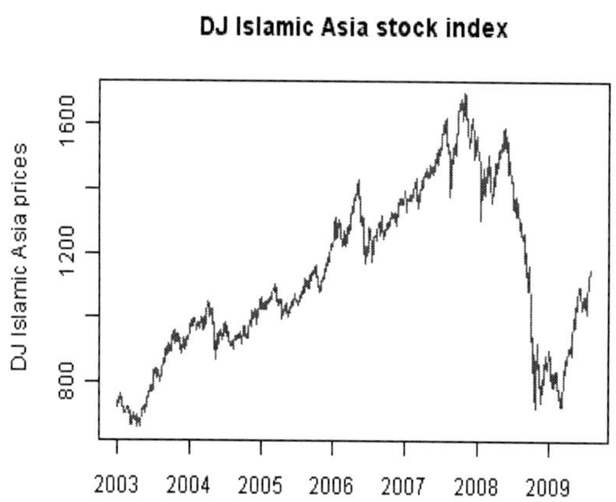

Figure 5.b

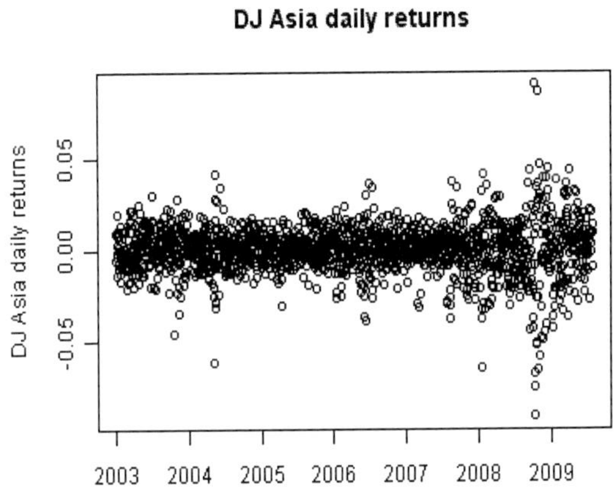

Figure 5.c

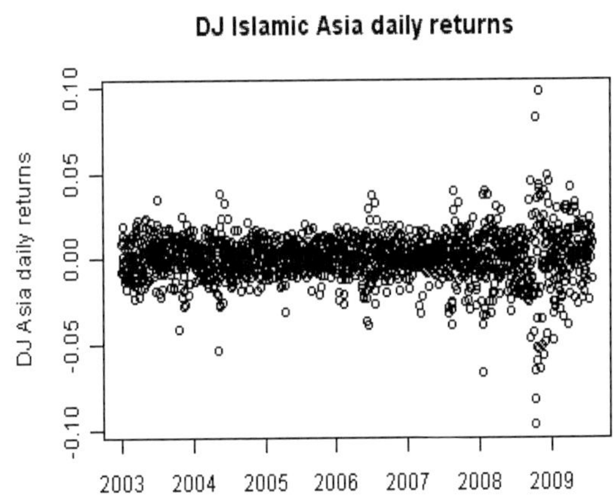

Figure 5.d

EUROPE

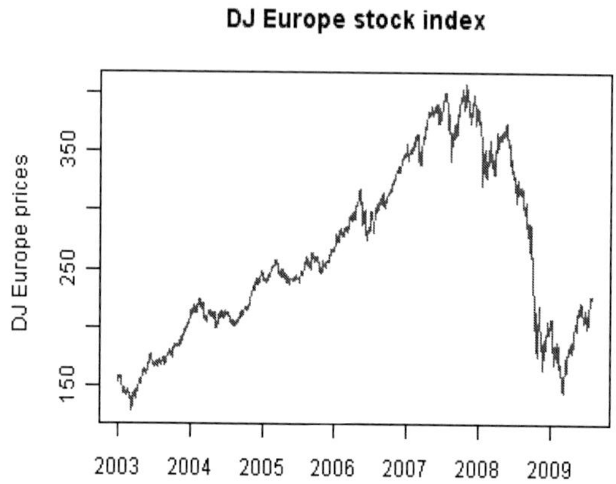

Figure 6.a

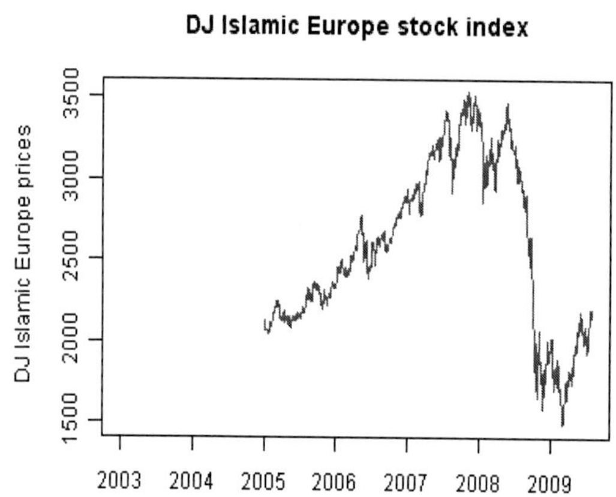

Figure 6.b

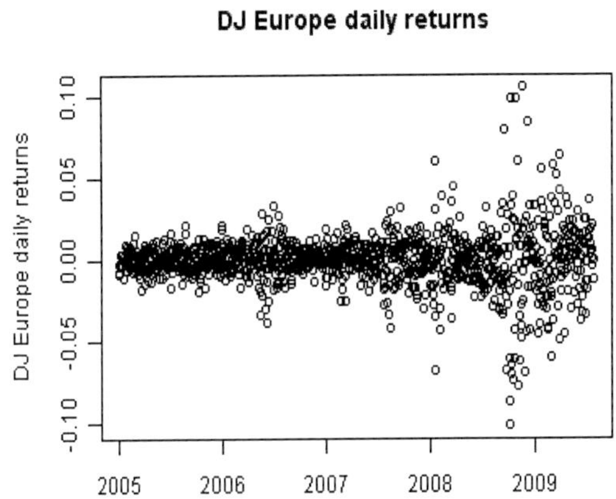

Figure 6.c

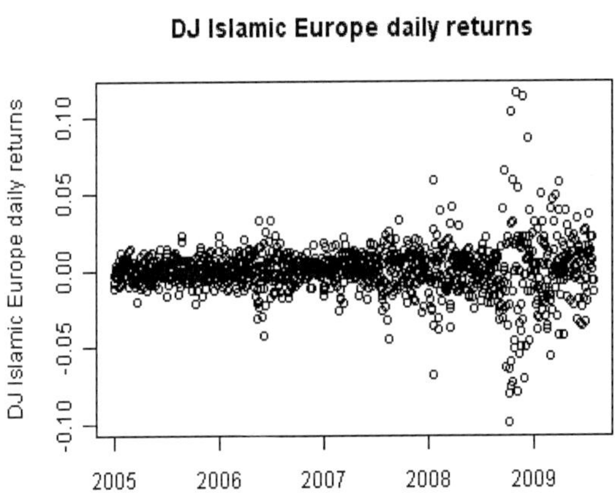

Figure 6.d

Comparison between VaR estimation Islamic against Conventional to detect the adverse trend over the two sub periods

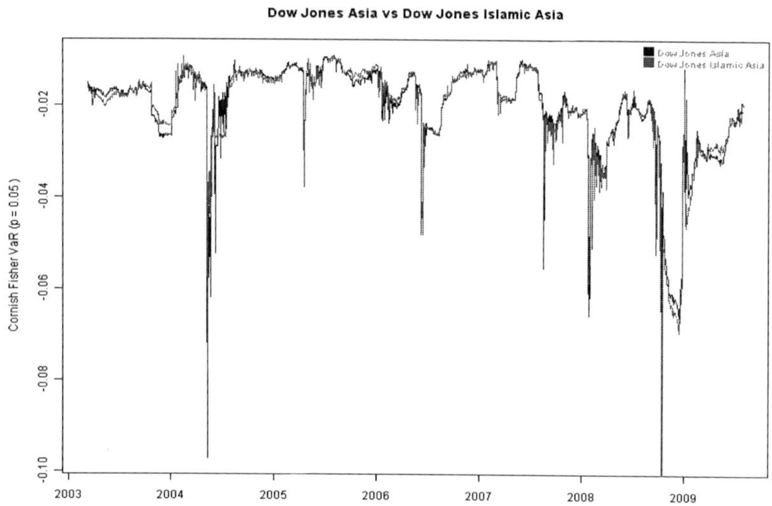

Figure 7.a

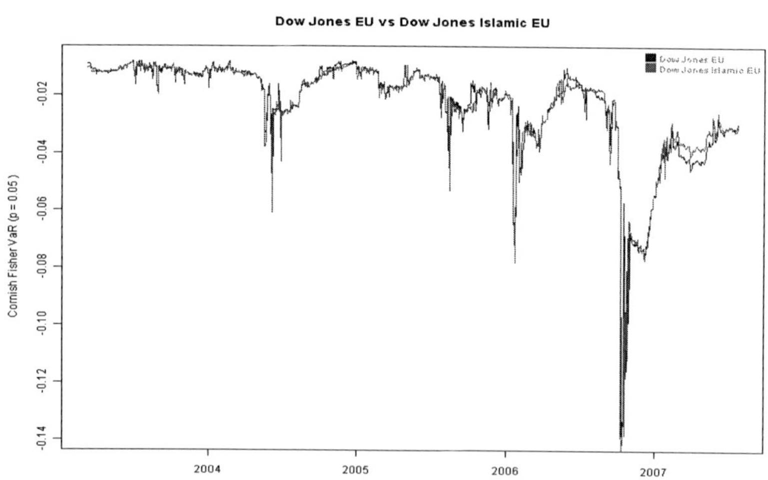

Figure 7.b

Figure 7.c

Europe Islamic DJ

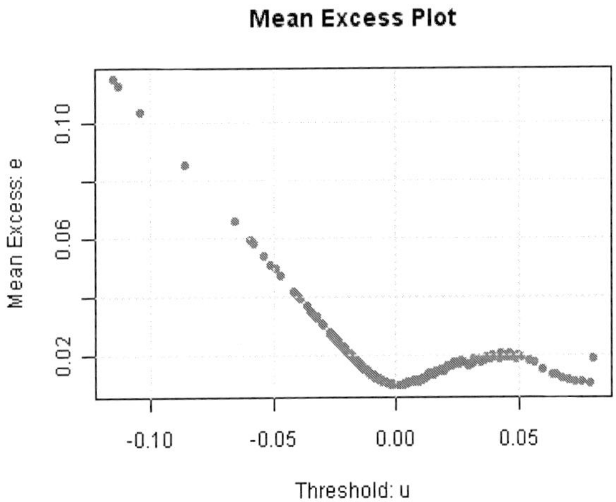

Figure 8.a

Europe DJ

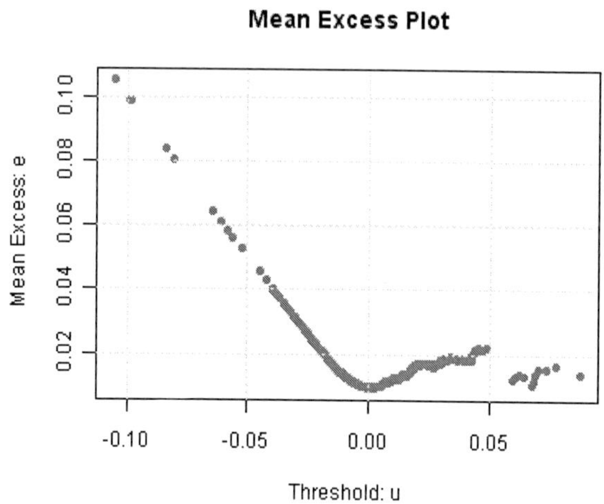

Figure 8.b

US Islamic DJ

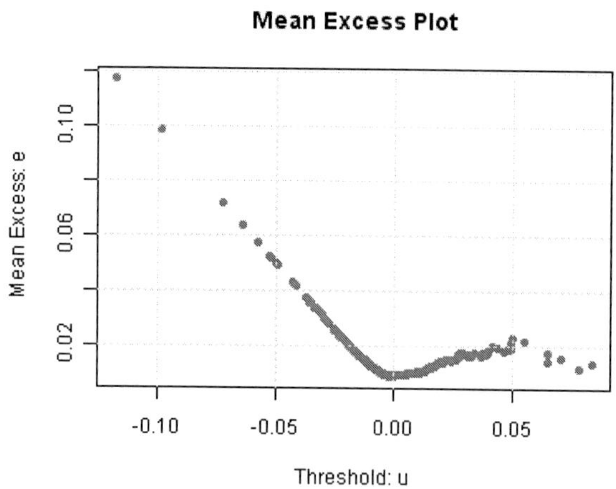

Figure 9.a

US DJ

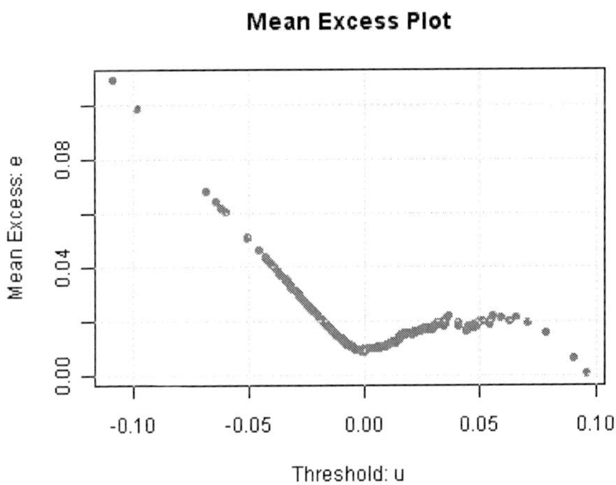

Figure 10.a

Asia Islamic DJ

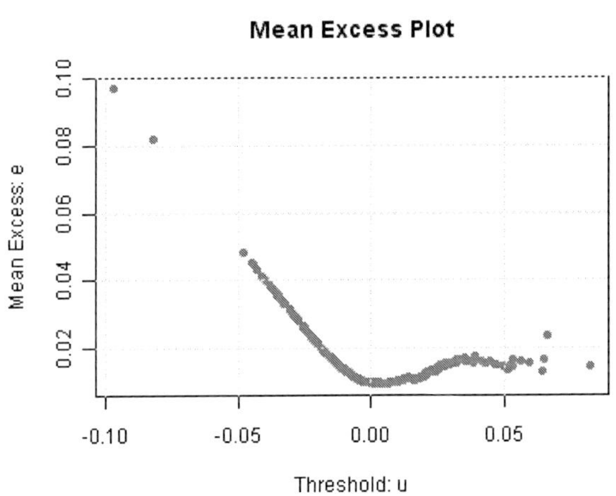

Figure 10.b

Asia DJ

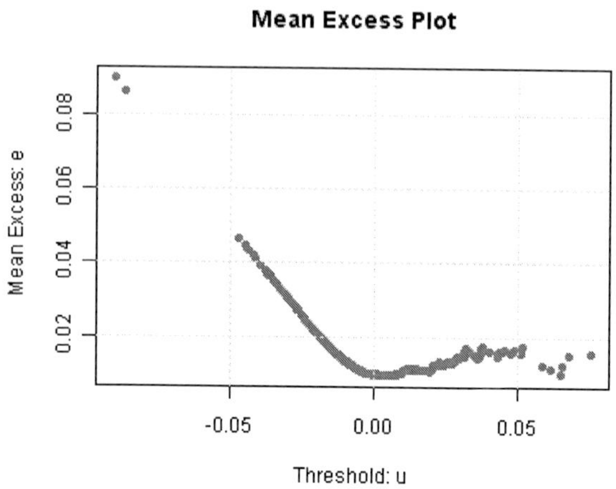

Figure 10.c

Annex

Country Allocation

		Dow Jones Islamic market World index	**Dow Jones market World index**
Country Allocation	United States	52.00%	40.32%
	Japan	6.64%	9.85%
	United Kingdom	6.62%	8.08%
	Canada	4.31%	4.08%
	France	3.48%	4.27%
	Switzerland	3.39%	3.35%
	Australia	2.80%	3.28%
	India	2.51%	1.70%
	Taiwan	1.96%	1.64%
	Germany	1.89%	3.07%
	South Korea	1.64%	1.70%
	Russia	1.51%	0.82%
	China	1.16%	1.80%
	Brazil	1.05%	1.88%
	South Africa	0.92%	1.70%
	Hong Kong	0.81%	1.27%
	Sweden	0.80%	1.08%
	Finland	0.71%	0.53%
	Italy	0.67%	1.55%
	Denmark	0.57%	0.41%
	Netherlands	0.57%	1.06%
	Mexico	0.45%	0.47%
	Singapore	0.41%	0.67%
	Norway	0.34%	0.38%
	Spain	0.33%	1.77%
	Malaysia	0.30%	0.33%
	Indonesia	0.30%	0.25%
	Chile	0.21%	0.20%
	Kuwait	0.21%	0.18%
	Thailand	0.20%	0.19%
	Belgium	0.17%	0.40%
	Russia	1.51%	**0.82%**
	South Africa	–	**0.75%**
	Ireland	0.06%	**0.42%**
	Israel	–	**0.32%**
	Greece	0.06%	**0.28%**
	Turkey	0.12%	**0.21%**

	Austria	0.12%	**0.20%**
	Portugal	0.05%	**0.17%**
	Poland	0.15%	**0.17%**
	Colombia	–	**0.10%**
	Egypt	**0.05%**	**0.08%**
	New Zealand	0.05%	**0.07%**
	UAE	0.04%	**0.07%**
	Philippines	0.05%	**0.07%**
	Qatar	**0.07%**	**0.07%**
	Peru	–	0.06%
	Czech Republic	0.11%	**0.05%**
	Hungary	0.03%	**0.05%**
	Morocco	0.04%	0.05%
	Jordan	0.01%	0.03%
	Pakistan	–	0.03%
	Cyprus	–	0.03%
	Argentina	–	0.02%
	Slovenia	0.04%	0.02%
	Oman	0.02%	0.02%
	Bahrain	0.01%	0.02%
	Mauritius	–	0.01%
	Malta	–	0.01%
	Estonia	–	0.01%
	Bulgaria	–	0.01%
	Iceland	–	0.01%
	Lithuania	–	0.01%
	Romania	0.01%	0.01%
	Siri Lanka	0.01%	0.01%
	Component Number	605	11767
Market Capitalization	**Full**	6,414.7	37,195.5
	Float adjusted	6,026.6	28,530.7
	Mean	10	2.4
Country Allocation		**Dow Jones Islamic Europe index**	**Dow Jones Europe index**
	United Kingdom	31.89%	28.45%
	France	18.48%	15.04%
	Switzerland	17.51%	11.79%
	Germany	9.84%	10.82%
	Sweden	3.84%	3.81%

	Finland	3.69%	1.86%
	Italy	3.51%	5.47%
	Netherlands	2.96%	3.74%
	Denmark	2.71%	1.44%
	Norway	1.78%	1.32%
	Spain	1.51%	6.24%
	Belgium	0.88%	1.39%
	Austria	0.63%	0.71%
	Greece	0.32%	1.00%
	Ireland	0.27%	1.49%
	Portugal	0.17%	0.58%
	Turkey	0.0%	0.73%
	Poland	0.0%	0.58%
	Czech Republic	0.0%	0.19%
	Hungary	0.0%	0.19%
	Cyprus	0.0%	0.10%
	Slovenia	0.0%	0.08%
	Romania	0.0%	0.02%
	Malta	0.0%	0.01%
	Estonia	0.0%	0.01%
	Bulgaria	0.0%	0.01%
	Iceland	0.0%	0.01%
	Lithuania	0.0%	0.01%
Market Capitalization	**Component Number**	278	1997
	Full	2,971.7	11,209.7
	Float adjusted	2,269.6	8,101.0
	Mean	8.2	4.1
Country Allocation		**Dow Jones Islamic Asia/Pacific index**	**Dow Jones Asia/Pacific index**
	Japan	34.25%	43.07%
	Australia	15.01%	14.36%
	India	12.72%	7.43%
	Taiwan	11.57%	7.16%
	South Korea	9.32%	7.43%
	China	6.02%	7.89%
	Hong Kong	4.39%	5.53%
	Singapore	2.19%	2.92%
	Malaysia	1.54%	1.46%
	Indonesia	1.45%	1.08%
	Thailand	1.07%	0.84%

	New Zealand	0.24%	0.32%
	Philippines	0.23%	0.31%
	Sri Lanka	0.01%	0.03%
	Pakistan	0.0%	0.15%
Market Capitalization	**Component Number**	1070	4250
	Float adjusted	2,236.2	6,521.7
	Mean	2.1	1.5

Sector Allocation

ASIA ISLAMIC		ASIA CONVENTIONAL	
Industrials	20.76%	Financials	25.54%
Basic Materials	18.33%	Industrials	16.95%
Technology	17.85%	Consumer Goods	14.24%
Consumer Goods	10.82%	Basic Materials	10.75%
Oil & Gas	8.50%	Technology	8.66%
Telecommunications	8.50%	Consumer Services	7.82%
Health Care	8.14%	Oil & Gas	4.37%
Consumer Services	4.05%	Utilities	4.12%
Utilities	2.61%	Telecommunications	3.90%
Financials	0.45%	Health Care	3.64%

EUROPE ISLAMIC		EUROPE CONVENTIONAL	
Health Care	27.07%	Financials	25.40%
Oil & Gas	23.44%	Oil & Gas	12.46%
Industrials	14.25%	Consumer Goods	12.04%
Basic Materials	13.96%	Industrials	11.88%
Technology	9.04%	Health Care	8.83%
Consumer Goods	6.45%	Basic Materials	7.60%
Consumer Services	3.50%	Consumer Services	6.47%
Utilities	1.34%	Telecommunications	6.17%
Telecommunications	0.95%	Utilities	6.01%
Financials	0.00%	Technology	3.13%

US ISLAMIC		US CONVENTIONAL	
Technology	25.88%	Financials	17.27%
Health Care	20.89%	Technology	16.34%
Oil & Gas	17.23%	Health Care	12.27%
Industrials	10.90%	Industrials	12.14%
Consumer Services	8.75%	Consumer Services	11.49%
Consumer Goods	8.70%	Oil & Gas	10.73%
Basic Materials	4.00%	Consumer Goods	9.94%
Telecommunications	2.76%	Utilities	3.84%
Utilities	0.79%	Basic Materials	3.25%
Financials	0.11%	Telecommunications	2.73%

References

A. Al-Zoubi, I. Maghyereh. (2007), "The Relative Risk Performance Of Islamic Finance: A New Guide To Less Risky Investments," International Journal of Theoretical and Applied Finance (IJTAF), vol. 10(02), pages 235-249.

Ayub, M., (2007) "Understanding Islamic Finance" (Wiley Finance).

Bollerslev, T. (1986), "Modeling the coherence in short-run nominal exchange rates: a multivariate generalized ARCH model", Review of Economics and Statistics, Vol. 72, pp. 498-505.

Campbell, R, Huisman, R & Koedijk, K (2001), "Optimal Portfolio Selection in a Value at Risk Framework", *Journal of Banking and Finance*, Vol.25, pp.1789-1804.

El-Gamal, M. A., (2006) "Islamic Finance Law, Economics and Practice".

Eugene F. Fama, (1972) "Components of Investment Performance", Journal of Finance 27, no.3, 588.

Favre, L & Galeano, JA (2002) "Mean-Modified Value-at-Risk Optimization with Hedge Funds", *Journal of Alternative Investment,* Vol.5, No.2, pp.2-21.

Ferson, W., and M. Qian. (2004). Conditional performance evaluation: Revisited. Working Paper, Boston College.

Ferson, W., and R. Schadt. (1996). Measuring fund strategy and performance in changing economic conditions. Journal of Finance 51: 425–61.

Ferson, W., and V. Warther. (1996). Evaluating fund performance in a dynamic market. Financial Analysts Journal 52:20–28.

Giot, P. and Laurent, S. (2003), "Value-at-risk for long and short trading positions", Journal of Applied Econometrics, Vol. 18, pp. 641-63.

Giot, P. and Laurent, S. (2004), "Modeling daily value-at-risk using realized volatility and ARCH type models", Journal of Empirical Finance, Vol. 11, pp. 379-98.

Greg, N. (2009) "The VaR implementation handbook", McGraw-Hill.

Jorion, P. (1997), "Value-at-Risk: The New Benchmark for Controlling Market Risk", McGraw-Hill.

Jorion, P. (2001), "Value at Risk", McGraw-Hill, New York, NY.

Kupiec, P. (1995), "Techniques for verifying the accuracy of risk measurement models", Journal of Derivatives, Vol. 2, pp. 173-84.

Zangari, P (1996), "A VaR Methodology for Portfolios that Include Options", *RiskMetricsMonitor*, First Quarter, pp.4-12.

BIBLIOGRAPHY

Websites

www.ameinfo.com

www.gata.org

Islamic Finance – cfapubs.org, www.cfapubs.org

Islamic Finance, www.islamic-finance.com

Islamic Financial Services Board (IFSB), www.ifsb.org

World Database for Islamic Banking and Finance, www.wdibf.com

International Islamic Financial Market, www.iifm.net

Islamic Finance News, www.islamicfinancenews.com

Global Islamic Finance Magazine, www.globalislamicfinancemagazine.com

Islamic Finance – Deloitte, www.deloitte.com/xd

Islamic Finance News – Bloomberg, topics.bloomberg.com/islamic-finance

Islamic finance: Banking on the ummah, www.economist.com

Islamic Finance, www.islamicfinance.de

Islamic financial institutions – Islamic Finance WIKI, wiki.islamicfinance.de/index.php/Islamic_financial_institutions

IslamicFinance Overview – Islamic Finance – FNB, https://www.fnb.co.za/islamic-finance/islamic-finance.html

Islamic banking – Wikipedia, the free encyclopedia, en.wikipedia.org/wiki/Islamicbanking

International Shari'ah Research Academy for Islamic Finance (ISRA), www.isra.my

Islamic Finance News, www.islamicfinancenews.com

Ethica Institute of Islamic Finance™, ethicainstitute.com/

Islamic Banking & Finance Institute Malaysia, www.ibfim.com/

IIUM Institute of Islamic Banking and Finance (IIiBF) www.iium.edu.my/iiibf

Bibliography and selected references

Abdallah, A. (1987), “Islamic banking”, Journal of Islamic Banking and Finance, January March, 4(1): 3156.

Abdul Gafoor (2000), “Interest – Free Commercial Banking”, A.S. Nordeen, KualaLumpur.

Al Arabi, M. A. (1966), “Contemporary banking transactions and Islam’s views thereon”, Islamic Review, London, May 1966.

Aldrich (1979), “Organizations and Environments”, Prentice-Hall: New York.

Aglietta M. (1995), “Normativité de la monnaie et indépendance des Banques Centrales”, Contribution au Colloque Economie Normative, CAESAR-GRESE-METIS, Octobre.

Ali, M. (1984), Papers on Islamic Banking, New Century Publishers, London.

Allen L. and Rai A. (1996), “Operational Efficiency in Banking: An International Comparison”, Journal of Banking and Finance 20, 655-672.

Al- MISRI R. (1975), “Islam et Monnaie”, Djeddah: Institut International de Recherche en Economie Islamique, Université de Djeddah, Arabie Saoudite.

Altunbas, Y. et Chakravarty S.P. (1998), Efficiency measures and the banking structure in Europe, Economics Letters 60, 205-208.

Andrews, K. R. (1980), “Director’s responsibility for corporate strategy”, Harvard Business Review, p. 30-42.

Ariff, M. (1982), “Monetary policy in an interest free Islamic economy nature and scope’ in M. Ariff, (ed.), Monetary and Fiscal Economics of Islam, International Centre for Research in Islamic Economics, Jeddah.

—. (1988), “Islamic Banking in Southeast Asia”, Institute of Southeast Asian Studies, Singapore.

Arshadi, N. et Lawrence E. C. (1987) “An Empirical Investigation of New Bank Performance.” Journal of Banking and Finance 11: 33–48.

Barth James R. et R. Dan Brumbaugh Jr. (1994), “Moral Hazardand Agency Problems: Understanding Depository Institution Failure Costs”, dans G.G. Kaufman (Ed.) Research in Financial Services (pp:61-102), Greenwich, CT: JAI Press Inc.

Bartholdy, Boyle et Stover (1997), “Deposit Insurance, Bank Regulation, and Interest Rates: Some International Evidence.” University of Otago, New Zealand.

Barth, Nolle et Rice (1997), "Commercial Banking Structure, Regulation, and Performance: An International Comparison", OCC Working Paper 97-6, March 1997.

Bataille, F. (1999), "Compétence collective et performance", Revue de Gestion des Ressources, Humaines, 40, 66-81.

Battese G. and Coelli T. (1995), "A Model for Technical Inefficiency Effects in a Stochastic Frontier Production Function and Panel Data", Empirical Economics, Vol. 20, 325-332.

Baumol, William J., John C. Panzar and Robert D. Willig, (1982), "Contestable Markets and the Theory of Industry Structure", San Diego: Harcourt Brace Jovanovich.

Blaug M. (1992), "The methodology of economics. Or how economists explain", Cambridge University Press, Cambridge, 1992.

Berger A.N. (1993), "Distribution-Free Estimates of Efficiency in U.S. Banking Industry and Tests of the Standard Distributional Assumptions," *Journal of Productivity Analysis*, 4, pp. 261-292.

—. (1995), "The profit-structure relationship in banking – tests of market-power and efficient structure hypotheses", *Journal of Money, Credit and Banking* 27, 404-431.

Berger, A. (1995), "The Relationship between Capital and Earnings in Banking." *Journal of Money, Credit and Banking* Vol. 27: 432-456.

Berger, Allen N. and Mester J. (1995), "Inside the Black Box: What Explains Differences in the Efficiencies of Financial Institutions?" Journal of Banking and Finance 21: 895-947.

Berger A. and Humphrey D. (1997), "Efficiency of Financial Institutions: International Survey and Directions for Future Research", European Journal of Operational Research 98, 175-212.

Berger, Davies et Flannery (1998), "Comparing Market and Supervisory Assessments of Bank Performance: Who Knows What When?, Finance and Economics discussion Paper, 98/32, Board of Governors of the Federal Reserve System.

Berger, Hancock et Humphrey (1993),"Bank Efficiency Derived from the Profit Function." Journal of Banking and Finance 17(2-3): 317-347.

Berger, Kashyap, Scalise (1995), "The Transformation of the U.S. Banking Industry: What a Long, Strange Trip It's Been," Brookings Papers on Economic Activity 2, 55-218.

Beshir A. (1993), "Equity Capital, Profit Sharing Contracts, and Investment: Theory and Evidence", Journal of Business and Accounting, 20(5) Sept. 1993.

—. (1999). "Risk and Profitability Measures in Islamic Banks: The Case of Two Sudanese Banks", Islamic Economic Studies, Vol. 6, No. 2: 1-24.

—. (2000), "Assessing the Performance of Islamic Banks: Some Evidence from the Middle East".

Bessire D. (1999), "Définir la performance", Comptabilité Contrôle Audit, tome. 5, vol. 2, 127-150.

Bhla et Raj (1992), "Perspectives on Risk-Based Capital: a guide to the new risk-based capital adequacy rules", Tokyo: Toppan C. Ltd., 1992.

Bierwag et Kaufman (1977), "Coping with the Risk of Interest Rate Fluctuations: A Note", Journal of Business 50, 364-370.

Bizot A. (1985), "La pratique bancaire française en matière de financement sur le marché intérieur", Revue banque éditions.

Bourguignon A. (1995), "Peut-on définir la performance", Revue Française de comptabilité, n°269, juillet –août, p.200-217.

—. (1997), Sous les pavés la plage…ou les multiples fonctions du vocabulaire comptable: l'exemple de la performance, Comptabilité-Contrôle – Audit, tome 3, vol.1, mars, p.89-101.

Bourke P. (1989), "Concentration and other determinants of bank profitability in Europe, North America and Australia", Journal of Banking and Finance.

Bourke (1990), "An Introduction to Bank Lending", Editor with Shanmugan, B., Addison-Wesley, 1990.

—. (1990), "The Management of Financial Institutions". (Editor with Shanmugan, B.), Addison-Wesley. 1990.

Brealey et Myers (1997), "Principes de gestion financière des sociétés", McGraw Hill.

Brealey, Richard and Stewart Myers, (1997), Principles of Corporate Finance, 5th ed., New York, NY, McGraw-Hill.

Brewer, and Mondschean (1994), "An Empirical Test of the Incentive Effects of Deposit Insurance: The Case of Junk Bonds at Savings and Loan Associations." *Journal of Money, Credit and Banking 26*: 146-164.

Bruce, N.C. (986), "Islamic banking moves east", Euromoney, July: 1425.

Brucker, E. "A Microeconomic Approach to Banking Competition", *Journal of Finance,* Vol.25, Issue 5.

Chapra (1970), "The Economic System of Islam: A Discussion of its Goals and Nature", The Islamic Quarterly, vol 14, Londres 1970.

—. (1985), "Toward a Just Monetary System: The Islamic Foundation", Leicester.

Dar et Presley (1999), "Islamic Finance: A Western Perspective", *International Journal of Islamic Financial Services* 1(1), 3-11.

Darmon O. (1998), "Stratégie bancaire et gestion de bilan", Economica.

Daryl O. McKee, P. Rajan Varadarajan, William M. Pride (1989), "Strategic Adaptability and Firm Performance: A Market-Contingent Perspective", *Journal of Marketing*, Vol. 53, No. 3 (Jul., 1989).

De Coussergues.S. (1994), "La banque: structure, marchés, gestion", Dalloz.

—. (1996), "Gestion de la banque", 1996, Dunod.2 édition Paris.

De La Villarmois, O. (1998), "Le concept de performance et sa mesure", Actes des XIVèmes Journées des IAE, Nantes, t.2, vol.2, 199-216.

Demirguc-Kunt, et Huizinga (1997), "Determinants of commercial bank interest margins and profitability: some international evidence", Working Paper, Development Research Group, World Bank, Washington, D.C.

Demsetz. H. (1973), "Industry structure, market rivalry, and price policy", The Journal of Law and Economics, vol 16, April, pp. 1-9.

Demsetz (1983), "The Structure of Ownership and The Theory of The Firm", Journal of Law and Economics, Vol: 26, Juin, pp: 375-390.

Dietsch, Dow (1996), "Why the banking system should be regulated", The Economic Journal, 106, may, pp. 698-707.

Dietsch. M (1992), "Coûts et concurrence dans l'industrie bancaire", Rapport pour le Conseil National du Crédit et l'Association Française des Banques, Mars, 98 p.

Dietsch (1996), "Efficience et prise de risque dans les banques en France", Revue Economique, mai 1996.

Dietsch & Anna (2000), "How the environment determines banking efficiency: A comparison between French and Spanish industries," Journal of Banking & Finance, Elsevier, vol. 24(6), pages 985-1004, June.

Demirgüç-Kunt, Aslı, and Huizinga (1993), "Official Credits to Developing Countries: Implicit Transfers to the Banks", Journal of Money, Credit, and Banking 25(3):430–44.

Demirgüç-Kunt A. et Huizinga (1999), "Determinants of Commercial Bank Interest Margins and Profitability: Some International Evidence", *World Bank Economic Review*, Vol:13, No 2, pp 379-408.

Edwards, R. and Heggestad A. (1973), "Uncertainty, market structure and performance: The Galbraith-caves hypothesis and managerial motives in banking", *Quarterly Journal of Economics*.

Eldin, A.K. (1986), "Ten years of Islamic banking", Journal of Islamic Banking and Finance, July-September, 3(3):4966.

Elasker, A.A.F. (1987), "The Islamic Business Enterprise", Croom Helm, London.

Emery (1971), "Risk, Returns, and the Morphology of Commercial Banking", Journal of Financial and Quantitative Analysis, Vol. 6, N°. 2, March, pp. 763-776.

Erol, et El-Bdour (1989), "Attitudes, Behaviour and Patronage Factor of Bank Customers Towards Islamic Banks", International Journal of Bank Marketing 7(6), 31-39.

Fama et Jensen (1983), "Separation of Ownership and Control", *Journal of Law and Economics*, Vol:26, No:2, June, pp:301-325.

Fraser et autres (1974), "A Canonical Analysis of Bank Performance", *Journal of Financial and Quantitative Analysis*, 9, 287- 295.

Fraser et Rose (1972), "Bank Entry and Bank Performance", *Journal of Finance*, Vol. 21, N°1 (March), 65- 78.

Gambling, T. and Karim, R.A.A. (1991), "Business and Accounting Ethics in Islam", London: Mansell.

Gambling and Karim (1998), "Islam and Accounting", Journal of Business Finance and Accounting, V.13, 1986 spring.

Garsuault P. et Priami S. (1992), "La banque: fonctionnement et stratégie", Techniques bancaires, Section 2.

Gattoufi S. and Reisman A. (2004), "A taxonomy for data envelopment analysis", Muhittin Oral, Socio-Economic Planning Sciences, 38 pp. 141-158.

Gerrad, P. et J.B. Cunningham (1997): "Islamic Banking: A Study in Singapore", *International Journal of Bank Marketing* 15(6), 204-216.

Ghosh, A. and Steven Phillips (1998), "Warning: Inflation May Be Harmful to Your Growth," IMF Staff Papers, International Monetary Fund, Vol. 45, No. 4, pp. 672–710.

Gilbert R.A. (1984), "Bank Market structure and competition: a survey", Journal of Money Credit and Banking, part II, 16 (4), p.617-645.

Goyeau, D., A. Sauviat et A. Tarazi (1998), "Taille, rentabilité et risque bancaire: évaluation empirique et enseignements pour la réglementation prudentielle", *Revue d'Economie Politique*, vol 108, n° 3.

Goyeau et Tarazi (1992), "Evaluation du risque de défaillance bancaire en Europe", Revue d'économie politique, n°102.(2), mars-avril, pp.249-280.

Goyeau, Sauviat et Tarazi (1998), "Risk and Optimal interest margins: The case of commercial banks in Central Europe", p. 342, mars.

Goyeau, Sauviat et Tarazi (2000), "Marché financier et évaluation du risque bancaire Les agences de notation contribuent-elles à améliorer la discipline de marché?"

Graciela L., K. et Carmen M. R. (1996) "The Twin Crises: The Causes of Banking and Balance of Payments Problems," forthcoming in American Economic Review.

Halim, A. (1986), "Sources and uses of funds: a study of Bank Islam Malaysia Berhad," paper presented to the Seminar on Developing a System of Islamic Financial Instruments, organized by the Ministry of Finance Malaysia and the Islamic Development Bank, Kuala Lumpur.

Hannan, M.T. and Freeman, J. (1984). "Structural inertia and organizational change". American Sociological Review, 49: 149–164.

Hannan, Michael T. and John Freeman (1989), "Organizational Ecology", Cambridge, MA: Harvard University Press.

Hanson et Rocha (1986), "High interest rates, spreads, and the cost of intermediation, two studies", Industry and Finance Series 18, World Bank.

Hao, Hunter et Yang (1999), "Deregulation and Efficiency: The Case of Private Korean Banks," working paper, Federal Reserve Bank of Chicago.

Haron, S., N. Ahmad et S. Planisek (1994), "Bank Patronage Factors of Muslim and Non-Muslim Customers", International Journal of Bank Marketing 12(1), 32-40.

Haron S. (1993), "The effects of management policy on the performance of Islamic banks" Asia Pacific Journal of Management Vol 13, NO 2: 63-76.

Hasan Y.D. (1996), "al-Riqabah al-Shari yyah fi al-Masarif al-Islamiyyah, Cairo, Egypte: International Institute of Islamique Thought.

Hassoune A. (2002), "Islamic banks' profitability in an interest rate cycle", International Journal of Islamic Financial Services, Vol.4, No.2.

Heffernan S. (1996), "Banking", Chapter in International Encyclopaedia of Business and Management 1, 303-311.

Heggested (1977), "Market structure, risk and profitability in commercial banking", Journal of finance, n°4.

Heggested et Mingo (1976), "Price, Non-prices, and Concentration in Commercial Banking", Journal of Money, Credit and Banking, 8 February, pp.107- 17.

Hester et Zoellner 1966, "The Relation Between Bank Portfolios and Earnings": An Econometric Analysis, Review of Economics and Statistics, 48, 372- 386.

Hirschey (1999), "Managerial Equity Ownership and Bank Performance," Economic Letters, 64:209-213.

Homoud, S. (1980), "The Theory and Practice of Islamic Banking in the Modern World", Conférence de l'Association des Banquiers Arabes et de la Chambre de Commerce arabo-britannique, Londres, Avril 1980.

—. (1985), "Islamic Banking", Arab Information, London, 1985.

Humayon A. Dar and Presley (2002), "Lack of profit loss sharing in Islamic Banking": Management and control imbalances, International Journal of Islamic Financial Services Vol. 2 No.2.

Humayon A. Dar and John R. Presley (1999)," Islamic Finance: A Western Perspective", *International Journal of Islamic Financial Services* Vol. 1 No.1.

International Institute of Islamic Thought (1996), A committee of experts on economics Shari ah sciences and banking, "Taqwin Amal Hayha at-Shari iyah fi al-Masarif al-Islamiyyah", Cairo, Egypt.

Iqbal, Z. (1997), "Islamic financial systems" Finance & Development, Vol. 34, Issue 2, pp. 42-45.

Iqbal et al. (1998), "Challenges Facing Islamic Banks", Jeddah: IRTI.

Iqbal Z. (2001), "Profit and loss sharing ratios a holistic approach to corporate finance", *International Journal of Islamic Financial Services*, Volume 3, Number 2.

Iqbal, Z. et A. Mirakhor (1987), Islamic Banking International Monetary Fund Occasional" Paper no 49, W.C.

Irshad, S.A. (1964), "Interest Free Banking", Orient Press of Pakistan, Karachi.

Issa, M. A. (1985), "Effets des variations de la valeur de la monnaie et son traitement dans une économie islamique", Thèse de Magistère, Université de Um al –Qura, La Mecque, 1985.

Ittner et Larcker, (1998), Innovations in performance measurement: trends and research implications", *Journal of Management Accounting Research,* p.205-238.

Jensen et Meckling (1976), "Theory of the Firm: Managerial Behavior, Agency Costs and Ownership Structure", *Journal of Financial Economics*, Vol 3, pp:305-360.

Kahf, Monzer (1982a), "Saving and investment functions in a twosector Islamic economy", in M. Ariff (ed.).

—. (1982b), "Fiscal and monetary policies in an Islamic economy", in Ariff (ed.).

Karsten, I. (1982), "Islam and financial intermediation", IMF Staff Papers, March, 29 (1):10842.

Kerr, Malcolm H. (1996), "Islamic Reform: The political and legal theories of Muhammed Abduh and Rashid Rida", Cambridge and California University press.
Khan et Mirakhor, (1987), "Theoretical Studies in Islamic Banking and Finance", The Institute for Research and Islamic Studies, Houston.
Khan M.S. (1986), "The Framework and Practice of Islamic Banking", Finance and Development, New-York, V.23, 1986.
—. (1986), "Islamic Interest-free Banking: A Theoretical Analysis", International Monetary Fund Staff Papers, No. 33, pp. 1-27.
Khan, A. J. (1986), "Noninterest banking in Pakistan: a case study", paper presented to the Seminar on Developing a System of Islamic Financial Instruments, organized by the Ministry of Finance Malaysia and the Islamic Development Bank, Kuala Lumpur.
Khan, M. F. (1983), "Islamic banking as practised now in the world" in Ziauddin, Ahmad et al. (eds.).
Khan, M. S. (1987), "Principles of monetary policy in an Islamic framework", paper presented to the International Institute of Islamic Economics, Islamabad, Pakistan, July.
Khan, M. S. and Mirakhor, A. (1986), "The framework and practice of Islamic banking", Finance and Development, September.
Khan, M. S. and Mirakhor, A. (1988), "The financial system and monetary policy in an Islamic economy", Journal of Research in Islamic Economics.
Khan, M. A. (1968), "Theory of employment in Islam", Islamic Literature, Karachi, XIV (4): 516.
Khan, W. M. (1985), "Towards an Interest Free Islamic Economic System", The Islamic Foundation, Leicester.
Khan (1983), "Comments on Volker Nienhaus: Profitability of Islamic Banks Competing with Interest banks", Journal of Research in Islamic Economics, Vol. 1, N° 2 (Winter), pp. 73-78.
Khan, M S. (1986), "Islamic interest-free banking: A Theoretical Analysis", IMF Staff Papers, Vol. 33, No. 1, pp. 1-25.
Khoury, R.G.K (1979), "Islamic Banking- yes to profit-sharing, not interest" The Middle East, ndeg. 59, Londres, sept. 1979 (Special Survey "Banking and Finance") "How an Islamic Bank will do Without Usury", Financial Times, Londres, 22 mars 1979.
Kurshid, A. (1980), "Economic Development in an Islamic Framework", Studies in Islamic Economics, International Center for Research in Islamic Economics, Djedda.
Lawrence et Lorsh, (1989), "Adapter les Structures de l'Entreprise: Intégration ou Différentiation", Éditions d'Organisation, Paris

(Traduction autorisée de Organization and Environment, Copyright 1986, Harvard Business School Press, Traduction par J. Ledru).
Leibenstein, H. (1966), "Allocative efficiency versus X-efficiency", American Economic Review, 56(3): 392-415.
Lubatkin, M. & Shrieves, M. (1986), "Towards Reconciliation of Market Performance Measures to Strategic Management Research". Academy of Management Review, 11(3), 497.
Man, Z. (1988), "Islamic banking: the Malaysian experience", in M. Ariff (ed.).
Mannan, M. (1970), "Islamic Economics, Theory and Practice", Lahore 1970, Nouvelle édition en 1986 chez Hodder & Stoughton, Sevenoaks.
Mannan, M. A. (1986), "Islamic Economics: Theory Practice", Cambridge: Hodder and Stoughton.
Mannan M. (1980), "Islamic economics: Theory and Practice", India, 1980.
Martens A. (2001), "Finance islamqiue: fondements et realites", Cahier 20-2001.
Mathé (1999), "Intention stratégique et types de performances de l'entreprise", Revue Française de Gestion, n° 122 Janvier- Février 1999.
Mester L. J. (1993), "Efficiency in the Savings and Loan Industry," Journal of Banking and Finance, 17, April, pp. 267-286.
—. (1996), "A Study of Bank Efficiency Taking into Account Risk-Preferences", Journal of Banking and Finance 20, 1025-1045.
Metawa et Almossawy (1988), "Banking Behaviour of Islamic Bank. Customers: Perspectives and Implications", International Journal of Bank.
Mokashi (1998), "Les banques à l'ère de la mondialisation", 1998.
Modigliani et Miller (1958), "The cost of Capital, Corporation Finance and the theory of Investment", American Economic Review 48, 1958, pp. 261–297.
Mokhtarul W. et Wahida Y. (2003), "Competitiveness and Returns to Scale in Bangladeshi Banking Industry: With a Closer Look into Profitability of Islamic Banking", *International Islamic Banking Conference 2003.*
Mohsin, M (1982), "Interest rate and intertemporal allocative efficiency in an Islamic economy", in M. Ariff (ed.).
—. (1982), "Profile of riba-free banking", in M. Ariff (ed.).
Molyneux, P. & Thornton, J. (1992), "Determinants of European bank profitability: A note", *Journal of banking and finance* 16. 1173 –1178.
Muazzam A. (1982): "Islamic Banks and Strategies of Economy", London, New Century Publishers, 1982.

Naughton, S.A.J. and Tahir, M.A. (1988), "Islamic banking and financial development", Journal of Islamic Banking and Finance, 5 (2).

Naulleau, G. (1988), "Banques Islamiques et Banques coopératives", Cahiers Internationaux de Sociologie Économique et Culturelle (Paris), Octobre 1988.

Nienhaus V. (1982), "Islamic Economics – Policy between Pragmatism and Utopia", Economics, V.25, Tubingen, 1982.

—. (1983), "Profitability of Islamic PLS banks competing with interest banks: problems and prospects", Journal of Research in Islamic Economics, 1 (l):3747.

—. (1986), "Islamic economics, finance and banking theory and practice", *Journal of Islamic Banking and Finance*, 3(2):3654.

Nisse-Jason, (1987), "No Interest", Banker (UK) V.137, oct.1987.

Ory (2003), "La démarche RAROC utilisée en banque est-elle transposable à l'assurance-vie", Revue Financier, Numéro 137-138, 2003.

Qureshi, (1967), "Islam and the theory of Interest", Ashraf, Lahore.

Qureshi, Iqbal (1967), "Islam and the Theory of Interest – with a New Chapter on Interest-Free Banking", Lahore, 2deg. édition 1967.

Qureshi, Anwar Iqbal, (1946), "Islam and the Theory of Interest-with a new chapter on interest Free banking", Lahore, 2ème edition.

Rahman, Fazalur, (1981), "Riba and interest", Islamic Studies, Karachi, 3(l):143.

Robinson J. (1952), "The Generalization of the General Theory", dans The Rate of Interest and Other Essays, London: Macmillan, pp. 67-142.

Rosa, D.A. (1986), "Islamic financial policies and domestic resource mobilisation", Savings and Development, 2:14353.

Saunders A., Strock E. et Nickolaos G. Travlos (1990), "Ownership Structure, Deregulation and Bank Risk Taking", *Journal of Finance*, No: 2, June, pp: 643-654.

Siddiqi, M.N. (1982), "Islamic Approaches to Money, Banking and Monetary Policy: A Review", in M. Ariff (ed.), above.

—. (1983a), "Banking Without Interest", The Islamic Foundation, Leicester.

—. (1983b), "Issues in Islamic Banking", Islamic Foundation, Leicester.

—. (1985), "Partnership and Profit Sharing in Islamic Law", Islamic Foundation, Leicester.

—. (1988), "Banking without Interest", Leicester: The Islamic Foundation.

Short Brock K. (1979), "The Relation Between Commercial Bank Profit Rates and Banking Concentration in Canada, Western Europe and Japan", *Journal of Banking and Finance*, Vol:3.

Udovitch A. (1981), "Bankers without Banks: Commerce, Banking and Society in the Islamic World of Middle Ages", Princeton Near East Paper No. 30, Princeton, NJ: Princeton University Press.

Véronique M. (1998), "Vers une redéfinition de la mesure de la performance des entreprises", *Revue Financier*, n°117.

Wilson, Rodney (ed.) (1990), "Islamic Financial Markets", London: Routledge.